MARY C. J... ...esearch at Oxford after gaining a First Class Honours degree in history at the University of York. She then taught history at Aylesbury High School and is now a part-time tutor in history for the Workers' Education Association. She has been an A-level examiner in history for ten years. Her husband Lawrence, who wrote part of this book, teaches history at Merchant Taylor's School and is an O-level paper setter and awarder. Mary James is also the author of *Model Answers: History, Social and Economic (1815-1939)* and co-author of *Multiple Choice: History, Social and Economic (1815-1951)* both of which are in the Key Facts series (Charles Letts & Co Ltd).

key facts

GCE O-Level Passbooks

BIOLOGY, R. Whitaker, B.Sc. and
J. M. Kelly, B.Sc., M.I.Biol.

CHEMISTRY, C. W. Lapham, M.Sc.

ECONOMICS, J. E. Waszek, B.Sc.(Econ.)

ENGLISH LANGUAGE, Robert L. Wilson,
M.A.

FRENCH, G. Butler, B.A.

GEOGRAPHY, R. Knowles, M.A.

GEOGRAPHY, BRITISH ISLES,
D. Bryant, B.A. and R. Knowles, M.A.

HISTORY, Political and Constitutional
(1815-1951), L. E. James, B.A., M.Litt.

HISTORY, Social and Economic
(1815-1951), M. C. James, B.A.
and L. E. James, B.A., M.Litt.

MODERN MATHEMATICS, A. J. Sly, B.A.

PHYSICS, B. P. Brindle, B.Sc.

TECHNICAL DRAWING, P. Barnett,
D.S.C., M.C.C.Ed., Adv.Dip.Ed.

GCE O-Level Passbook

History,

Social and Economic
(1815-1951)

M. C. James, B.A.
and L. E. James, B.A., M.Litt.

Published by Charles Letts & Co Ltd
London, Edinburgh and New York

First published 1980 by Intercontinental Book Productions

Published 1982 by Charles Letts & Co Ltd
Diary House, Borough Road, London SE1 1DW

2nd edition 2nd impression
© Charles Letts & Co Ltd
Made and printed by Charles Letts (Scotland) Ltd
ISBN 0 85097 544 1

Contents

Introduction, 7

1 England in 1815, 9

2 Rural Society, 1815–1939, 26

3 The Poor, 48

4 Industrial Society, 78

5 Communications, 94

6 Reform of Working Conditions, 108

7 Public Health and Medicine, 117

8 Crime and Punishment, 124

9 Trade Unions, 132

10 The Changing Status of Women, 140

11 Education, 153

12 Local Government, 167

13 1939–1945 The Second World War, 171

14 Brave New World 1945–1951, 183

1815–1951. Summary and Comment, 199

Key Terms, 202

Suggested Reading, 203

Index, 204

Examination Hints, 208

Introduction

One objection often levelled against history is that since it is concerned with the past it has no relevance to the present: but history can be defended from this charge on at least two counts.

Since it concerns itself with the beliefs, actions and circumstances of people, it provides interesting insights into the working of the human mind. Thus it can be said to have much of the appeal of literature. It gives account of the manner in which people respond to different circumstances in the light of a different scale of values, and of the way in which particular men were able to change and shape not merely their own lives but that of the nation. We can none of us experience all things but the study of history enables us to expand our knowledge and understanding vicariously (indirectly).

It also enables us to understand many of the issues of our own day. The language used in much political and social debate presupposes a knowledge of history. Take, for instance, the case of the Shrewsbury pickets in 1973, the two men sent to prison following a dispute in the building industry and their alleged breach of the law on peaceful picketing. The case became a *cause célèbre* and the men were compared by some to the Tolpuddle Martyrs. Those who applied the description supposed the general public to be well enough versed in history to understand that the men were being cast in the role of martyr and that the whole Trade Union movement was being attacked through them. Thus a direct historical parallel was being drawn and its meaning and its validity could only be understood if one knew enough history to take the reference up.

To take a more general event, consider the case of the economic situation of the 1970s and the question of unemployment. A large part of the attitude of all political parties is explained by historical memory. Those who resist unemployment frequently refer to the large-scale suffering experienced during the Great Depression of 1921–39. Those who argue that a certain amount, even a large amount, of unemployment is the price we must pay to end the crisis, insist that the Depression image is a bogey and that the historical parallel is invalid. But both points of view take cognisance of a past event in the debate about a present problem. And if you think that only very recent history matters, remember that Mr Enoch Powell opposed continued British membership of the Common Market with reference to six hundred years of parliamentary history!

Thus one has to live with history, so one may as well attempt to understand it. A CSE or GCE O-level course helps one to do this because the study is on a broad enough basis for one to perceive the general pattern of development towards the present, and at a deep enough level to be informative.

In this revised edition of the Key Facts History Passbook, the main themes of nineteenth- and twentieth-century history are clearly laid out and the book is planned as a useful aid to examinations. The first twelve chapters deal thematically with the period 1815–1939. The new material in the final two chapters extends the coverage of these themes to 1951 and provides a concise account of the Second World War and its aftermath. Examination syllabuses vary from board to board and it is impossible to provide for *all* contingencies: this book will satisfy the requirements of those boards offering a nineteenth- and twentieth-century social and economic history paper, and the topics treated are the key topics in respect of it. A list of 'key terms' – that is, words basic to a general understanding of history during this period – is included (on page 202).

Acknowledgements

I should like to thank my husband Lawrence for his help. He has written four chapters of this book and the examination hints, and has been a constant source of encouragement. I should also like to thank Mrs Chesworth, who did most of the typing.

Chapter 1
England in 1815

It is interesting to speculate on the reaction of a person living in the 1970s, suddenly set down in the England of 1815. How would the landscape strike him? How easy would he find it to adjust to the social and political values of the age? Would he find the structure of society and the conditions of life very different and if so in what respect? What of the cultural tastes of the age and the general tone? What features would strike him most?

Landscape

The landscape he would find reassuring. The England of 1815 would be instantly recognisable, presuming of course that our traveller in time is a country dweller, for towns of any size were a novelty though they were fast ceasing to be so. England was predominantly a rural country. That is the great difference between then and now, but the appearance of the landscape was otherwise similar. There were no great primeval forests or great wastes as on the continent at this time. The land was extensively cultivated and shaped and patterned as today. The same patch-work of fields existed, the result of continuous enclosure begun in the Middle Ages and speeded up since the end of the eighteenth century. The forests had disappeared too during the same period and many of the wet lands had been drained. Not all however. A German observer remarked that the land between Ely and Cambridge for a distance of about thirteen miles was still under water and the same was true of parts of Lincolnshire and East Anglia. Another difference which might strike the outsider was the quietude, and perhaps the isolation, of the various regions and villages of England. These features are best understood with reference to the system of communications.

Communications

In 1815 passenger travel was limited to the road. Considerable improvements had taken place in the late eighteenth century at the instigation of the **Turnpike Trusts**, companies which built roads and then charged travellers for the use of them. The trusts employed the famous road engineers **Telford, McAdam,** and **Metcalfe** who gave scientific thought to aspects of road building which had often been neglected, such as camber, drainage, foundation and surfacing. But the fact that so many separate trusts existed varying in size and solvency meant that there was a lack of co-ordination in road building. Also, the procedure whereby trusts had to apply to Parliament for permission to construct was expensive and the costs were passed on to the road users. Regulations designed to protect the road, specifying wheel diameter and minimum loads, also inconvenienced travellers. Lastly it is important to remember, since much is made of the trust roads as a factor in an improved transport system, that turnpike roads were the minority. Out of 125,000 miles of road in 1820 only 21,000 were turnpike. In most areas the old mud tracks, which depended for maintenance upon the spasmodic labours of paupers in the parishes they ran through, survived.

Travel was therefore a hazardous and momentous undertaking. How hazardous may be gathered from Oliver Goldsmith's play *She Stoops to Conquer*, where the road is so lost sight of that the coach party inadvertently returns to its point of departure. How momentous is suggested in Jane Austen's novel *Emma*. When Emma Woodhouse's sister visits Hartfield from London, a journey of some sixteen miles, it is an important event, occasioning great excitement and taking time. The time involved in travel was certainly considerable. A journey from York to London in 1815 would take two days and from Edinburgh about four or five days.

These peculiar conditions had an important and interesting social effect in so far as they bred a **parochialism** which we see only remnants of today. Small communities were very isolated and self-sufficient in terms of goods and ideas, and someone coming from another village would be regarded as a foreigner. The isolation was not total. Newspapers existed and were passed round and of course people did leave and return. But contact was spasmodic and on the whole the pattern of existence remained unchanged, in small close-knit communities whose identity was sometimes defined by particular modes of dress (agricultural smock patterns differed from area to area) and habits of speech. In these communities everyone had an identity and the tempo of life was measured and slow.

There were intimations of change: the first steamship would cross the Atlantic in 1819 and Stephenson had already designed his locomotive. The world was opening up, but all this seemed remote to the typical villages and hamlets of England in 1815.

The towns

Towns were an important part of Britain's transformation too and they were increasing rapidly. In 1810 only eleven towns existed with a population in excess of 50,000 and three of more than 100,000 – London, Dublin and Manchester. In 1820 there were fifteen with more than 50,000 and seven of 100,000. To the others were added Edinburgh, Glasgow, Liverpool and Birmingham.

The reason for this phenomenal growth is two-fold. It reflects the growing importance of these areas industrially, and it reflects the rapid increase in population.

Economic structure

Population

The word 'explosion' is often used in connection with population figures at this time. The population of the United Kingdom in 1700 stood at 5½ million. By 1750 it was 7 million and by 1815 it had nearly doubled and stood at 13 million, over a million living in London. The **reasons** behind this rapid expansion have been hotly debated. It is thought that a series of good harvests in the mid-eighteenth century allowed the initial breakthrough, since famine had been the most effective check to population. The increase was maintained on account of the employment which growing industrialisation provided and the successful response of agriculture to the demand for more food.

Another factor in the expansion has been thought to be the working of the **Poor Law**. The number of children one had determined one's claim upon the poor rate and this may have provided a positive incentive for people to have children – though a more likely inducement to large families was probably the **demand for child labour** by both industry and agriculture. The decline in the **death rate** must also be taken into account. In 1780 the death rate was 1 in every 40, in 1810 it was 1 in 54 and in 1830 1 in 60, in spite of the appalling conditions of life in the new factory towns. The conquest of smallpox and the increased prosperity which reduced starvation partly explain the reduction. Hunger brings many diseases in its wake and lowers resistance to them.

Thomas Malthus

Although essential to continued industrial expansion the population increase did cause concern, since the numbers coming to depend upon the poor rate for the means of survival were increasing rapidly. That this might be the consequence of an inadequate wage structure rather than evidence of too large a population did not readily occur to many contemporaries who believed what Thomas Malthus had to say in his influential *Essay on Population.*

Malthus insisted that a balance must be kept between population and resources and argued that it had been upset. Population was increasing at a much faster rate than resources. Remedies must be applied. The lower classes should practise sexual restraint and the poor law system should be reformed so that children could no longer be a charge upon the rate. Malthus was the doom-watcher of his day and his influence was immense. The subject of population created great anxiety in the early nineteenth century though it became thereafter a source of pride.

Economic theory

Malthus was one influential theorist in 1815, others were **Adam Smith** and **David Ricardo**. Smith had been dead for twenty-five years but his influence was very strong. His outlook was much more optimistic than Malthus's. He had great hope for the future since Great Britain's potential was immense. The eighteenth century had witnessed the expansion and consolidation of her great colonial empire. India and Canada had been brought under British control and British possessions in the West Indies were augmented. On the industrial front great strides were being made. The textile, coal and iron industries had all benefited from the new inventions and processes which enabled them to expand, and a financial structure existed which facilitated investment in both industry and agriculture. The Bank of England and the county banks were the repositories of a surplus wealth which could be tapped at low rates of interest (about 4 per cent). The economy was then extremely buoyant (though the same could not be said of government finances) and the scope for expansion seemed unlimited – to Smith at any rate, for his importance to economic philosophy lay in perceiving these facts and in suggesting the means by which the nation could benefit. To this end he developed his free trade theory.

Mercantilism
The most influential economic theory prevailing before Smith outlined the principles of free trade was mercantilism. Mercantilists believed not that trade could expand limitlessly but that

only a fixed amount was available. The trade potential of the world remained unaltered and unalterable. Governments therefore had a duty to protect native commodities from outside competition by means of duties and tariffs and to increase the nation's share of world trade as far as possible by diplomatic and martial enterprise. They had a duty too to regulate wages and prices so that goods could be sold competitively.

Free trade

Smith thought that the mercantilist theory was mistaken and that market forces should be given free play. Tariffs and duties, wage- and price-regulation should be abandoned. They kept prices artificially high. Left to their own devices manufacturers would have to reduce prices in order to sell their goods competitively. As goods became cheaper more people would be able to buy them. Increased demand would increase production which would increase employment which would in time increase the market, since more people would have the means of purchase. Demonstrably, then, trade was unlimited. Markets could expand indefinitely so long as the price was low and the goods available. Supply and demand created their own momentum. Smith's importance lay in explaining in scientific and rational terms what many manufacturers and traders had always believed.

David Ricardo (1772–1823) was very much Smith's disciple as far as free trade and *laissez faire* was concerned, but he developed for himself the notion of Natural Laws in economics which he believed should be left to work unhindered. They would regulate the balance between price and demand and act as price regulators. Ricardo also believed a state of harmony existed between the individual and the state and that what benefited the former was advantageous also to the latter. These arguments too were designed to encourage economic *laissez faire*.

The role of the state

Economic policy

The phrase *laissez faire* which had been introduced describes the policy of government non-intervention already prevailing in respect of social conditions which economists now espoused.

But it seems clear that although the arguments against state interference were very influential they were not universally applied. As far as trade was concerned the old system of tariffs and dues existed to protect British industry and agriculture. The Corn Laws passed in 1815, which prohibited the importation of foreign corn until English corn had reached 80s. a quarter ton, is the best-known example of protectionism but the importation of silk was wholly forbidden; the duty on earthenware was 79 per cent of the value, on glass 114 per cent, and on woollen goods 50 per cent. Ten years later these duties were substantially reduced to an average of 20 per cent by the then secretary to the Board of Trade, **William Huskisson**, but the idea of protection was tenaciously adhered to, especially by the small agriculturists whose profit margins were small. Manufacturers producing goods which other countries wanted but could not themselves produce could afford to be more sanguine on the question of free trade.

The state intervened too in maintaining the system of **bounty** as an enticement to export, for it was part of traditional mercantilist theory that a favourable balance of trade should exist. Thus sugar exporters, for example, were in receipt of a bounty of 5s. a hundredweight. This practice of giving bounties was beginning to lapse, however.

Shipping
Shipping too was protected, by the **old navigation laws** which had operated since the mid-seventeenth century. These laws stipulated that goods could be carried only in the ships of the country of origin or in British ships. In 1825 these laws came in for amendment and it was agreed that goods could be carried in ships belonging to the importing country. Since the importing country might not be the country of origin, restrictions were being lifted to a small extent and perhaps some concession was being made to the idea of free trade. But the laws were still in operation as late as 1840 and certainly no *carte blanche* had been issued to prospective rivals in the carrying trade. The principle of protection still operated.

Industry
The position as far as industry was concerned was somewhat different. The government seemed to subscribe to *laissez faire* principles in so far as the old statute of labourers which regulated wages in industry was not operated. And where the state did intervene it was to repeal old legislation which committed the government to continued intervention. Thus in 1821 the **Sealing and Stamping Acts** which had operated in Yorkshire but not elsewhere to regulate the length of cloth and size of bales of wool

were repealed. Similar regulations affecting **Scottish linen** were also dispensed with.

The development towards *laissez faire* in economics was therefore gradual and protection was not lightly abandoned. Free trade in respect of corn did not come in until 1846 and even then there was strong opposition to the repeal of the Corn Laws. But even in 1815 the principle of non-intervention was coming to be accepted, and Lord Liverpool, Prime Minister at the time, remarked when the Corn Laws were passed that trade should on the whole be left to regulate itself.

Social policy

Where social policy was concerned *laissez faire* operated to a very much greater degree. That this was so aroused little criticism. Traditional views of freedom and an ancient system of local administration both contributed to the view that the main function of government lay in providing for the nation's security with the result, as Halevy, the celebrated nineteenth-century historian, remarked, 'the central government did nothing to secure the public safety, provided no schools, made no roads, gave no relief to the poor. With the solitary exception of the postal service the state performed no function of immediate benefit to the tax payer. In the eyes of the public the state appeared only as the power that enlisted men and levied taxes.'

Even where the last function was concerned the government had to tread carefully, for the English conception of liberty rested on the idea of free property ownership. It was believed that the state ought to protect property (by which was meant landed wealth) and any attempt to diminish it, or to introduce any principle which seemed to admit that anyone other than the holder of it had a claim upon it, was regarded with grave suspicion. The civil war in England during the seventeenth century had occurred as a direct result of attempts to oppose royal taxation which was regarded as an assault upon property. And though the civil war might seem remote to the nineteenth century the events which followed confirmed these ideas of freedom. The **Revolution Settlement** of 1688 which laid down the terms on which William III and any succeeding monarch might reign made this very clear. And in 1815, all political parties regarded the Revolution Settlement as having provided the classic definition of the rights of the governed and the limitations within which governments must exercise power. Thus although during the wartime emergency, Parliament was prepared to agree to income tax, as soon as the war was over it was repealed, not because it was thought inequitable in financial terms but because the admission of income tax in ordinary peacetime would constitute a threat to property. Government acting upon this precedent could make further depredations.

Another check upon the power of the government was provided by the system of local administration. The system was very loose. No formal bodies such as county, town or parish councils existed. The counties were governed by the great landowners and respected gentlemen who maintained order in their capacity as Justices of the Peace, having links with the central administration through the Sheriff and Lord Lieutenant, officers appointed generally from the local aristocracy by the government. But even here the freedom of choice was limited and a government seeking to impose an outsider would arouse strong opposition, as James II found to his cost. The great landowners regarded government of the localities as their concern and guarded their preserve, using mounted volunteers to maintain order.

Thus the **role of central government was limited**. Social welfare which we regard as a crucial area of government concern was left to philanthropists and religious organisations, whilst the parish administrators operating the old poor law and in the south the newer Speenhamland system kept starvation at bay. The paternalist concern of the landowners themselves made some contribution but such a system was very ragged and had a limited effectuality. As for education, religious organisations and private monetary gifts provided the educational needs of the day. Transport was provided by the parishes, turnpike trusts and canal companies.

The challenge to *laissez faire*
The ideas of Jeremy Bentham were becoming influential in 1815 and in some respects they presented a challenge to the exclusive notions of liberty which have been outlined above. He suggested that it should be the object of government to provide the **greatest good for the greatest number**; an idea which questioned the belief that what was good for the owners of property was automatically in the best interests of the nation. Changing economic circumstance and the increased social complexity arising from industrialism and a rapidly increasing population were also beginning to undermine the idea of *laissez faire*.

Greater co-ordination and rationalisation was needed in many areas of life. Public health was one obvious example. Factory conditions, education and transport were others.

Social structure

Society in 1815 differed substantially in appearance from today. Basically it was two-tiered, consisting of **upper** and **lower classes**.

The **upper classes** comprised the **titled aristocracy** and the **gentry**; a group defined mainly by their right to a coat of arms. As a group the gentry could be very diverse, rich with an income of thousands of pounds a year, connected by birth or marriage with the aristocracy, or at the lower end struggling to maintain their position in society on a few hundreds. A gentleman could earn his living but was limited to employment in the professions. The Church, the Law, the armed services and the Civil Service were the only occupations open to him if he was to retain his right to the description of 'gentleman'. It must be understood that the term 'gentleman' denoted specific social standing and was not used as the mere courtesy address of today.

The upper classes were also the **landowning classes** and status was to a large extent bound up with this fact. They were also the governing classes in so far as they controlled the political and administrative systems. They had the right to vote (the franchise) and the right to sit as M.P.s. The Civil Service was controlled by them through a system of patronage, for positions in the Civil Service were not then gained on merit. They could be purchased from or given by members of the upper classes who had acquired or inherited the right to dispose of them. And we have already seen how the upper classes governed the localities. The hold of the upper classes over the populace was also strengthened by virtue of the fact that they owned most of the land. About four-fifths of the nation's land was owned by 7,000 families. Thus most of the population in both town and country were tenants and therefore dependants of the landed classes.

Thus the power of the upper classes, although they probably constituted no more than 5 per cent of the nation, was immense. They were the politicians, administrators, legal officers and landlords and in all these capacities they ruled the nation. They dominated also in the sense that they were the arbiters of taste and social convention, and set the cultural tone of the age.

The lower classes

They were the majority. They were the agricultural and industrial workers, the skilled craftsmen and small shopkeepers forming an aristocracy among them. For the mere labourers life was harsh. They lived exposed to calamities such as famine and disease which took a heavy toll among them. Life expectancy was short, on average not more than twenty-nine years. Conditions were worst in the towns and the drawings of **Hogarth** provide the best illustration of the prevailing squalor and its brutalising effects.

The middle classes

The upper and lower classes formed the two main social categories in 1815 but another class was emerging to join them – the middle class. The **entrepreneurs**, the **manufacturers**, the large and small **tradesmen** were increasing in numbers and influence. Industrialisation had given them the scope for development and in their wake followed the lawyers who dealt with their legal affairs and the clerks who handled their paperwork. It would be wrong to give the impression that these people came magically into existence in the late eighteenth century. Of course, there had always been tradesmen and manufacturers, lawyers, clerks and shopkeepers, but the numbers had been small and their influence minimal. The Industrial Revolution gave them a considerable economic importance. They were beginning to realise their strength and to press for greater political and social power. The intellectuals among them were even beginning to persuade the lower classes to challenge the established order too.

The distinguishing mark of the middle class was its energy and dynamism. Another important facet of its character was the progressive nature of its members. The upper class looked to the past as their inspiration. The more ancient a family, the more respect it commanded and the ideas which influenced them were rooted in tradition. The middle classes however looked to the future and took great pride in the present. Change was sought and they were not fearful of it. Some members of course readily defected to the upper classes. They bought land, adopted upper-class attitudes and sought to disguise their origins, but many other members took pride in their station, believing their morality and taste superior to that of the upper classes.

Political attitudes

Upper classes

The attitude of the upper classes towards politics was simple enough. They controlled society and it was right that they should do so. As landowners they had a vested interest in the nation's property. What benefited them was advantageous to the nation. They believed that landownership also provided security for the future since land inherited was land which would be handed on to one's descendants, and one had a positive duty to hand it on intact. In fact a political system based, as ours is, upon the individual ideas and personal ambitions of representatives was considered vulnerable, since it was felt that conflicting ambitions would threaten the stability of the state.

In any case, the landed classes could argue that the majority were effectually represented. Through their dependence upon the land they were directly linked with the landowners who could therefore claim to represent their '**interest**'. The same would be said of other sections of the community. Members of the upper classes often controlled industrial and commercial enterprises so that the interests of those employed in these spheres could also be said to be represented. It was not necessary to represent persons, if interests were accounted for.

The upper classes were thus against the granting of political power merely on the grounds that since we are all governed we all have a right to govern or at least to choose our governors ourselves. Such a principle would deliver power into the hands of the 'mob', and there would be no check to riotous self-interest. Each man would be for himself and there would be such a confusion of colliding interests that chaos would ensue. This was an opinion only confirmed by the events of revolutionary France.

What was more, it was thought by the upper classes that their education fitted them peculiarly for government. An education based upon study of the classics provided a special insight into the responsibilities of government. From Greek and Latin texts the upper classes understood what constituted a free and just society, and that it was their duty to maintain and defend it.

How effective in practice?

But did what was good for the landed classes really benefit the nation as a whole? Did the upper classes really rule in a disinterested and dispassionate way? The **Corn Laws** seem to indicate that they did not, for the laws were intended to **protect** the **landed interest** and had they operated as they were intended (which they did not — corn rarely reached 80s. after

1815) they would have caused even greater hardship than in fact materialised. It is worth remarking, however, that the middle classes opposed the laws for equally selfish reasons, for they considered that the laws would be detrimental to manufacturing interests.

On the other hand the upper classes did sometimes act in a very disinterested way. It should be remembered that some of the strongest advocates of parliamentary reform were members of the upper classes such as Lords Brougham, Grey, and Russell, even though the reform envisaged and effected in 1832 aimed to diminish the legislative power of their class.

The idea that the upper classes were aware of their duties in respect of government is borne out by both fiction and fact. In the political novels of Anthony Trollope, Mr Palliser, later Duke of Omnium, is an example. And Lord David Cecil tells how his grandfather, the Prime Minister Lord Salisbury, displayed the same kind of motivation.

But times were changing and the whole notion of upper-class government was weakened by the fact that the **landed interest was ceasing to be predominant**. Industry and manufacture were gaining in importance and those involved in these enterprises felt the need for their representation. They did not accept that the upper classes were able to judge in their interest. Though they might invest money in industry and involve themselves in trade they were primarily the landed classes. Their first loyalty was to land and their best knowledge of it.

Middle classes

Thus the middle classes' political attitude is quickly explained. They felt the system was unrepresentative. Although it was possible for the more substantial among them to vote in elections, few had the right to sit as M.P.s on account of the stringent property qualifications in force.

Lower classes

As for the lower classes they had been on the whole politically dormant throughout history, coming to life of their own accord during periods of exceptional crisis like the Civil War or prodded into wakefulness by a political agitator like John Wilkes who had used the mob in his vendetta against the king during the 1760s.

In 1815 they were particularly wakeful, and had formed themselves in the various towns of England into political groups known as **corresponding societies**. Here were discussed the ideas unleashed by the French Revolution and given English expression by writers such as **Tom Paine** who wrote *The Rights of Man*. They espoused the ideals of **equality, brotherhood** and **freedom**, which would be achieved through political domination by the lower classes. The existing order of society should be upset. Perhaps reason would prevail to change it but violent action might have to be resorted to and should not be scrupled at.

Other political societies followed in the wake of the corresponding societies: the **Hampden Clubs** named after John Hampden who had defied Charles I on the question of ship money, which aimed at parliamentary reform, and small almost lunatic fringe groups like the **Spencean Philanthropists** who recounted the gospel of Thomas Spence (a Newcastle schoolmaster who had died in 1814). The Spenceans believed that land should be given to the people to cure 'the poor man's poverty and the rich man's gout'.

Newspapers existed too, such as the scurrilous *Black Dwarf* and the more respectable *Political Register*, to fan the growing political consciousness of the lower orders. These propagandised the revolutionary ideas which were given intellectual respectability by the middle-class orators; radicals such as William Cobbett and 'Orator' Hunt, who wrote for these journals and addressed audiences on the question of greater political power and freedom.

Lower-class disturbances 1815–30

Causes
In 1815 there had been much talk but, apart from the machine-breaking by the Luddites in 1812, not a great deal of action. Patriotism had prevented the lower orders from making a direct assault upon the government in time of war, and high wages and full employment had taken the edge off revolutionary fervour.

In 1815 they stood ready for action. The war had ended bringing **widespread unemployment**. Britain and her allies had no further need for the vast supplies of munitions and uniforms which had stretched the textile, iron and coal industries. Nor did she need a large army. Thus soldiers were added to the ranks of the unemployed. At the same time the price of food, and in particular bread, was high since the landed classes, anticipating a price collapse as a result of resumed imports of cheap continental corn, protected themselves with the **Corn Laws**. Another factor which contributed to distress was **high taxation**. England had had to maintain herself during the war and had had to subsidise her allies. The war had lasted for twenty-two years and the national debt stood at £860 million. The interest charges on this amounted to £35 million a year. Since direct taxation based on income was unacceptable to the landed class an elaborate system of indirect taxation was devised which amounted to purchase tax. Many essential items carried it. A contemporary complained how there are 'taxes upon every article which enters into the mouth or covers the back or is placed under the foot ... taxes on the sauce which pampers man's appetite and the drug which restores him to health; on the ermine which decorates the judge and the rope which hangs the criminal; on the poor man's salt and the rich man's spice; on the brass nails of a coffin and the ribands of the bride.' All these circumstances contributed to the desperate hardship which caused these years to be known as 'The **Years of Distress**' and which became a spur to violence. In addition the old Luddite resentments must be considered, since the process of mechanisation which had gained a galloping momentum during the war years continued in spite of the slump. The fall in prices and the decreased profit margins encouraged machinery, making the skilled handloom weavers and stockingers redundant.

Events

1816 was the year of highest unemployment and it was the year of the **Spa Fields Riot**. The disturbances occurred in December when Orator Hunt confronted a crowd which he had addressed a month earlier. He came to present a report on the fate of a petition which he had intended to present to the Prince Regent, outlining the demand of Londoners for radical reform: universal suffrage and a secret ballot featured in the petition. His attempts to present the petition had been unsuccessful and he intended to discuss the next move with the crowd. When he arrived he found the meeting attended by Spenceans full of revolutionary fervour and waving tricolours (the flag of revolutionary France). They suggested that the occasion was suitable for an attack upon the English 'Bastille', the **Tower of London**. Accordingly, a mob set off but was halted and the leaders arrested before they had proceeded far.

1817 witnessed two more episodes in what the government conceived as the march to revolution. The first event was the **Blanketeer March** from Manchester to London. Six to seven hundred weavers were to march in groups of ten, 'each man with a blanket on his back and a petition to the Prince Regent requesting aid for the cotton industry, on his arm'. The marchers were turned back by yeomanry on the way. Few got further than Derbyshire and only one marcher reached London. Thus the government's fear that the marchers would form a rallying point for disaffected members of the lower classes who would join them as they marched never materialised. Nor did the **Pentrich Revolution** which was to have taken place in the summer of 1817. Led by **Jeremiah Brandreth**, a stockinger, demonstrators intended to storm **Nottingham** and set up a provisional government. As with the Blanketeers the grievances of the Pentrich rebels were not political, although the act of rebellion against the government was. Brandreth understood by the term 'provisional government' not a temporary government but one which would literally supply provisions. He and his marchers wanted food, drink and entertainment as their reward and recruits were enticed with the promise: 'You will be kept on roast beef and ale while you are along with us.'

The attack was a fiasco. There were many desertions and the 'army' went into retreat when a party of hussars appeared.

Peterloo

1818 was a year of strikes rather than political demonstration but in 1819 the political remedy was once again being sought. Poor harvest and glut in the textile market provide the backcloth to the meeting which was arranged for 9 August in St Peter's Fields, Manchester. A crowd of some 60,000 came to hear Henry Hunt speak on parliamentary reform. The meeting was orderly and peaceful. Women and children attended, but when the arrest of Mr Hunt was being effected the yeomanry cavalry, inexperienced volunteers, panicked, sabreing the crowd. There were eleven deaths and many injuries. The event became known as Peterloo, a satirical reference to Wellington's glorious victory at Waterloo.

The last important incidents manifesting lower-class unrest were the **Cato Street Conspiracy** of **1820** and the **agricultural riots** of **1830** which are described in chapter 2. The Cato Street Conspiracy was a plot thought up by a leading Spencean **Arthur Thistlewood** who conceived it as an act of revenge for Peterloo.

'I resolved', he said, 'that the instigators of the massacre should atone for the souls of murdered innocents'. He planned to murder the Cabinet whilst at dinner, but the conspirators were discovered in the nick of time, armed and ready to undertake their deadly enterprise.

Reaction of the government

The government responded sternly to all these incidents. There were arrests after Spa Fields, the Blanketeers were turned back, four of the Pentrich rebels and the leaders of the Cato Street Conspiracy were executed. Members of the crowd at St Peter's Fields were sabred and Hunt arrested. The agricultural rebels also suffered. Execution and transportation were the punishments meted out to those thought to be the leaders.

The **Habeas Corpus Act** which guarded against imprisonment without trial was **suspended** in **1817** enabling the government to arrest suspected revolutionaries arbitrarily. A heavy **tax** was imposed upon cheap newspapers in an attempt to prevent the publication of pamphlets urging reform and in consequence the 'Political Register' closed. Limitations were placed upon political public meetings and magistrates were given the right of entry and search to premises considered likely hiding places for arms. These restrictions and others in a similar vein were outlined in six parliamentary acts, sometimes called the **Gag Acts** and passed in 1819.

All these innovations were designed to deter prospective rebels and to preclude the possibility of rebellion. Inflammatory ideas could no longer be disseminated at gatherings such as Spa and St Peter's Fields, nor was it easy to circulate them through news-papers. The protection of the law against arrest had been removed and heavy punishment meted out to those who actively opposed the government. Precautions had also been taken against the amassing of arms. Finally, an elaborate **spy network** acted as a check upon the disruptive capacities of prospective rebels. The Pentrich and Cato Street risings had both been frustrated on account of information passed to the government by informants who had infiltrated suspect organisations.

All these precautions may seem extravagantly elaborate in view of the ludicrous and often non-political nature of many of these demonstrations which seem to indicate lack of unity and effective organisation. We are, however, looking with hindsight and cannot enter into the tense and highly charged atmosphere of post-Napoleonic England. From the contemporary point of view the motive behind any demonstration was immaterial: a definite threat was presented to the established political and social order. It manifested itself physically at Spa Fields, Nottingham and Cato Street and it was implied in all the political writings and meetings where the need for political reform was urged. The French Revolution had shown after all what tolerance of this sort of behaviour and attitude would lead to. The mob could succeed in taking over government. That had happened in France and must be prevented here at all costs. What would be the sense in having fought a long war to ward off the imposition of revolutionary ideas from outside (for the aim of Napoleon's France was to spread the Revolution throughout Europe), only to allow revolution to be accomplished from within? Thus the government could not view these disturbances with our detachment. To them they did not appear as ludicrous, isolated, often pitiful episodes. They appeared as part of a coherent and unified plan to topple the government. Had Brandreth taken Nottingham, this would have been the signal for a general uprising. Had the Blanketeers reached London, what a following might they have acquired on the way. Or so the government argued. Rumour was rife and it fanned anxiety. The government heard of plans to burn Manchester, the fire to act as a rallying signal to the lower classes in the north-west. And it was unnerved by the leadership afforded to the workers by middle-class agitators like Hunt and Cobbett who gave the economic discontent of the lower orders a political coherence and intellectual respectability.

Thus one must be wary of representing the governors of England as reactionary ogres mindlessly defending an outdated political system. They feared the real possibility of mob rule and were frightened of what it would bring. No one could know how responsibly the Brandreths and Thistlewoods would rule, but fearful speculation was perhaps not unwarranted.

Conclusion

Thus England in 1815 was a nation in a state of transition and uncertainty. Many traditional ideas and values were being questioned, and enormous economic and social changes were taking place. Superficially its appearance was peaceful and tranquil, but underneath were uncertainty and turmoil.

Chapter 2
Rural Society, 1815–1939

The rural areas of Great Britain saw many changes during this period. Traditional social relationships altered, agricultural practice changed, but some aspects of rustic life remained untouched. There was little difference between the tempo and quality of the life lived by the agricultural labourer in 1815 and his counterpart in 1900. Photographs might show him unchanged even in appearance. Dressed in a smock or cords, he might be seen leaning against a pitchfork at either date. Thereafter of course changes were discernible.

Changing farming practice

The Napoleonic Wars had given great impetus to change to the whole concept of farming. The high prices commanded by agricultural goods had encouraged farmers to expand where they could and to resort to devices and practices which would increase production and lower costs. Thus the ideas which had gained currency in the eighteenth century such as **crop rotation**, **artificial fertiliser, drainage**, and in particular **enclosure**, were put into practice. Tracts of land hitherto uncultivated were brought under the plough and **animal husbandry** improved too. All these changes accelerated during the war years and our period begins with the countryside in the throes of change, though its nature and pace varied from area to area.

Enclosure
This was probably the most important change to take place. Between 1770 and 1850 some 6,000 million acres were enclosed, and although the bulk was over by 1815 it was not until 1875 that it might be judged complete. Most of the enclosure after 1830 was of moorland and down, the enclosure of the open field parishes having been completed by then.

The **advantages** of enclosure were mainly **economic**. Where cultivation had been formerly on the open field strip system it increased the size of the basic units for cultivation, facilitated the introduction of machinery and made improvements such as drainage more practical propositions. The **social significance** has been disputed. It was thought by many contemporaries and by early historians that the effect it had upon the lower orders was wholly deleterious. It was thought that the independence of the lowest strata of society, the 'peasants' who lived by grazing pigs, geese, and perhaps the odd cow upon common land, was ended as a direct result of enclosure since the principle that each man should be given a strip of land proportionate in size to the use he had made of the commons before enclosure was not always applied; the rich and influential receiving the best and largest share, sometimes by dint of bribery. Thus the picture was drawn by poets such as **Goldsmith** and contemporary commentators like **William Cobbett** and **Arthur Young** of an independent peasantry transformed into a class of drudges, degraded, downtrodden and destitute.

There is no doubt that the life of the nineteenth-century farmworker was hard, that he did live often on the verge of destitution, but the question is how far **enclosure** contributed to this state of affairs. Modern economic historians such as J. H. Clapham, and more recently J. D. Chambers and G. E. Mingay, say that the **population increase**, which was a rural as well as an urban phenomenon, and the operation of the **Speenhamland** system which contributed towards depressed wages, were the main contributors to poverty. They admit that enclosure sometimes affected the lower classes adversely since the pieces of land given in compensation for loss of commons rights were sometimes inconveniently sited or too small to be of use, and were soon sold, but they point out that many cottagers were without commons rights and therefore had nothing to lose by enclosure. They point out too that the proportion of paupers was as high in those counties least affected by enclosure, such as Kent and Sussex, as in the areas of new enclosure, Northamptonshire, Leicestershire, Rutland and Nottinghamshire. It is worth noting too that hardship and destitution were no new experience for the rural lower classes. They had always lived precariously, exposed to climatic whims which could destroy crops, create shortages and push up prices beyond their means. Enclosure seems not to have affected this time honoured pattern of existence. In fact it could ease the traditional hardship a little by creating employment. The actual process of enclosure, the erection of fences and digging of ditches, created work, and the increased production which followed enclosure increased the demand for labour too. Heavier crops meant more work in connection with harvesting, more animals reared meant an increase in the occupations associated with animal husbandry, such as bacon curing and tanning.

Another misapprehension which has arisen in connection with enclosure concerns the **small farmer**. It was said that the small farmer could not afford the expenses which enclosure involved: the payment of fees to the commissioners and the cost of erecting fences were beyond the means of such men who were squeezed out, causing the agricultural scene to be dominated by large-scale farmers. The solid English yeoman, the small independent freeholder, began to disappear. Modern historians dispute this view also. The **Census of 1851** reveals the great extent to which the small farmer survived enclosure, since two-thirds of the farms were found to be under 100 acres. Many farmers had in fact taken full advantage of the benefits afforded by enclosure and were able to do so especially during the war years 1793–1815 on account of the easy availability of credit and the practice of long-term repayment.

Why then have these two 'myths', that the lower classes were made destitute and dependent and the small farmer destroyed, gained credence? The answer must lie partly in human nature. People often dislike change mainly because it upsets a known routine or tradition. And enclosure undoubtedly had a great effect; **it transformed the appearance of the landscape**, introducing the patchwork of fields which we recognise today, and **it facilitated new practices in agriculture**, upsetting many of the old habits of rural existence. It was a new, dramatic and noticeable change, and it was easier to attribute prevalent social ills to it than to perceive them as parallel developments. Changes affecting conditions of rural life for the worse were taking place at the same time as enclosure but independently of it.

Drainage

Alongside enclosure, drainage must rank as one of the most significant contributors to the revolution in agriculture since it released new land and provided greater scope for the implementation of new farming techniques. Certainly it was an innovation which conscientious landlords thought desirable and in Mrs Gaskell's novel *Wives and Daughters*, Squire Hamley suffers loss of esteem at his inability to finish a drainage scheme. But the practice was slow to spread outside the fens, since the known systems were expensive and the principles not widely understood. **James Smith**, a Scotsman, increased public knowledge of the question when in 1831 he published *Remarks on Thorough Drainage and Deep Ploughing*, and urged a system whereby stone-filled trenches were laid underground. His work was well received and advertised but it did not overcome the problem of expense. Stones, readily available in Scotland, were scarce in the heavy clay areas where drainage was most needed and his process

28

was laborious. But in **1851** at the **Great Exhibition** great excitement was caused by **Fowler's drainage plough**, a device which could lay pipes easily. Pipes were cheaper by two-thirds than the flat-bottomed and arched tiles which had been widely used as an alternative to Smith's scheme. The cost of drainage was now reduced from about £12 to £4 an acre. This fact, allied to the government grant scheme inaugurated in 1846 whereby loans were made for the express purpose of drainage, encouraged improvement. Even so, a House of Lords select committee reporting on the improvement of land for agricultural purposes estimated that by the 1870s only 3 million acres of the 20 million needing drainage actually benefited from it. A great gap existed between needed and actual improvement. Why? Partly on account of the ignorance and apathy and traditionalism which were endemic in nineteenth-century British agriculture. Partly too on account of the system of land tenure which perhaps discouraged expensive innovation. Many farmers did not possess leases but rented their farms from year to year, nor was a tenant farmer entitled to compensation for any improvements he made until 1875, when the **Agricultural Holdings Act** was passed. Even then the landlord was free from obligation to compensate if the tenancy had commenced on the understanding that he would not do so. He was able to opt out in this way, until an **Act of 1883** made it illegal for him to do so.

Science and agriculture

The gradual change in the attitude towards land and productivity meant that earnest agriculturists were keen to ultilise any means beneficial to that end. Science was an obvious focus for their attention. Knowledge of soil composition helped the farmer to judge crop suitability, even elementary knowledge of geometry was useful in any surveying or levelling project, and acquaintance with the principles of hydraulics was of incalculable use in drainage and irrigation. Physics, chemistry, botany, these subjects too had an important place in the repertoire of farming knowledge. The importance of these subjects had always been urged by the **Royal Agricultural Society** which included scientific articles pertinent to agriculture in its own periodicals. Then in 1846 the first **Royal College** of Agriculture was founded at **Cirencester**. Its express aim was to combine a theoretical scientific education with practical knowledge. The importance of this development was that such knowledge was given wider scope. The Royal Agricultural Society had been well intentioned but its membership was comparatively small and comprised an educated elite who perhaps did not have much in common with the ordinary farmer. It is of course arguable whether many 'ordinary' farmers or their sons could avail themselves of the early agricultural colleges either, since £30 was required as an initial registration fee for a two-year course for which a charge of £30 a year was made. Sir James Caird, surveying the agricultural scene in 1850, noted that no sons of tenant farmers, the class he remarked for whom the college had been intended, were students at the college when he visited it. Nevertheless, a start had been made and knowledge was beginning to fan out, even if only gradually.

Crop rotation

The principle of crop rotation was a scientific principle which had been long understood. **Lord Townsend** had reintroduced the practice into Norfolk in the eighteenth century and had set the fashion for it. The traditional system of cultivation had been to raise two crops on a piece of land and then to let it lie fallow for a year to avoid soil exhaustion. But agricultural theorists argued that soil exhaustion would be prevented and productivity increased if cereal and fodder crops were alternated. Thus on a field being rotated in the classical manner, a farmer would raise perhaps wheat, turnips, barley and clover. At the end of four years the cycle would be repeated. The system, known as the **Norfolk System**, had advantages beyond the obvious one of avoiding an unproductive year. The high nitrogenous content of the grasses, clover, lucerne, sainfoin and trefoil increased soil fertility. As for the turnips, swedes or mangel wurzels, they derived nourishment from a different stratum of the soil from the other crops and so in a way did not displace the old idea that it was good to rest the soil from time to time. Another obvious advantage of the fodder crops lay in the contribution which they made to animal husbandry which could now be practised on a much larger scale. But in spite of these advantages the spread of this new system of crop rotation was slow and uneven. In districts such as the Midlands where heavy clay predominated and where drainage was a problem, the new roots and grasses were not suitable and the traditional system of two crops did not begin to gain ascendancy in these areas until drainage was accomplished.

Fertilisers

The eighteenth century saw some interesting developments where fertilisers were concerned, and to the ordinary farm manure and bone dust already used was added **guano** (bird droppings) and **superphosphate**. Both were introduced in the

1840s, and by 1846 guano was being imported at the rate of 300,000 tons a year. Extravagant claims were made for it. Lord George Bentinck claimed that from 100,000 tons of guano nearly 100 million pounds of mutton could be produced, so greatly did it enrich the soil. Even so, many farmers were ignorant or careless of the benefits of fertiliser. Sir James Caird remarked on the amount of 'antiquated farming' which he saw in his travels in 1850. Even farmyard manure was regarded as a mere nuisance in many areas and fertiliser was generally applied only in Northumberland, Lincolnshire and Norfolk.

Machinery

The theme of indifference or of resistance to innovation and change continues in this account of the spread of machinery in agriculture. Many new implements had been contrived by 1815, such as the **Rotherham plough**, the main feature of which was a curved mouldboard in place of the straight board which had been prevalent. The advantage consisted in the smallness and lightness. Few draught animals were needed to draw it and the superior metal cutting edge meant that heavy soils could be ploughed with ease. Nevertheless the old-fashioned wooden plough was in frequent use as late as 1850. **Seed drills** too had been invented in the eighteenth century, and **horse hoes**. The benefit of these machines were obvious. The old method of sowing seeds, casting them from side to side as one walked down a field, was wasteful. The seed was easy prey for the birds and the wind. The drill injected seed into the earth in rows, whilst the hoe helped the farmer to keep weeds at bay. Even so, the broadcast method remained in use since the drill and hoe were operable only in well-drained and easily cultivated soils. The harvesting of crops was assisted by mid-century by the **reaper**. The principles upon which such a machine would work had been established as early as 1812, but reapers did not come into commercial use until the famous **McCormick steam prototype** was shown at the **Great Exhibition**. Its advantages were so numerous that it was widely adopted in some areas. It minimised grain loss and maximised straw production and above all recommended itself to farmers on account of its speed, which released them to some extent from anxiety about the weather. **Threshing machines** too were well established by mid-century and were much favoured by farmers on account of the laboriousness and therefore expensiveness of the ancient biblical system of flailing the grain with sticks and winnowing it (i.e. separating the grain from the chaff) by throwing it into the air. Sir James Caird calculated a saving of 75 per cent at least when he observed a Mr Thomas of Lidlington in Bedfordshire threshing his wheat for 1*d*. a bushel. 'We found other farmers paying four or five times as much for the same operation not so well done by hand.'

Machinery spread also to the dairy industry and was used in connection both with milking and butter-making by the 1870s, a development which upset some romantic observers who mourned the loss of the picturesque milkmaid.

> 'So Dolly thou to fate must bow
> And our regret grows keener
> As thy poetic figure joins
> The thresher and the gleaner
> Acadia is again bereft
> And bands in sorrow mutter
> There's nothing now idyllic left
> Connected with our butter.'

But of course there was. Though many farmers espoused the new machines enthusiastically, as is indicated by a contemporary estimate that between 1846 and 1863 many thousands of steam engines were purchased for agricultural use, many farmers eschewed them and were proud to continue old practices. John Grout, a Suffolk farmer who recalls his life on the land in Ronald Blythe's book *Akenfield*, remembers the harvest being reaped by hand. 'You could count thirty mowers in the same field, each followed by his partner who did the sheaving', and Flora Thompson in her book *Lark Rise to Candleford*, describing rural Oxfordshire at the turn of the century, recalls bevies of farmworkers mowing the hay by hand. Photographic evidence confirms this kind of recollection.

Why was machinery opposed? Mainly it would seem on account of expense. Capital was needed for this initial outlay, but we have seen that farming in Great Britain was on the whole conducted on a small scale. (The estates running into the thousands of acres of the great aristocracy and gentry must not be overlooked however, and it was they of course who often initiated trends and improvements in farming.) Also labour was cheap. Traditionalism too provides an explanation. The countryside always responds sluggishly to change and in the nineteenth century the attitude of those who were well established on the land was complex. It was not merely a means of livelihood. It was a mark of status, and a means of defining social relationships. Land was not regarded in a purely commercial light. The main aim of those who cultivated it was not necessarily the maximisation of profit, and it is worth remarking that many of the most notable innovators were new to farming. John Joseph Melchi for instance, whose estate at Tiptree in Essex was famous, was a businessman who turned to agriculture having made his fortune from razor blades. He applied the principles which had made him successful in business to farming, writing his formula for success in a pamphlet entitled *How to Farm Profitably*. The land had no mystique for him, and since his origins lay elsewhere he could regard farming as a purely commercial enterprise.

Developments affecting agriculture

The kind of attitude evinced by Melchi however was being taken up by many of those farmers who had in the past been content to emphasise the social rather than the economic aspects of their landowning role. Events which took place from the end of the eighteenth century made it impossible for them to remain financially casual.

The Napoleonic Wars and the population increase

Both factors were especially formative in changing attitudes, since both events revealed the scope for economic enterprise on the land. Population increase meant a heavy demand for agricultural products. The Napoleonic Wars reduced outside competition, and secured for British agriculturists a virtually captive market. Prices were high (wheat reached 126s. a quarter during the war) and every incentive to expand existed. Another important event in the history of agriculture was the **repeal of the Corn Laws in 1846** which ended the protection which had kept corn at an artificially high price, cushioning farmers against economic reality. Imports of foreign corn were only allowed upon payment of duty, the amount depending upon the price English corn could command. If a high price, such as 73s. a quarter, was achieved then the duty was slight at 1s., but if the price was low, say 64s., the duty payable was 25s. 8d. This **sliding scale** of duty had been brought in in 1828 after it was apparent that the original Corn Law passed in 1815, forbidding foreign imports until English corn reached 80s., was unrealistic. But like its predecessor, the 1828 law aroused strong opposition from those who believed in the principle of free trade and from those who disliked the suffering caused by dear bread, and the **Anti-Corn Law League** was founded to achieve its destruction. The effect of repeal was crucial in changing attitudes since it threw the British farmer into a fierce competitive world. He had to increase efficiency, reduce costs and maximise profits if he was to make an adequate living. And so the concept of **high farming** was introduced.

High farming

Basically, the term 'high farming' describes merely the more commercial practice of farming which prevailed from the 1840s till 1870. The farm was looked upon as an investment which must yield profit. The emphasis was upon efficiency, and such farmers seized readily upon whatever mechanical devices or scientific principles would increase production. Sir James Caird explained what was entailed in high farming when he declared that the farmer's business 'is to grow the heaviest crops of the most remunerative kind his soil can be made to carry ... the better he farms the more capable his land becomes of growing the higher qualities of grain; of supporting the most valuable breeds of stock and of being readily adapted to the growth of any kind of agricultural produce, which railway facilities or increasing population may render most remunerative. In this country the agricultural improver cannot stand still. If he tries to do so, he will soon fall into the list of obsolete men, being passed by eager competitors willing to seize the current of events and turn them to their advantage.' **The Great Depression** which set in during the 1870s also had an important effect upon agricultural practices, reducing as it did the importance of farming as an industry. Between 1871 and 1901 the agricultural labour force decreased by 300,000 and the area of grain cultivation declined by 3 million acres. Land which had been reclaimed fell back into disuse. Farm buildings decayed. Many farmers and labourers emigrated. The whole pattern of farming changed. Since the Depression had been caused by cheap grain imports from America coinciding with a series of bad harvests, the trend turned away from corn production into pasture and fruit farming. Between 1870 and 1900 land under pasture increased by over 4 million acres. The land involved in fruit farming increased too; by 26,696 acres between 1872 and 1882.

The railways

These also left their mark upon the agricultural scene, increasing the viability of dairy farming and also the raising of animals for slaughter. Quick distribution opened up new markets for milk and eggs in the towns and it was remarked that 'by 1850 when the rail had got through to Norfolk the 28lbs by which a bullock fell in weight on the march from Castle Acre, a waste entirely lost to everybody, was saved!' The old system of driving animals across the countryside was now obsolete.

First World War

War, especially on the scale of 1914–18, was bound to make a significant impact upon British agriculture. As had been the case during the period 1793–1815, there was a desperate need for increased production, particularly of foodstuffs, the shortage of which was exacerbated after 1916 when U-boats began to take a heavy toll of merchant shipping. The **Corn Production Act** of 1917 was therefore intended to reverse the continuing trend towards pasture. The Act empowered the Board of Agriculture to enforce the ploughing up of pasture and the revival of arable farming. In return, farmers were guaranteed a minimum price for corn. The effect of the Act was shortlived, however, for in 1921 the **Agriculture Act** which had superseded the Corn Production Act, extending its provisions considerably to cover labour relations and land tenure agreements, was repealed. The newly revived arable lands reverted again to pasture and the agricultural depression was resumed. It lasted until the outbreak of the Second World War.

Agriculture in the twentieth century

The intervention of the war years, though ineffectual, is important because indicative of the growing assumption of responsibility by governments. Acts of intervention had occurred in nineteenth-century agriculture; the passing and repeal of the Corn Laws are cases in point. But government intervention was looked upon as an extraordinary event. It was not thought to be the proper province of governments to concern themselves with the organisational problems of an industry or occupation, nor with the personal relationships within it.

Farmers had been glad of government help where the regulation of prices was concerned, and also where public order was affected, but interference in other matters threatened basic concepts of liberty. Liberty left a man to do with his own as he wished and forced him to do nothing against his will. By the twentieth century this view had to be tempered and amended. Society had become far too complex and the social ramifications of any large economic enterprise far too wide for governments to practise *laissez faire*. This was true of industry and to a lesser extent it was true of agriculture, and some far-reaching reforms in agriculture took place in the twentieth century.

The **Agriculture Act** has already been mentioned but not the provisions which righted the imbalance in the relationship between landlord and tenant, which so inhibited land improvement. Outgoing tenants now had the right to harvest crops planted before the expiry of their tenancy and had to have at least twelve months' notice.

The establishment of **district wages boards** constituted another important social reform. These boards, another wartime innovation, regulated hours of work and laid down a minimum wage. Their efficacy, however, depended very much upon the general economic climate. They achieved success when the climate was propitious and agriculture flourished, but wages fell sharply in spite of their recommendations after 1921. By the end of the year labourers were getting 27s. 6d. where only months earlier they had been ambitious of 50s. and likely to get it. But by the end of the year slump had set in and it was clear that no organisation was in a position to dictate wages.

What of **prices**? The maintenance of prices was time-honoured government policy, and the government did what it could to protect and to aid agriculture.

The **1917 Corn Production Act** was one example of government intervention on behalf of British farming. The **1932 Wheat Act** which imposed a levy on all foreign wheat and guaranteed a fixed price was another. But these new Corn Laws had no better effect than the old (1815). Like them, they kept the price of bread artificially high and they had a stultifying rather than energising effect. One very welcome innovation which did positively benefit agriculture however was the establishment in the 1930s of **marketing boards** specialising in the distribution of particular products such as eggs, potatoes, bacon and milk. These boards established qualitative standards and recommended prices, establishing uniformity in both these areas. They also relieved the farmer of the perennial headache of glut in one area and scarcity in another. The volatile price system resulting from this pattern prevented the farmer from having any very certain idea of his cash expectations. And from the national point of view reform was beneficial in avoiding waste.

Relationship between town and country

Another very important development in the twentieth century was the blending of town and country. Throughout history the two ways of life had continued separately and there was little cross-reference. That this is so is illustrated by the recurring theme in drama and in real life of the country bumpkin being outsmarted by town tricksters able to play upon his rustic ignorance. The advent of the railways had closed the gap between town and country to some extent and in *Lark Rise to Candleford*, for instance, one sees the social influences of the town being felt by the end of the century.

But in the twentieth century one saw a new phenomenon in the positive desire on the part of the town dweller to get to know the countryside. The **Ramblers' Association** was established and organised cheap excursions in collaboration with the Metropolitan Railway, and in 1930 the **Youth Hostel Association** was founded, the first hostel being opened at Pennant Hill in North Wales. The increase in numbers of private motors – by 1939 there were over 2 million – also contributed to the invasion of the countryside.

The reason behind this desire for rustic escape lies in the increased leisure available, but some saw it as a reflection of a general state of disillusionment with urban and industrial life. **G. M. Trevelyan**, founder president of the Youth Hostel Association, thought that contact with the countryside enabled people to cope with their confused and disorientated sensibilities. He explained how in the past the 'presence of nature reconciled man to his life. The modern Englishman though he is taught more in school and reads and hears more than his forefathers, lacks something which they had in ages past. The physiological ailments of our time and our discontent and failure to accept and enjoy life are largely due to this sudden imprisonment of our population in cities far from natural sights and sounds.' This nostalgic and romantic view of the countryside and of rustic life recurs frequently throughout the nineteenth and twentieth centuries. Poets, painters and photographers depicted idyllic scenes of picturesque cottages and imprinted an image of tranquillity and peace. Field workers mused gently in the noonday sun. Women in their Sunday best smilingly raked the hay.

Was it a false image? Dorothea, the ardent heroine of George Eliot's novel *Middlemarch*, set in the 1830s, thought it was and energetically rejected it. 'Think of Kit Downes' uncle, who lives with his wife and seven children in a house with a sitting room and a bedroom hardly larger than the table, and those poor Dagleys in their tumbledown house where they live in the back kitchen and leave the other room to the rats. That is one reason why I do not like the pictures here, dear uncle, which you think me so stupid about. I used to come home with all that coarse ugliness like a pain within me, and the simpering pictures in the drawing room seemed like a wicked attempt to find delight in what is false.' How false we shall see. But let us turn first to consider the composition and organisation of agricultural labour.

Rural life

The labour force

There were many sorts of workpeople employed on the land, the 'aristocrats' such as the ploughmen, shepherds and wheelwrights, men with a particular skill and able to take on a specific responsibility, and the main body of mere labourers: men, women and children who often offered themselves for employment on a casual basis at times of seasonal necessity, such as harvesting, shearing, threshing, etc. Sometimes they travelled from a distance in droves, coming perhaps from Dorset or Somerset to the Isle of Wight to help with the harvest or from London to the hopfields of Kent. These traditional and seasonal **migrations** were one means of recruiting labour. Another source was the **agricultural gang** which was particularly prevalent in the Midlands and East Anglia. A gang comprised a troop of field workers, men, women and children, under the leadership of a **gang master** who would negotiate terms of employment with a farmer on their behalf. They worked for a pittance and were an attractive proposition for the farmer because he had no responsibility for them. He need provide no accommodation, since they slept in barns or in the open, and could employ them just as he needed them. Obviously the gang system was open to abuse particularly where the women and children were concerned, and in **1868** an act was brought in to regulate it. The **Gangs Act** made the employment of children under eight illegal, stipulated that women should be employed only if a licensed gang mistress was present, and required gang masters to be licensed.

Life was hard for all agricultural labourers. They had few rights, though obviously the labourer who hired himself at a **fair** had some security in so far as he had his employment for a year until the next hiring and certain rights as to food, shelter and a wage enshrined in a contract and sealed by the offer and acceptance of what was called **God's penny**, a sum of money (the amount varied, originally it had been a penny) traditionally preferred by the farmer once terms had been agreed. The casual labourer, however, had no such assurances. A sensible and farsighted farmer might provide him with a house, an allotment, free milk, cheap coal and a quota of free beer, but many did not and it was common practice to lay off labour during wet weather, at a time when no unemployment benefit existed. The village friendly society, if he belonged to it, could cushion the labourer against this hardship, as also the extra earnings brought in at harvest, haymaking or threshing. If he was provident and put them by, these could help his survival, but even so poverty was a very real experience and whilst historians are prone to disagree violently on the question of urban poverty, they concur in their acceptance of its rural counterpart centring debates on its causes not its factual existence. Even so it is difficult to establish a uniform picture since so many differentials exist. Regional variations in wages, in the quality of houses, the number and ages of children, fluctuations in prices and the cost of living, changes in agricultural practice, all these were factors which affected the material conditions of the rural lower classes.

Wages

Wages had risen substantially during the Napoleonic Wars, rising from 7s. to 8s. a week to 15s. and even 18s. in some places, but then the cost of living had increased too. The price of corn (which governed the price of bread) regularly reached 90s. a quarter, whereas 40s. had been regarded as a good price before the war. After 1815 wages settled at between 10s. and 12s., but thereafter fell steadily. It will be remembered that the Tolpuddle labourers who in 1833 joined Robert Owen's union were prompted to do so because their wages had been reduced to 7s. In the 1850s 9s. was the average in the southern counties, but even at the end of the century in rural Oxfordshire Flora Thompson reckoned a labourer's wage was 10s., a figure which Leonard Thompson, a Suffolk labourer, confirmed for his area. By 1907 wages were up to 12s. and even 14s. in some parts of Oxfordshire and 14s. to 15s. elsewhere, but the cost of living had risen by 10 per cent since 1897 as against a wage rise of only 3 per cent. These figures are a fairly accurate reflection of the state of affairs throughout the period and economic historians are agreed that though it is impossible to be precise about the relationship between wages and the cost of living, it would be broadly true to say that the agricultural labourer never achieved a wage commensurate with the increase in the cost of living. Wages always lagged behind.

Wages were of course lowest in the southern and eastern

counties. In the industrial north and Midlands they were higher perhaps even by as much as 30 per cent, since farmers had to compete with the factories for labour.

Supplements to income

Economic hardship was sometimes tempered by traditional rights such as gleaning, largesse (a bonus paid to labourers when the harvest was in) and free beer (sometimes as much as twenty-six pints a day!), which Richard Jeffries, a Wiltshire farmer in the mid-nineteenth century, said could cost the farmer £50–£60 a year for all his labourers. Flora Thompson tells of the tradition whereby labouring families received a side of beef every Christmas. In addition to these traditional gifts the labourer could often rely on his cottage garden or allotment, although a rent was charged. (It was £4 a year in Wiltshire during the 1860s.) An allotment was reckoned by the Poor Law Commissioners to be worth about 4s. a week. On the other hand it should be remarked that many farmers opposed the allotment schemes because they felt that the cultivation of them drained the labourer of energy which could be put to better use on the farm, and they were not universal. They are not mentioned in Akenfield in Suffolk, for instance, though Flora Thompson remembers them in Lark Rise, Oxfordshire and emphasises their importance to the domestic economy of the labouring classes.

The **tied** or **farm cottage** too must be taken into any account of rural lower-class economy for often these were supplied at a very nominal rent. One shilling a week was typical in mid-century Wiltshire, although Richard Jeffries contends that an economic rent from the farmer's point of view was nearer 4s. They were not universally provided however, and some farmers as payers of the poor rate were anxious to have their workers living outside the parish rather than on the farm. Flora Thompson reminds us, too, how ambivalent a benefit the tied cottage was, and says that in Lark Rise it was not liked simply because it was 'tied' and occupation of it circumscribed the freedom of the labourer.

Keeping a pig was also regarded as a sensible means to more comfortable survival and great importance was attached to the pig in Lark Rise. The whole hamlet contributed to its maintenance in expectation of reward at killing time. In some areas, however, the problem of feeding it was considered to outweigh the advantage of having it at last to eat.

The **most decisive factor** in the fight which the rural labourer waged against poverty was the **size of his family** and its capacity for work. Both women and children were in demand upon the land. Hay-making, reaping and stone-picking were the most common occupations, for which they earned $\frac{1}{3}-\frac{1}{2}$ of the wages paid to the men. The wages paid to children depended on their age and capability and the availability of child labour did not decrease noticeably after the education acts. The report kept by successive school-mistresses in Akenfield from 1870 when the board school was established testifies to this. High absenteeism, sometimes as high as 50 per cent, provides a constant lament. Leonard Thompson, who was a boy in Akenfield at the end of the nineteenth century, describes too how 'the farmers came and took the boys away ... when they felt like it'. Nor could parents ask them to desist. In Leonard Thompson's family the ability of his two elder brothers to work increased the family income by 100 per cent, bringing it to £1 a week on which to keep nine people. Two economic historians Chambers and Mingay bear out this percentile estimate for an earlier period. 'Some figures for labouring families in the North and South for 1839, show that a family with four children over the age of ten earned altogether twice as much as a single man.'

In spite of all these contrivances to boost income, in some southern parishes in the mid-nineteenth century every single labourer's family was drawing upon the poor rate.

Domestic life

Housing
A great deal of debate centres on the quality of housing and the degree of domestic comfort enjoyed by the rural lower classes. Rural slums undoubtedly existed. The agricultural labourers during their rising in 1830 specified poor housing as one of their grievances. **Edwin Chadwick** making his report on *The Sanitary Conditions of the Labouring Population* in 1842 described 'earth floors, no drainage, houses built below road level and therefore, liable to floods. Single rooms to house entire families. Houses without windows and fireplaces.' In Somerset he found barracks in which each family was apportioned a room, most of which had no private access.

William Cobbett too had been horrified by what he had found in his journey across the country in 1830. 'Look at those hovels of mud and straw; bits of glass or of old cast off windows without frames or hinges frequently but merely stuck in the mud wall. Enter them and look at the bits of chairs or stools the wretched boards tacked together to serve for a table, the floor of pebble, broken brick or of the bare ground. Look at the thing called a bed and survey the rags on the backs of the wretched inhabitants.' Leonard Thompson too leaves us with a stark impression. He describes his own home as a child as 'a cottage empty except for people' comprising a living room, larder and two bedrooms. Nine people lived there. There was a scrubbed brick floor and just one rug made from scraps of old clothes pegged on to a sack. There was no oven in the house and no water. 'All had to be fetched from the foot of a hill nearly a mile away.' Some rural communities were more fortunate and water was brought round in a horse-drawn container.

These were the worst sort of conditions and Richard Jeffries was inclined to think them exaggerated. He dismissed the sort of hovel which Cobbett had described as the abode of the squatter not the bona fide labourer and he challenged his readers to find in Wiltshire 'a single bad cottage on any large estate, so well and thoroughly have the landed proprietors done their work'. The typical cottage he described as having three bedrooms 'and every appliance and comfort compatible with their small size'. Other commentators commended the cottages being erected by model landlords such as the Duke of Bedford. It is worth noting too that Flora Thompson leaves us with a warm and comfortable impression of cottage interiors. Polished brass, rag rugs and unpretentious but well-scrubbed furniture and above all a fire in the grate, feature in her descriptions.

Domestic economy
The diet of the agricultural labourer's family was monotonous and scanty throughout the period. **Suet**, **bacon**, **bread** and **cheese** were the **staple foods**, though those who cultivated allotments would supplement them with cabbages, onions and potatoes in particular. Amounts were meagre and it was difficult to make do. Flora Thompson tells of mothers foregoing food to feed growing children. Every effort was made to provide the men with a sufficiency since the family depended upon their capacity for work, but even they were malnourished. Sir James Caird, surveying British agriculture in the 1850s, remarked on this and on the resulting lassitude of the Wiltshire labourers he saw. 'Their appearance showed ... a want of vigour and activity', which he put down to 'meagre diet'.

Flora Thompson says that in Lark Rise 'nobody starved' but in other areas where perhaps the women were not so adept at household economy or where there was no allotment or cottage garden to eke out basic supplies or where perhaps there were too many children too young to earn, they did. The district nurse in Akenfield recalled the collapse of a young mother – 'I knew perfectly well what the trouble was; she was hungry ... we brought her some ordinary good food. That was all the medicine she needed.' Emily Legget, another elderly villager, recalls how when she was a child 'Nobody could get enough to eat no matter how they tried.'

It is a matter not merely of anecdotal recollection but of statistical fact that many labouring families were living below subsistence level at the turn of the century. Two surveys, one covering a Bedfordshire village and another the Wiltshire village of Corsley, concluded that one-third of the populace lived below the 'poverty line', the level laid down by Joseph Rowntree in his pioneer survey of York below which life could not be adequately maintained. Miss Davies who examined Corsley supplies a specimen budget of a labouring family consisting of a couple and their seven children during one week in 1906. Two points are worth noting before it is regarded in detail. The first is that the items are more varied and exotic than would have been the case fifty years earlier. Oranges, processed oats and oil would have been absent, otherwise purchases would have been similar. The other point concerns amounts. One must bear in mind that these purchases were meant to sustain nine human beings.

The budget

½lb. tea 8*d*., 3lb. sugar 5½*d*., 1½lb. butter, bacon 1*s*. 4*d*., Quaker oats 5½*d*., 2 oz. tobacco 6*d*., cheese 9*d*., ½lb. lard, ¼lb. suet 2*d*., baking powder 1*d*., papers 2*d*., 1lb. soap 3*d*., baking powder 2*d*., ½lb. currants 1½*d*., 1 pint of beer 2*d*., coal 1*s*. 2½*d*., loaf 2¼*d*., milk 6½*d*., butter 4*d*., sugar 2¼*d*., oil 2½*d*., stockings 6½*d*., bread bill 3*s*. Total: 13*s*. 4¾*d*.

Other aspects of household management such as the supply of clothing and warmth also posed problems. In respect of clothing, charity seems to have had an important part to play. Anthony Trollope depicts Lord Brotherton's sisters making calico shifts for the local tenantry in his novel *Is he Popenjoy?* and Flora Thompson in her real-life account recalls the charitable offices of the rector's daughter and of Mrs Bracewell the squire's mother

She remembers too the importance of the clothing parcels sent by the girls in 'service' to their families and the **baby box** upon which the mothers of Lark Rise could depend for the first weeks of a baby's life. The box supplied by the rectory contained a complete layette. Marjorie Jope, the district nurse in Akenfield, remembers that a committee existed there in the early years of the century to provide clothes for small children, but Leonard Thompson remembers boys at school with nothing under their top clothes, and Fred Mitchell, a fellow villager, explained that a choice had to be made, 'food or clothes', and that clothes were a secondary consideration to his mind. Certainly many period photographs show children in particular having to 'make do' wearing adult clothes hitched up or boys of quite advanced age in their sisters' frocks.

Conclusion

No one can deny then that the life of the English labourer was hard. He lived throughout the period poised on the edge of destitution. His wages lagged behind the increase in the cost of living and he had little protection against the exigencies of the weather and the changing economic scene. Both could put him out of work and leave him unprovided for. The workhouse, the friendly society and the compassion of his employer were his only aids in the event of misfortune. But he was lucky in so far as he had these. The compassion of his employer was a variable in his life. But joining the friendly society was his own insurance against misfortune, and the workhouse, though much vilified, did stand between him and starvation. Sir James Clapham in his *Economic History of Britain* points out that widespread starvation of peasants in Silesia and in parts of France did take place during this period and remarks that there is no comparable incident in British history.

Self-help

The labouring classes did not lie prone under the great weight of their poverty and distress. They may have left Sir James Caird with an impression of lassitude and inertia but, in fact, the British labourer was prepared to test several remedies.

The Swing riots

Violent insurrection was one obvious response and in the summer of 1830 uprisings took place in the southern and western counties of England. The riots began in Kent. There was no organised leadership, but the labourers adopted 'Captain Swing' as the *persona* who issued challenges and threats to the local magistrates and landlords on their behalf.

Main grievances

The demands are revealing. Increased wages were asked for and the labourers were anxious to secure a guaranteed 2s. a day and no lay-offs in the event of bad weather. Objections were also raised to the **threshing machine** which though common in the north was only just beginning to gain a hold upon the south. The rioters were anxious to prevent its advance. A man could earn 15s. to 20s. a week during the winter by threshing and 'need never require poor relief' claimed one Kentish landowner, which explains why the machines were destroyed *en masse*. Housing and in particular the practice by farmers of closing parishes as a result of enclosure or as an expedient to avoid the poor rate also provided grounds for complaint since closure meant that the labourer was forced to live at a distance from his work. The operation of the game and poor laws also came in for criticism. The penalties for poaching had by this time become very severe and were frequently enforced.

Outcome of the revolt

The revolt met with little resistance at first but gradually the confidence of the magistracy grew and with the help of troops the rising was suppressed. By December it was over and the price paid. Six men had been executed, 400 transported and 400 imprisoned at home.

Trade unionism

The attempt by agricultural labourers to solve their problems through trade unionism also failed. The dramatic case of the **Tolpuddle Martyrs**, the Dorset labourers who in 1834 tried to form a branch of Robert Owen's National Union and were transported, is famous. Since the implications of the case touched all working men, the agricultural labourers were not alone in facing this setback to their hopes. They were alone however when in 1874 their next attempt at trade unionism failed since trade unionism elsewhere was rapidly gaining strength.

Joseph Arch and the National Agricultural Labourers' Union

The first national agricultural union was founded in 1872 by Joseph Arch, a Warwickshire hedge layer, and it was designed to co-ordinate the small local branches of labourers' unions which were springing up throughout the country. The union was based on the **New Models** and combined the function of trade union and friendly society. The **aims** were broad: 'To raise wages, shorten the hours and make a man out of a land-tied slave.' The political franchise and land for labourers also emerged as objectives. The union's following was large and by **1874**, the high point, membership stood at **150,000** and some improvement in wages had been achieved; 12s. had been conceded by employers in several areas. But there were ominous signs that success would be shortlived and by the summer of 1874, farmers in the eastern counties had established **a lockout** of some 6,000 union members, employing blackleg labour in their place.

The strike pay needed to maintain the labourers placed an impossible strain upon the union and the voluntary contributions by well-wishers were insufficient. In any case the labourers themselves began to break ranks and to drift back to work. Those who remained out were advised by the union to capitulate.

The **decline** of agricultural unionism was swift. By **1877** membership had fallen to **55,000**. The **reason** for this failure must be found in the economic climate. There had been bad harvests during 1872–73 and farmers felt they could not afford better wages and conditions for the agricultural labourer. By the mid-1870s it was clear that the whole industry was in a state of slump. Men were being turned off the land at a fast rate. There were more seeking jobs than jobs existing to be filled. This was not a climate in which unionism could thrive, though it did revive in the agricultural sector in 1906 when **George Edwards**, an East Anglian farm worker, established a new union, the **National Union of Agricultural Workers**. The Transport and General Workers Union also founded an agricultural section in the early years of the twentieth century and some advance was made towards the establishment of a minimum wage.

Emigration
Many workers however did not wait to see the revival of their hopes for better conditions on the land. Disillusioned, they had emigrated, helped by union funds before the union collapsed and thereafter on their own initiative, feeling that the nation had nothing to offer. Indeed, by 1850 the economic balance had swung away from agriculture to industry, and agriculture had less and less to offer in the way of prospects. The advance of mechanisation which reduced the need for labour was slow but

inexorable. The amount of land under cultivation declined and towns encroached steadily upon the countryside. By 1901 only 12 per cent of the adult male labour force was engaged in agriculture as against 25 per cent in 1850. By 1939 the percentage had dropped to 6 per cent. Propagandists portrayed a melancholy picture of a labourer's family, thin, wan, pale, dejected and bowed, and contrasted it with the same family removed to Canada, now stalwart, robust and smiling. Emigration societies existed too throughout the nineteenth century, often attached to village friendly societies, their purpose to provide prospective emigrants with accurate information on life abroad. Information was based on the experiences of former members who had emigrated and established a new way of life, much better they thought than the old.

Chapter 3
The Poor

Attitudes towards the poor

The maxim 'the poor are always with us' is a famous one. The problem of the poor is one which every society in every period has had to contend with, but it was a problem particularly to the forefront of nineteenth-century consciousness because the particular moral, economic and social developments of the period gave it a peculiar character. Not only was it numerically a larger problem than it had ever been before, it also aroused a great deal of moral concern, though that was centred not on the question of whether society could accept the idea of poverty but on how individuals themselves should avoid it. This idea of individual responsibility and the moral challenge inherent in it is so alien to our thinking that the historian must make a more particular effort than usual to understand a very different scale of values, which were influenced very much by the religious ideas of the period.

Poverty and religion
Firstly it must be understood that many religiously minded people of the day accepted society as it stood. 'The rich man in his castle, the poor man at his gate: God made them high and lowly and ordered their estate.' This is a verse of a famous Victorian hymn, and it explains a great deal. God had created the world, and all its seeming imperfections and inequalities had a rationality. God had made them and they served some kind of purpose in His overall plan for mankind. Each station in life presented some kind of challenge. It was the duty of each Christian to rise to the challenge and to succeed in the role God had given him.

Poverty was also a means through which Christian charity and compassion could be displayed. All Christians are members of the same family, therefore each has a duty to help the other. Thus poverty's worst discomforts could be eased through charitable works.

The idea of poverty was therefore perfectly acceptable on one plane of religious thought. On another level of thinking it became less so, but the responsibility for ending it was laid largely at the door of the poor themselves.

Evangelicalism

In the eighteenth century great changes had taken place in religion. There had been a great religious revival and Methodism and Evangelicalism became very influential. Both Methodists and Evangelicals were dominated by the idea of man's sinfulness. Adam had sinned against God in the Garden of Eden and succeeding generations of mankind inherited the taint of this **original sin**. Thus man had to strive hard against the evil tendencies in his nature which might deny him a place in heaven. He was helped in his struggle by God's grace, but grace was not automatically given. It had to be earned. A man must demonstrate his worthiness of it. Hard work, thrift, diligence, sobriety and self-discipline were virtues pleasing to God and therefore likely to incline him to mercy. Idleness, extravagance, laziness and drunkenness were sins to be avoided at all costs.

The practice of 'evangelical' virtues very often brought economic prosperity and social success which were regarded as signs of God's approval and manifestations of His grace. The next step was to regard the unsuccessful as deficient in virtue and therefore responsible themselves for their predicament. Had they worked hard, had they been thrifty with their resources, had they too practised self-restraint, they too could be prosperous. But on account of moral weakness, they had not striven against sin. They preferred idleness to work. They wasted what little they had on drink and exacerbated their poverty by a lack of sexual self-restraint which burdened them with children.

Thus religion contributed two important ideas to the question of the poor. The first that they were part of God's plan, thus that society as a whole had no responsibility for them, and the second that the remedy lay within the bounds of individual endeavour. The individual could go far in preventing poverty for himself and the individuals dispensing charity could do much to help the pauper alleviate his want, though in the latter case great care must be taken to prevent dependence upon charity. That was no kindness since in bringing material comfort the charitable might place obstacles in the way of religious salvation. It was the duty of those dispensing charity to help the pauper to a position where he might help himself.

The Poor Law

The state could not absolve itself of responsibility entirely however. There were far too many paupers for an informal system wholly dependent upon personal endeavour and individual philanthropy to suffice, though these ideas figure in the background and had a great bearing upon the way the Poor Law worked and the manner of its reform. Thus our period begins with a system in force which reluctantly doled out aid to the poor, but it was an incoherent and unwieldy system, disorganised and inefficient, and known as the **Poor Law**.

There was **no central organisation**. The administration of the Poor Law was handled by the parishes, and although **Gilbert's Act** passed in 1782 had empowered parishes to band together into unions, few had done so. Thus in 1815, 15,000 separate authorities administered the Poor Law in England and Wales. The **overseers** of the poor, officers appointed by the local J.P.s, gave monetary relief to those on the verge of destitution. Funds were raised in the parishes by means of an obligatory levy and were augmented by voluntary gifts and endowments. But the system was harsh. **Houses of correction** and **workhouses** had been erected to house the able-bodied poor, who were considered able but unwilling to fend for themselves, and **Settlement Laws** existed which gave the parish authorities the right to remove any stranger within forty days of his arrival if he could not produce evidence of his ability to maintain himself without recourse to poor relief. Thus the Poor Law officers were obliged to accept responsibility for the paupers in their own parish but had no obligation in respect of the itinerant poor.

The settlement laws were stringently applied and had the unfortunate effect of inhibiting the mobility of the labour force and concentrating the problem of pauperdom in particular areas. People were discouraged from venturing away to seek work in case they might find themselves unprovided for in the event of not finding work or losing it. Such payments as were made to those who qualified for it were minimal, sufficient only to ward off starvation, since the overseer had a duty to the parish to see that the poor rate was kept down.

The Speenhamland system

By 1796 it was clear that the Poor Law was not maintaining the poor adequately. The rural lower classes in particular were in dire need on account of meagre wages and high prices. The informal system of deciding who qualified for relief and how much they should have was arbitrary and ineffectual. So a group of J.P.s met at Speenhamland in Berkshire to evolve a more rational system of poor relief. There it was decided that when a quartern loaf cost 1s. a labourer needed for subsistence 3s. for himself and 1s. 6d. for each member of his family. For every 1d. increase in the price of bread above 1s. he needed an extra 3d. for himself and 1d. for each member of his family. Thus a labourer earning 7s. with a wife and six children needed 13s. 6d. to maintain himself and his family at subsistence level. The parish would provide the difference between the 7s. wage and that sum, and so he would be entitled to 6s. 6d. relief. Should bread rise to 1s. 3d., then he would merit 9s. relief. This plan of estimating relief on the basis of the price of bread and the size of family was adopted throughout the southern counties. It did not displace the old Poor Law which remained on the statute book, but it altered its working.

Poor Law reform

Background

The Speenhamland system was humanitarian in intent but it had some unfortunate effects. It was disliked by many, in particular by Thomas Malthus and his disciples because it seemed a positive encouragement of large families which constituted a danger to individuals and the state.

Certainly the poor seemed to be costing the nation a good deal. In 1803 expenditure in poor relief was estimated at £4 million. In 1818 it was £8 million, and it seemed to contemporaries that it was an ever-increasing spiral. In fact expenditure was never so high again. By 1832 it had dropped to £6½ million, a fairly negligible figure if one set it beside the £35 million interest paid yearly on the national debt. But those in the parishes having to pay the poor rate were receptive to alarmist statistics put out by Malthusians who predicted ever-increasing numbers of paupers, and they were reluctant to continue to shoulder the burden.

Another consideration was the **moral one**. It was felt that dependence upon the poor rate was morally debilitating. Since the Poor Law system guaranteed a basic level of subsistence the labourer had no incentive to reach that level and beyond by his own efforts. Thus the system was thought positively to encourage idleness, thriftlessness and sexual excess. At the same time it discouraged employers from facing up to the moral obligation they had to pay a living wage. Thus the poor must become self-sufficient for the economic and moral good of the nation and a commission was appointed to work out details for the reform of the Poor Law.

The Poor Law Amendment Act
In 1834 the Poor Law Commission which was led by **Edwin Chadwick** and **Nassau Senior** made its recommendations. It aimed to unify the existing Poor Law in the interests of efficiency and it made a clear distinction between what it conceived as the **deserving** and undeserving poor; that is between those who were unable to work on account of age or infirmity and those who were physically capable of work but were disinclined to support themselves. In **1834** the Poor Law Amendment Act was passed which put the main recommendations of the commissioners into effect.

Organisation of the Poor Law
The Act established a Central Poor Law Department run by a secretary (the first was Chadwick) and three commissioners. The department was to direct the Poor Law guardians (the men elected by the ratepayers to be responsible for the working of the Poor Law) and it laid down rules and regulations for them to follow in the parishes or unions (for once again the idea of combining the parishes was attempted. This time the commissioners had power to effect it). The existence of this new central organisation gave a greater coherence to the working of the Poor Law.

Treatment of the poor
The commissioners intended to discourage the able-bodied poor from seeking relief and the inference was plainly drawn that those who were physically capable of work and did not do it were shirkers and malingerers. Thus **no outdoor relief** was to be given to people in the **able-bodied** category. They could obtain indoor relief; that is they could enter a workhouse and be maintained there at public expense, but within the workhouse they could expect only minimal comfort and the loss of their personal freedom. Conditions were intentionally harsh. Food was scanty and some workhouse inmates actually starved. The public was shocked by the **Andover case of 1847** when inmates of the workhouse there, employed in bone crushing, competed for a share of the putrid marrow and gristle.

Regulations existed, restricting freedom in every particular. Husbands and wives were separated, times stipulated for going to bed and rising, drinking and smoking were forbidden, letters often opened, and harsh punishment meted out to those held to be disruptive or disobedient.

Less bitterness might have been felt on the question of the new Poor Law had the workhouse received only the able-bodied and 'idle' poor, but many who did not come within the able-bodied category found themselves in the workhouse if the amount afforded them by the board of guardians was insufficient for them to maintain themselves in their own homes or those of their families. This applied particularly to the old, the very young and the sick. The commissioners had intended that these people should receive outdoor relief, and if forced into the workhouse that they should be distinguished from the 'indigent' poor and housed in separate buildings. The local boards considered the plan too expensive, and so workhouses were **mixed**, the rules and regulations drawn up with an eye to deterring the idle.

Effects of the Act

Political
Politically the Act was of great importance in arousing the active hostility of the lower classes. It had been the intention of the commissioners to attach shame to the idea of pauperdom and the workhouse, and all inmates carried the taint of it, though as has been seen, not all deserved it. Not only had the Act failed to make humane provision for the sick, the elderly and the young, it also failed to take into account the seasonal trade fluctuation which created periods of temporary unemployment, and provisions had to be made following the act to provide for this contingency. The Chartists owed much of their following to the dissatisfaction attending the Poor Law Amendment Act.

Economic
On the economic front the Act seemed to have been vindicated. The number of dependants upon the Poor Law decreased. Employers appeared to be paying more realistic wages and the poor rate was no longer regarded as an integral part of wages. But the growth of the railways provided extra employment and the relaxation of the Settlement Laws encouraged the poor to take advantage of new employment. Harvests too were good in the years immediately after the Act. Thus it is difficult to gauge how far the Amendment Act was responsible for the easing of the Poor

Law burden and how much economic trends, and in particular the lapsing of the Settlement Laws which created a more flexible labour market, contributed.

Changes in the law 1834–1906

After 1834 changes took place amending the Amendment Act itself, and the fact that these changes were necessary sheds further light on the weaknesses inherent in the Act. In 1834 the **Outdoor Labour Test** was brought in which gave guardians the right to dispense outdoor relief to able-bodied men engaged on work outside the workhouse such as stone breaking, oakham picking and what was specified as 'spade husbandry'. This was an attempt to make the Poor Law more flexible and to provide for the able-bodied willing to work but unable to obtain regular employment. Even these provisions were found inadequate however, and when a crisis struck the cotton industry during the 1860s (the American Civil War had prevented supplies of raw cotton from reaching this country), **outdoor relief** was given to 'able-bodied' men out of work, without the terms of the Labour Test order being complied with. Thus adaptations were made within the Poor Law system which made its working more humane and some Poor Law guardians, in fact, realised that the bald distinction between the able-bodied and disabled poor was unrealistic. Physical capability ought not always to be the determining factor where relief was concerned.

Other amendments eased some of the petty restrictions which circumscribed the liberty of the workhouse poor and exposed them to humiliation. Elderly husbands and wives were **no longer separated** and following the Andover scandal efforts were made to improve the quantity and quality of food. Consideration was also given to the health of the poor. In 1867 the **Metropolitan Poor Act** gave London unions the power to establish hospitals for the poor. And this example was soon followed in other major towns.

The process of centralising the administration of the Poor Law also continued and in 1847 the **Poor Law Board** was set up replacing the **department**. The Poor Law was now directed by a government minister in Parliament. This was an important step in the assumption of state responsibility and the abandonment of *laissez faire*. But in spite of all these changes the basic attitude enshrined in the Poor Law, that the responsibility for the avoidance of poverty rested with the individual, remained. And it was an attitude to which most organisations and individuals involved in charity work subscribed.

Charity and the poor

The formal provisions laid down by Acts of Parliament were not the only facilities in existence to help the poor. Charitable organisations also played an important part. The most influential organisation was probably the **Charity Organisation Society** (C.O.S.) founded in 1869 which aimed to promote 'the habits of providence and self-reliance and of those social and sanitary principles, the observance of which is essential to the well being of the poor and the community at large'. The 'Charity' in its title was something of a misnomer, since charity in the sense of unconditional aid was what the C.O.S. opposed. The poor must be placed in a position to help themselves. To our way of thinking the view of the C.O.S. seems unremittingly harsh. But above all the C.O.S. feared the corrupting influence of monetary 'hand-outs'. The organisation was prepared to help with practical gifts such as a sewing machine or a horse which might help individual poor to establish a trade and an independence but felt that indiscriminate charity would undermine self-respect and encourage idleness, endangering the wealth of the nation and the soul's salvation.

Other charitable organisations existed, as also numerous individuals who dedicated their lives to the plight of the poor. Octavia Hill worked in slums of East London, and Josephine Butler gave her attention to the problems of prostitutes, for sometimes prostitution seemed to many women the only way to avoid destitution. Religious organisations such as the Salvation Army also had an important part to play.

Self-help

The poor were prepared to help themselves, though not always in the approved evangelical manner. Self-denial and thrift were all very well but many soon realised that there was a limit to what individuals could achieve for themselves. Combination and co-operation were much more effective means of combating poverty.

Friendly societies

Friendly societies had existed since the seventeenth century, achieving official recognition in 1793. They combined the function of social club, insurance company and savings bank, and were a means by which the poor could provide against unemployment and sickness and could meet expenses such as funerals.

A small weekly contribution was paid to the society to cover these contingencies. The facilities offered by the various friendly societies, formed very often on a village basis, differed. There was no uniform contribution and cash expectation. Probably only the thrifty and self-disciplined poor took advantage of them, though conscientious employers would sometimes make partial contributions on behalf of their employees, and make their membership a condition of their work contract. By 1815 membership of friendly societies stood at a million and membership increased steadily throughout the nineteenth century. They went into decline after the passing of the National Insurance Act in 1911 which removed their main *raison d'être*.

Co-operative movement

Co-operation was an idea developed by Robert Owen, a philanthropist industrialist. Owen believed that if men co-operated instead of competing in industrial life enough wealth would be generated to end poverty. Owen wished to impose the idea of co-operation upon the whole of industrial society and he used his own mills at New Lanark in Scotland as a proving ground for the feasibility of his plans. But the idea was regarded as being socially subversive and Owen aroused distrust too on the grounds of his atheism. For both reasons other manufacturers were reluctant to follow his lead.

His ideas did appeal to many members of the lower classes however. **Co-operative societies** were established in many areas during the 1820s and by 1830 there were reckoned to be 300 of them. They were very diverse. Some functioned as political clubs and members of them merely discussed and advertised Owen's plan for a co-operative society. Others functioned at a more practical level and ran stores and shops, setting their profits aside to finance the establishment of 'villages of co-operation' (communities in which workers would organise their own social and economic life) which Owen had envisaged. Thus the early co-operative idea was comprehensive and political. In it was outlined the means by which society could be revolutionised and wealth redistributed along more egalitarian lines.

Owen's concept of co-operation did not survive much after 1830 probably because it was too grandiose and idealistic. It involved too radical a social change, and presented too great a challenge and responsibility to the lower classes who were on the whole far less ambitious themselves than Owen was on their behalf. Greater political influence they may have wished for, as the post-war disturbances and the support given to the Chartists indicate, but political control and social domination were different questions altogether. Thus when the co-operative idea was revived it was on a much more mundane and practical level, as a venture to keep prices down and to encourage saving.

The Rochdale Pioneers, 1844

In 1844 seven Rochdale weavers began a co-operative society. The 2d. subscriptions paid by members were used to buy stock, which was sold through co-operative shops at slightly less than normal retail prices. The profit made by the shop belonged to the members of the co-operative who were entitled to a share in the form of a dividend which could be cashed or reinvested. This idea soon caught on. By 1850 there were over 100 co-operative societies and by 1875 1,266 with nearly half a million members. In 1863 the **Co-operative Wholesale Society** (C.W.S.) was formed as a central organisation from which the individual societies could purchase supplies at a favourable price. The movement is still in force today, though less important than once it was, since so many facilities for saving exist today. Co-operatives in the nineteenth century also performed a useful social function in so far as many established libraries and organised classes, helping the lower classes to an avenue of escape from poverty through education. In many ways the co-operatives resembled friendly societies and in 1846 were given the right to register as such.

Political movements

Chartism

The attempt of the working classes to end poverty via political action in the post Napoleonic War years has already been discussed (chapter 1), but the Chartist Movement has not.

Origins

Chartism arose in the 1830s, in response to the many frustrations felt by working men. The Parliamentary Reform Act of 1832 had not extended the franchise as much as they had hoped and government remained the prerogative of the upper classes. Robert Owen's G.N.C.T.U. had failed. His dreams of a co-operative society had not materialised, and implicit in the Poor Law

Amendment Act which had just been passed was the idea of the moral inferiority of the poor. Furthermore the 1830s and '40s were decades of particular challenge and hardship for the poor employed in agriculture and industry; a fact which is revealed by study of wages and price indexes, and by the great writers of the period. Charles Kingsley wrote *Yeast* and *Alton Locke*, novels describing the acute suffering in rural and manufacturing areas, Mrs Gaskell wrote *Mary Barton* and *North and South*, readable and romantic tales describing conditions in the North Midland cotton areas, and Benjamin Disraeli (who later became Prime Minister) wrote his famous novel *Sybil*, a long rambling tale chiefly famous for the observation within it, that in England resided two nations, the rich and the poor, who had no contact and therefore no knowledge and understanding of each other. Charles Dickens' *Hard Times* also described the lot of the poor during these years. Thus it is well known that it was against a background of particular economic distress that Chartism grew up. Furthermore the success of those novels indicated a gathering swell of sympathy for the poor in their predicament, a sympathy which the Chartists did not exploit to their advantage.

Beliefs

Until working men gained control of the political system, their condition would remain unchanged. This was the argument put forward by **William Lovett**, secretary of the **London Working-men's Association**, when in 1836 he drew up the charter from which the movement derived its name. This view was endorsed by **Thomas Attwood**, leader of the **Birmingham Political Union**, when in 1839 he presented the charter in the form of a petition to parliament.

There were **six main points** to the charter which demanded: universal male suffrage, annual parliaments, a secret ballot, equal electoral districts, payment of M.P.s, and the abolition of the property qualification for M.P.s. These principles, if put into operation, would secure a system of government which would favour the lower classes. Only one million adult males had the vote in 1836 and even then a free vote was by no means secure. The system of public declamation of one's vote at the hustings encouraged bribery and left voters susceptible to pressure. The facts that M.P.s were unpaid and that a man was only eligible to stand for Parliament if a quite substantial property owner excluded the possibility of lower-class M.P.s, whilst the fact that constituencies were very uneven, small in the rural south and large in the industrial north placed manufacturing areas and industrial workers at an electoral disadvantage.

Organisation

The ideas of the Chartists were disseminated through newspapers such as the *Morning Star* and the movement brought itself to the notice of the public by means of torchlit processions and large-scale meetings and strikes. The movement organised itself nationally by calling conventions to which members came from all corners to discuss general strategy and to formulate policy.

Strengths and weaknesses

Chartism flourished for about twelve years and was a powerful political force in so far as it provided an umbrella beneath which lower-class grievances could gather. But the **diversity of support** was a fatal **weakness** too since the leaders never managed to harness the different motives for support to a uniform policy and theme, in spite of the Charter. Dissidents were prepared to use the machinery of the movement, its facilities for propaganda, etc., to further their own particular aims but were not prepared to submit to the discipline which membership of a central organisation must inevitably impose. Nor were they prepared to commit themselves to policy and action which had not a direct bearing upon their own plight. The particularism of Chartist members was a very major cause of the failure of the movement as a whole.

The Birmingham Chartists under the leadership of Thomas Attwood, M.P., saw currency reform as the cure to all economic ills, believing that maintenance of the gold standard as the basis of the monetary system kept prices high and stultified trade. The industrial workers of the north were moved by the harsh working of the Poor Law, whilst those workers whose livelihood was threatened by machinery looked to Chartism as a means if not to end the threat at least to mitigate the effects of it. The Lancashire cotton workers supported the Chartists in the hope that through Chartism the terrible suffering occasioned by the cotton slump might be made known.

Since support for Chartism was prompted mainly by economic distress, membership was bound to fluctuate and the movement could not depend upon consistent support. Membership flourished when conditions were particularly bad. Over $1\frac{1}{4}$ million signed the petition presented to Parliament in 1839, outlining the main points of the charter, and over $3\frac{1}{4}$ million the successor in 1842.

Another fatal **weakness**, which perhaps goes a long way towards explaining the first which has been outlined, lay in the divided and unsatisfactory **leadership** of the movement.

Although William Lovett had inaugurated the charter his position as leader was challenged by Feargas O'Connor, a one-time Irish M.P. and proprietor of the *Northern Star*, the newspaper which became a vehicle for Chartist propaganda. Whilst Lovett believed that reason and moral persuason would attract influential support for the movement, O'Connor favoured a more violent approach, adopting for his slogan the words 'Peaceably if we may, forcibly if we must'. Thus he was behind a move to call a general strike during August 1839, the 'Sacred Month', following the failure of Attwood's Chartist petition to Parliament in July.

O'Connor's attitude towards violence is not as straightforward as has sometimes been believed however, since he combined with Lovett in November 1839 to oppose a plan formulated by Welsh Chartists to seize Newport and he abandoned the 'Sacred Month' when General Sir Charles Napier indicated that the government would crush the strike by force of arms. The same motive, fear of failure, also explained O'Connor's discouragement of the Newport plan (which proceeded nevertheless, illustrating the lack of discipline within the movement). O'Connor thought that the support of the local populace had been overestimated. 'I caution you', he wrote, 'against those who give exaggerated accounts of the spirit of the locality'. O'Connor could see the harm which would be done to the movement if its fire was drawn and found to be weak. An organisation is in a better position to gain its end if it is something of an unknown quantity in respect of its capacity for force. And as O'Connor had feared, the Newport *débâcle* was a failure.

On the other hand the strike called at Ashton-under-Lyne in Lancashire, after the failure of Attwood's second petition to Parliament in 1842, had the ingredients for success. Workers from areas as far afield as Scotland and Wales came out in sympathy and yet this action was also disowned by O'Connor. Here, jealousy that the Ashton strikers had acted spontaneously and not at his instigation may explain his attitude (although he himself explained it by claiming that the strike had been organised by the Anti-Corn Law League to discredit the Chartists). If so, the dangers of leadership in the hands of a fickle egoist are revealed.

There can be no doubt therefore that the movement suffered not only on account of the division of leadership but on account of its lack of altruism also. In this particular instance O'Connor's vanity was gratified by the collapse of the strike following his denunciation of it in the *Morning Star*. Thus leadership failed on two main counts: it failed to develop a coherent approach and it failed to exercise control over the local members who often ignored directives. The violence of the movement is another factor in explaining the failure of Chartism since it alienated the support of the influential middle classes. The failure of violence on the other hand (as at Newport) led the government to believe that Chartism was less of a threat than many had feared, therefore that Chartist demands could be safely overridden.

Other factors in the collapse of Chartism are said to be the preparedness of the government whose army was ready under the leadership of General Napier to oppose insurrection. Interestingly the government was able to take advantage of the newly improved system of communications in opposing the Chartists. The telegraph was used to transmit news of intended disturbance and the railway to move troops to the appropriate areas.

The existence of a **rival** and more respectable organisation, the **Anti-Corn Law League** has also been seen as a reason for the Chartists' failure. The League, led by William Cobden and Richard Bright, sought the repeal of the Corn Laws (achieved in 1846) and many supported it in the belief that the cheaper food prices which would follow would mitigate the extremity of poverty: thus that the political aims of the Chartists were unnecessary as a means to end destitution and want.

The end of Chartism
The movement slumped after 1842 and the failure of the incipient general strike, after which there were many arrests, always a discouragement to continued membership. It revived again briefly in 1847 when O'Connor was elected to Parliament and presented a new petition purportedly signed by 5 million. Again fear was aroused. Revolution was rife in Europe (in fact the governments of France, Germany and Austria were toppled in 1848) and in England there were bread riots and other violent incidents. There was fear that dissidents might combine and cohere under the Chartist flag, but although a mass rally was held in Hyde Park to launch the third petition the incident passed peaceably. The signatures on the petition were found to be less

than 2 million and many of them were forged. The petition was laughed out of the House and Chartism went into a permanent decline.

Conclusion

It has been said that the charter was too radical, that it was too far ahead of the times, but given Lovett's belief that only full political control by the lower classes would alleviate their lot, it made sense. Five of the points in the charter have become law, some of them within the lifespan of men who had been Chartists. The property qualification was dispensed with in the late 1850s. The secret ballot came in 1872 and universal male suffrage was achieved by the 1884 Reform Act. The Redistribution Act of 1885 did much to redress the imbalance of constituencies, though constant adjustments still have to be made as centres of population shift. Payment of M.P.s' salaries came in 1911, leaving only the demand for annual parliaments outstanding.

Chartism can then be accounted a success in so far as it brought these issues to the forefront of public consciousness and in so far as they ultimately became law, but as a means of solving the problem of poverty it failed. Those who believed that society could be pressurised into concern for the lower classes turned towards trade unionism which was making a comeback (see chapter 9) and later gave support to the emerging Labour movement.

But this assessment of the effectiveness of Chartism may be ungenerous. The government from the mid-nineteenth century did begin to accept some responsibility for the conditions of the poor and pursued some of the legislation which improved their life in the face of influential opposition (e.g. the Public Health Act of 1843). One cannot know how far the novelists of the period who wrote such affecting propaganda on the predicament of the poor are responsible for the stirring of national consciousness or how far the violence of Chartism in acting as a warning to governments prompted their action, but Chartism certainly demonstrated once again that the lower classes could act as a political force.

Poor Law reform
Background
Conditions in the workhouses had eased to some extent by 1900, and amendments had been made to the Act. The payment of

outdoor relief to the able-bodied was for instance a common practice. It was given at the discretion of the Poor Law guardians, but since they were now often working men themselves they viewed the matter liberally. (The property qualification for election to boards of guardians had been abolished in 1888.)

Reform of the Poor Law system was however felt to be necessary. Out-payments to the able-bodied may have become established practice but they needed formalising. The position of the aged, the imbecile and the very young within the workhouses also merited reconsideration, as also the question of the administration of the law in view of local government reform. As far as the old were concerned, many felt that the workhouse system was inhumane. Physical conditions had improved but the stigma of shame attached to the workhouse was deeply felt by many old people. Opinion was inclining in some quarters towards the idea of a pension to enable the old to remain independent. As for the workhouse children (there were 14,000 of them in 1906) and imbeciles, it was felt that the environment of the workhouse was unsuitable and that other provision should be made. The publication of two social surveys, Charles Booth's of London (1898) and Rowntree's of York (1901), also affected attitudes towards the poor and contributed to the feeling that the Poor Law should be re-examined. Both men estimated that one-third of the population lived below the poverty line, and Booth's survey was particularly chastening for those who believed that philanthropy could control poverty, for he illustrated the marginal effect of charitable work in the areas where it had been most concentrated.

Poor Law commission
In 1905 Lord George Hamilton was appointed as head of a commission to look into the working of the Poor Law and the principles upon which it was based, and to make recommendations for change. The members of the commission disagreed so violently however that in **1909 two reports** were presented representing the **majority** and **minority** views.

The majority report
It was agreed by **all** members of the commission that the boards of guardians should be dissolved and that the Poor Law should be administered by the new county and borough councils, but the **attitude** of the majority to the poor was rigorous in so far as they endorsed the prejudice of the 1834 commissioners against the able-bodied poor. They were in favour of outdoor payment in exceptional circumstances but against it as a matter of course.

They wished too to minimise the charge upon the rates and recommended local authorities to make use of charitable organisations and emigration agencies. In other words the majority commissioners were reluctant to advise the government to assume full responsibility for the poor and were unable to rid themselves of the idea that poverty was morally reprehensible and ought to be discouraged. Nevertheless they were sympathetic to the plight of children. They recommended an increase in the facilities for foster care and made the useful practical suggestion that labour exchanges should be established to help the unemployed.

The minority report
This was more radical, not surprisingly since its compilers were well-known Fabians, among them Beatrice Webb and George Lansbury. They wanted a break-up of the Poor Law administration to bring the various categories of paupers under the care of specialist local committees. A Health Committee would look after the old and the sick, an Education Committee after the interests of children. A Pensions Committee should also be established to provide for the old. The attitude of the minority was far more sympathetic to the poor and there was a greater readiness to urge the state to accept responsibility.

Both sets of recommendations were ignored by the government however, which was unable to reconcile the conflicting views, and the old Poor Law administration remained with its accoutrements of workhouses and boards of guardians, and its confusion of intention. Did it exist to punish the idle or to relieve the suffering of the needy? The question remained unanswered.

The Welfare State, 1906–14

Background
But whilst the government was unable to decide how to deal with paupers it was prepared to ease the general conditions of poverty and to prevent pauperdom where it could. Thus the Liberal Government in power after 1906 committed itself to a very radical programme of social reform. It was influenced partly by the changed political circumstance of the twentieth century which saw the working man with a majority vote and a new political party, the Labour Party, rising to champion his interests. Political survival for the Liberals depended upon concessions being made. It would be wrong, however, to explain the social

welfare programme purely in terms of political expediency. There can be no doubt that concern about poverty was increasing. It had been aroused by the social surveys which it was fashionable to conduct post-Booth and Rowntree, and was also a result of literary propaganda. Both **John Galsworthy** and **George Bernard Shaw** wrote plays about the working classes and the desperate effects of poverty. And the Boer War which had ended in 1902 was also important since the poor physical condition of the soldiers recruited into the ranks had become generally known. Finally it was increasingly accepted that the complexity of modern society, its scale (population had doubled between 1800 and 1900 and stood at about 28 million), and its economic structure made nonsense of the idea that each man could (and should) be wholly responsible for his own fate.

Old-age pensions

The idea of paying pensions to the elderly was translated into law in 1909. Five shillings a week could be given to anyone over seventy with an annual income of less than £21, though it could be withheld from those who had consistently refused to work. The pension was non-contributory and paid by the state. It was of immense importance in enabling the poor to retain their independence. Flora Thompson, who was a postmistress in Oxfordshire when the act was passed, described how tears of gratitude ran down the faces of those cashing their first pensions. 'There were flowers from their gardens and apples from their trees for the girl who merely handed them their money.'

National Insurance Act, 1911

The plan for national insurance was in two parts. Separate provision was made for the unemployed and the sick, but in both cases money could be drawn when work was impossible, contributions having been paid into a central fund by worker, employer and the state.

In the case of **unemployment benefit** each paid $2\frac{1}{2}d.$ ($7\frac{1}{2}d.$ in all) enabling a worker to draw 7s. a week for a maximum of fifteen weeks in any one year. It was hoped that unemployment would be minimised however since **Labour exchanges** had been established in 1909. They were regarded as an important adjunct to the Act.

The arrangements for **sickness benefit** were a little more complex. All workers earning less than £160 a year had to contribute 4*d*. to the central fund. The employer paid 3*d*. and the state 2*d*. This entitled the sick to 10*s*. a week and the services of a doctor. Women, if employed, were eligible for the scheme and could claim maternity benefit in addition.

The importance of the National Insurance Act was immense, increasing as it did the average working-class income by some 6 per cent. It has been criticised because there was no supplementary allowance for wives and children, because it did not cover all trades, and because it buckled to some extent under the pressures placed upon it during the post-war depression years, but it was a great breakthrough. The friendly societies and trade unions (which incidentally were used to administer the scheme) and the co-operative movement had done much to help the poor, but the relief afforded by the act could be on a much larger scale, since all parties were compelled to contribute to it.

These two pieces of legislation were probably the most crucial in staving off pauperdom, but it is worth while mentioning other legislation beneficial to the working classes here, since the growth of the welfare state and the assumption of responsibility by the government for the condition of the working classes is being touched on.

In general the government did much to improve their condition, especially in respect of employment. The Trade Union Acts of 1906 and 1913 (see page 136) in safeguarding the rights of trade unions gave working men greater political and economic scope. Legislation in the form of the **Trade Boards Act** (1909) also helped workers in trades where there was notoriously very little protection. Trade boards composed of employers, employees and a neutral chairman were given power to investigate conditions in what were called the **sweated trades**, such as tailoring and lace making, and to fix minimum rates of pay. The attempt was not wholly successful however and even today one comes across cases of long hours and poor remuneration for people working in these industries from a home base. The **Workmen's Compensation Act** and **Shop Hours Act**, passed in 1906 and 1912 respectively, were also important. The former entitled workers to compensation from their employers for injuries sustained in the course of work. This problem had been first tackled in 1897 but in 1906 the provisions of the earlier act were extended to cover additional trades. The Shop Hours Act entitled shop assistants to a half-day's holiday each week.

Legislation affecting children

The Liberal Government, horrified by accounts from all quarters regarding malnutrition and disease among poor children, was anxious also to improve conditions for them. In **1907** an act was brought in authorising local authorities to provide **school meals** for needy children. Provision was also made for **medical inspections**, each child to be seen at least three times during its school career. In this way it was hoped that diseases such as rickets could be detected and corrected.

In 1909 the **Children's Act**, better known perhaps as the Children's Charter, was passed. It aimed to protect children in various circumstances; against their employment in dangerous trades and against physical neglect or injury by parents or guardians. The charter also gave consideration to the moral dangers of poverty, since the conditions often encouraged bad habits and vice. Thus, the sale of tobacco and drink to young persons was restricted. Lastly the Act provided for the separate trial of young offenders in special juvenile courts and prevented the Press from naming them. Sentences were to be served in the newly established Borstals (1902) or approved schools, so as to avoid contact with the hardened criminals offenders might meet in prison. The Act is interesting in that it drew the same distinction between child and adult which had formerly operated in the middle and upper classes of society alone. In the lower ranks of society children had dressed as adults, and assumed many of their habits and responsibilities from a very early age.

Thus the period 1906–14 saw the final abandonment of *laissez faire*, as the government assumed responsibility for social conditions and tried to temper their worst effects (although there were some strange gaps in their endeavours: no efforts were made to improve housing, for instance). The welfare mission was not accomplished without opposition, however.

The People's Budget

Many resented the cost of reform and its social and political consequences. The state had assumed considerable commitments in pursuing its reform policy and **Lloyd George**, Chancellor of the Exchequer, had to tap new resources. His famous People's Budget (put forward in 1909) proposed increased taxation of the rich in the form of a super tax of 1*s*. 3*d*. in the pound on all incomes over £3,000. A land tax and increases in death duties were also envisaged, together with higher duties upon luxury items such as wines, spirits and petrol.

Resentment of the budget was felt on the grounds that it would tax the rich out of existence and that it was intended as a direct assault upon the social structure. The invective of Lloyd George against the 'privileged' classes did much to augment this impression. Thus the House of Lords rejected the Finance Bill in which the budget was enshrined. The Liberal Government thereupon appealed to public opinion by calling a general election in January 1910, which re-elected them. The budget was subsequently passed in April.

Parliament Act

The action of the House of Lords in frustrating passage of Lloyd George's Finance Bill confirmed many in their belief that its powers were anachronistic in a democratic age, and a Bill was drawn up to prevent any recurrence of its action. The proposed Parliament Bill sought to prevent the House of Lords from blocking financial Bills altogether and to limit the powers in respect of other legislation. Ironically the consent of the Lords was needed for this restrictive Bill to become law, and the House refused it. Another election was called in December 1910 as again the opinion of the electorate was sought. Again the Liberals were returned. They moved in for the kill, threatening with the King's connivance to flood the House of Lords with newly created Liberal peers in order to force passage of the Bill. The Lords had no alternative but to back down in the face of this threat and in 1911 the Parliament Bill became law. By terms of the Act, any Bill certified as a Money Bill receiving assent in the House of Commons automatically became law. Other legislation could be held up for two years, but once it had passed the Commons on three successive sessions it too became law. Thus all that was left to the Lords was the power (not an inconsiderable one) of amendment. The upper classes lost their last stronghold of domination by dint of the Act.

Thus the political and social ramifications of social reform were immense. The power structure had to change in line with the new priorities of government.

The economy, 1918–39

The fate of the British lower classes in the years following the First World War was tragic, as everyone knows. The hopes of creating a land fit for the returning war heroes and worthy of the sacrifice which millions had made were cruelly dashed, for although agriculture and industry flourished spectacularly between 1918 and 1921 the prosperity was bound to be shortlived since it depended upon the temporary dislocation of industry in post-war Europe. Once foreign industry revived, the British 'boom' ended.

The slump

The economic depression which lasted until the outbreak of the Second World War developed in two stages. It was the result of a cessation of demand for war commodities (ships, munitions, etc.), the lifting of the subsidies and price guarantees which had protected agriculture and industry, and the failure of investment which would have enabled British industry to modernise and adapt. All these factors contributed to a decline in the export market.

The heavy industrial areas in Wales and the north were worst hit. The shipbuilding industry virtually collapsed once the war ended and the peace began. 49 per cent of the shipyard workers in Barrow in Furness were out of work in 1922, 60 per cent of the workers in Hartlepool; in Jarrow the percentage was 43. The mining industry was also badly hit. The slump in the shipbuilding industry provoked a slump in the iron and steel industries and led to a reduction of demand for coal for smelting. The crisis in mining was heightened once the Polish and German mines began to function again and were able to compete in the export market. For three months during 1921 coal production in Britain actually ceased altogether. The textile industry too was in trouble, badly affected by competition from the Japanese. Agriculture suffered as well from the return to normality and the resumption of foreign grain imports. Grain prices nearly halved in two years and in 1922 wheat was fetching only 49s. 6d. a quarter. Wages sagged correspondingly. By the summer of 1921, 2 million men were out of work and the unemployment figures never went below 1 million until 1940.

There were signs of recovery by 1928. Unemployment figures in that year were the lowest they had been since 1921, and the pound had recently been on par with the dollar in the foreign exchange market.

The Wall Street crash

In 1929 however all hopes of recovery were dashed by news of the failure of the American stock market in Wall Street, New York. There had been an investment boom in the United States during the late 1920s and people began to speculate on the stock exchange without giving sufficient thought to the soundness of the industries in which they were investing or the state of the

69

commodity market. Goods began to stockpile and investors to panic. There was a rush to withdraw holdings and the house of cards came tumbling down.

The ramifications of the incident were widespread, since there had been large-scale American investment in Europe since the war. Now loans to European governments were likely to be recalled or not renewed and American investment in European industry to be withdrawn. The collapse of an important consumer market (12 million Americans were soon unemployed) was also disastrous. By 1932, unemployment in Britain had risen to 3 million and the rate of exports had fallen to 22 per cent of total production (in 1907 it had been 30·5 per cent).

Government policy

Governments were at a loss to know how to deal with the enormous problem they faced. And that it was enormous is beyond dispute for to the problem of sagging credit on account of declining exports was added the problem of the war debt. The wartime government had borrowed heavily, especially from the United States, to finance the war. Many overseas investments had been sold or transferred to reduce the debt but it still remained considerable and in selling the investments British credit in the world was still further reduced.

Thus throughout the period a consistent policy was followed and the theme was one of cutback and retrenchment. In order to keep the nation in credit at a time when earnings were low, national expenditure must be reduced. This was the advice of **Lord Geddes** in 1922 and of **Sir George May** in 1931, and on both occasions the advice was implemented.

The **Geddes Report** recommended cuts in expenditure on education and public health, and the abandonment of war pensions. Sir George May recommended a 10 per cent reduction of pay to public employees such as civil servants, teachers and the police. Few government advisors (Sir Oswald Mosley and Lloyd George apart) would give credence to the theories of **John Maynard Keynes**, a Cambridge economist who argued that such measures were self-defeating. The way out of a slump in his view was to increase government expenditure on public works such as roads or building. The employment which followed would stimulate consumption and bring about the revival of other industries. Keynes believed national indebtedness to be an unimportant consideration. It was to everyone's benefit to keep the wheels of trade and industry turning. After 1945 Keynes' theories were put into practice and became an established orthodoxy – politicians at the time of the slump being heavily criticised for ignoring him. However, in the late 1970s and early 1980s there was a swing away from Keynesian theory back to a policy of retrenchment and Keynes himself came in for much criticism.

The Gold Standard

Other expedients were tried in an effort to revive the flagging economy but the most unsuccessful must surely have been the reversion to the Gold Standard in 1925.

The Gold Standard is a means of measuring currency by reference to the gold reserves which a country has. Its currency may then be exchanged directly for gold. The advantage of the Gold Standard rests on the respect (not altogether rational) which gold commands on the international money market, and the reversion to the Gold Standard in 1925 (it had been abandoned during the war) was intended to increase confidence in British currency. The measure was, however, unfortunate, even disastrous, in its effect upon industry. The conversion rate for British gold was set far too high so that the pound was worth more against other currencies than before. British goods thus became expensive and Britain's position in the export market worsened.

The Gold Standard also had an unfortunate political effect in so far as it contributed to the General Strike. The wage cuts and increased hours of work which employers demanded to cancel out the price disadvantage accruing from the Gold Standard caused much bitterness and resentment.

Britain came off the Gold Standard in 1931 and the effect was the same as devaluation in lowering the price of British goods abroad. This beneficial effect was soon nullified however when other countries devalued their currencies.

Protection

It has been said that a nation can only afford free trade when in a position of industrial dominance. Certainly it was felt by many that Britain could no longer afford it by 1932. The **Trade Imports Act** thus imposed a 20 per cent import charge on most goods. Imperial goods were however exempted on the understanding that British goods would pay only minimal duties when entering the colonies. This understanding was formalised in the **Ottawa Agreement** of 1932.

In fact these arrangements were not beneficial. Britain was not alone in imposing heavy import duties and the result was a reduction of world trade at a time when everyone needed it to expand. As for the system of imperial preference developed at Ottawa, the colonies benefited from it to a greater extent than Britain. While exports to the Colonies rose by 5 per cent to 50 per cent, imports from the Empire rose from 30 per cent to 40 per cent.

Intervention in industry

Government policy was not altogether futile, however. Some useful legislation was implemented if belatedly to increase efficiency in the coal industry, for instance. The **Coal Mines Act** (1930) provided for the compulsory amalgamation of collieries into more efficient units. The newly established **Central Coal Board** in whom the powers of enforcement were vested was also authorised to draw up production targets. The legislation may have fallen short of the nationalisation which many miners wanted but it was a move in the right direction, and an important concession had been made to the idea that the state ought to have some control over home industries.

This idea was also enshrined in the **Public Corporation** scheme which brought several independent business enterprises under the control of public boards. Members of the boards, mainly employers and workers in the industries involved, were appointed by a government minister and were answerable to him. **The Central Electricity Board** was the first industry organised along these lines. The **British Sugar Corporation** followed.

The **marketing boards** (see chapter 2) designed to improve the quality of agricultural produce and to test the problems of distribution also testify to the assumption by governments of responsibility in respect of trade and industry. So also does the **Wheat Act**, although this differed from the other legislation just described in so far as it was designed not to increase efficiency but as a straight subsidy. Since the government's general economic policy was to cut back, subsidies were rarely given, but the government was obliged to make an exception in the case of agriculture since the system of imperial preference posed such a direct threat. (Most colonial imports were of agricultural produce.)

It is easy to give the impression that the inter-war period was one of unmitigated gloom on the economic front, but in fact several industries expanded and flourished. Against an overall annual increase in national industrial output of only 2 per cent must be set an increase of 10 per cent in car production and 15 per cent in artificial silk. The electricity industry and the electrical trades also expanded rapidly. So too did the building industry. There was expansion too in the distributive trades and in banking, insurance and various other local government and professional services. In the south-east where many of these trades and industries were based, population increased rapidly between the wars (by about 18 per cent as against 1 per cent in Lancashire and actual decline in the north-east and Wales). It is also worth noting that real wages increased during these years since the fall in prices was greater than average wage reductions. Thus for those in work the picture was one of increased prosperity. The point must therefore be understood that the main effects of the slump were regional, and resulted from the inability of **heavy** industry to adapt. The problem of what to do with these industries in ordinary peace time was never resolved. Given the state of British steel and shipbuilding now, perhaps it has not been yet. Rearmament which began in 1936 as a defence against the growing European instability solved the problem only temporarily.

Social effects of the Depression

'He was standing there as motionless as a statue, cap pulled over his eyes, gaze fixed on pavement, hands in pockets, shoulders hunched, the bitter wind blowing his thin trousers lightly against his legs. Waste paper and dust blew about him in spirals, the papers making harsh sounds as they slid on the pavement.' The importance of this description taken from **Walter Greenwood's** contemporary play *Love on the Dole* is immense, underlining as it does the effect of the slump upon individuals. The way in which it changed their physical surroundings and challenged their emotional and spiritual balance is most admirably portrayed here, though it is echoed abundantly elsewhere. The sense of physical desolation and decrepitude is something **George Orwell**, for instance, remarked upon. Peeling paint, rotting window frames, a general rundown seedy appearance was typical of the slump town, he thought. So too was a feeling of hopelessness and futility. 'Misery, despair, broken manhood and a profound doubt and cynicism' was **J. B. Priestley's** summary of the emotions to which the depression gave rise.

These feelings were most prevalent in the early years of the slump when the experience of being jobless was novel. Thereafter people were able to come to terms with the situation to a greater extent, since by 1931 the scale of unemployment was so vast and the phenomenon so well established that no one could consider it his fault to be out of work. This comfort was a small one however and could do nothing to mitigate the effects of poverty and the physical hardship to which it gave rise, nor the sense of frustration which came from having nothing to do.

Palliatives did exist for both conditions. **National Insurance** and, when that had run out, the **dole**, provided the means for basic subsistence and kept actual starvation at bay, but as J. B. Priestley remarked, the dole, whilst sufficient to keep a man alive, could not keep him alive **and** kicking especially during 1931–4 when the 10 per cent cut recommended by Sir George May was in force. The **means test** introduced in 1931 also had a harsh effect and brought the state subsidy down to an absolute minimum. The unemployed and their families may not have starved but they were certainly, in the opinion of George Orwell, a contemporary writer and journalist, 'underfed'.

As for the various social and occupational clubs introduced during these years run by trade unions and by religious (e.g. Y.M.C.A.) and state (e.g. National Council for Social Workers' Movement) organisations, they could provide nothing in the way of real occupation and members had to fall back on activities like basket weaving. The Quakers ran a useful allotment scheme but these strangely did not receive much backing from local authorities though they were enthusiastically adopted by working men, when available.

Undoubtedly these were harsh and demoralising years, and the condition of the poor was not without its **political dangers**. The **National Unemployed Workers' Movement** did attempt to stir up some kind of political action. Political instruction was offered and visiting political speakers of the left-wing variety were booked to address audiences of working men, but this aspect of the movement's activities did not receive much support. Some working men in the East End of London supported Oswald Mosley's right-wing **Union of British Fascists**, but on the whole the working classes exhibited little political interest during these years and Prime Minister Stanley Baldwin's fear that unemployment whilst 'eating away at the energies of the nation was breeding dangerous thoughts' was unfulfilled.

In some respects the lack of political initiative is hard to understand, since in the past, as has been seen, extreme material hardship suffered on a national scale had tended to provoke political action. The failure of the General Strike was a discouraging factor however and the scale of the economic problem also disinclined people to action. The Depression seemed too huge and depended (especially after 1929) largely upon external factors beyond national control. Until world trade began to pick up there was little that any political action in this country could achieve. Perhaps another explanation for political inertia lay, as George Orwell suggested, in the mass recourse to escapism. The cinema, the availability of cheap luxury items of food and clothing, the latter easily obtainable on hire purchase, and the establishment of the football pools along with other forms of organised gambling – all these facilities provided avenues of escape from the harsh realities of life. As George Orwell put it, 'You may have three halfpence in your pocket and not a prospect in the world and only the corner of a leaky bedroom to go home to but in your new clothes you can stand on the street corner, indulging in the private daydream of yourself as Clark Gable or Greta Garbo which compensates you for a great deal. And even at home there is generally a cup of tea going – "a nice cup of tea" – and Father, who has been out of work since 1929 is temporarily happy because he has a sure tip for the Cesarewitch.' He concludes, 'It is quite likely that cheap luxuries such as fish and chips, art silk stockings, tinned salmon, cut-price chocolates (five two-ounce bars for sixpence) the movies, the radio, strong tea and the football pools between them have averted revolution.'

Thus small physical comforts and the inspiration and opportunity for hope of escape meant that members of British working classes need never accept their fate. The casual glance from a film producer or a large win upon the football pools could lift them out of the mire of poverty and whisk them away to a life of luxury and fame. The dream of course rarely changed the reality, but this hope that it might made the hardship psychologically more bearable.

National Insurance and the dole

A great deal of store had been set by the National Insurance Act of 1911 but it came in for considerable amendment in the face of the prolonged and widespread unemployment for which it had never been intended to provide. Between 1920 and 1934, the main changes were to raise the rate of contributions (by 1922 workers were having to contribute 9*d*., employers 10*d*., and the state 6¾*d*.), and to extend the cover of the Act (from 1921, dependents also received relief) and the period of benefit (which in 1921 was extended to thirty-two weeks). A system known as the **dole** was also established to provide for unemployed workers once their National Insurance stamps had been exhausted. For the next twenty-six weeks of unemployment, responsibility for relief devolved upon the Unemployment Assistance Board (U.A.B.) which was financed by the government. Thereafter an unemployed worker and his family came under the care of a Public Assistance Board (P.A.B.), an arm of the old Poor Law (now reorganised and under the control of local authorities). Relief was theoretically paid out of the rates, but in fact the government made substantial contributions. The P.A.B. was gradually relieved of responsibility for the bulk of the unemployed however, who after 1936 remained under the care of the U.A.B.

Amount of relief

George Orwell reckoned that in the mid-1930s the average dole payment to a family of four was in the region of 30*s*. a week and that a quarter of this amount would generally have to go on rent, 'which is to say that the average person, child or adult has got to be fed, clothed, warmed and otherwise on 7/– a week'. Orwell estimated that some 20 million people, about one-third of the entire population, were living off the dole by the time all the unemployed and their dependents were taken into consideration. This may be an overestimate but probably not a substantial one.

The means test

In 1931 as part of the government plan to cut expenditure on unemployment benefit (£110 million was paid out in that year) the **means test** was introduced which placed the financial resources of those in receipt of the dole under close scrutiny. The U.A.B. which administered the test had the duty to enquire into the finances of each household. The earnings of a child doing a paper round or the contribution to the housekeeping of an elderly relative's pension would reduce the amount of benefit to which the family was entitled. Rigorous checks were also made on casual earnings.

The test had two particularly unfortunate effects. It created tensions within families and neighbourhoods. In the case of families one bad effect was upon the pride and authority of an unemployed man in his own household. Some felt very keenly the humiliation of dependence, however partial, upon a child's earnings. Another bad effect was upon the position of the old, since the pension which was contributed to the *ménage* would automatically reduce the relief to which it was entitled. Thus many old people were ousted and forced into lodgings or into the workhouse. Conditions in the former could be very harsh, as Orwell noted in the early chapters of *The Road to Wigan Pier*.

The test had a divisive effect upon neighbourhoods too. For as Orwell remarked, the system was 'an encouragement to the tattle tale and the informer, the writer of anonymous letters and the local blackmailer, to all sorts of unneighbourliness'. Certainly it was bitterly resented. Both the intrusion into privacy upon which the system depended and the doubts which the multitude of questions and checks seemed to cast upon the veracity of the working class were sources of humiliation.

Conclusion

Thus 1939 saw the poor, superficially at least, in very much the same position as in 1815. In both cases a post-war slump created an immense economic problem of which the main manifestation was widespread unemployment and to which officialdom reacted by seeking to cut expenses. Reduction of aid to the poor, and the application of a stern moral code which seemed to assume that it was the intention of the unemployed to exploit the available facilities for relief, was noticeable in both cases. The able-bodied test in 1834, the means test in 1931, both seem to testify to this attitude. Probably the proportional scale of the problem was similar in both cases too. But the whole moral atmosphere had changed by 1939. The idea that poverty represented a challenge to the individual and was a means by which he could prove his spiritual worth had certainly been abandoned by 1939. The notion of state responsibility had by then come into play. The means test was in fact an unfortunate expedient with a purely economic aim. An inherited sensitivity on the part of the working class was the largest factor in the sense of humiliation induced by the test which was not conceived as a trap to catch shirkers and 'skivers'. The workhouse test in 1831 was designed primarily of course to do this.

Thus there had been a significant change in attitude. The poor were still there but a greater understanding of economic forces gave rise to a larger compassion for them. Economic circumstances made it difficult to express, but it existed nevertheless.

Chapter 4
Industrial Society

250,000 tons of iron were produced in 1810, and 94 million tons of raw cotton were processed by the textile industry in 1815. Everywhere that coal was found, the mines were going deeper and the tonnage extracted was increasing. A map of Britain in 1815 would show the nation crossed by Brindley's canals along which the expanding industrial produce was being slowly transported. Thus Britain's metamorphosis from rural to industrial nation was well under way by the outset of our period. By 1815, the Industrial Revolution could be judged complete though some historians extend the date to 1840, for not until then, they argue, were all the features of modern industrialism apparent.

Industrial Revolution

What is meant by the term 'Industrial Revolution' and how is it relevant to the heading of this chapter? Briefly, it is a term used to describe the transition from an economy based on small-scale manufacture, organised by small masters and produced in workshops or the home (domestic system) to one based on large-scale mechanised industries organised by overseers in factories. The change from the **domestic system** of organisation to one based on the **factory** is the main feature of the industrial revolution but the phrase encompasses more than that, for it describes not merely the change in the method and nature of work but the transformation of a whole way of life, bringing people away from the villages and hamlets into the towns where the factories were sited. It therefore presupposes the change from rural to urban life as well.

Progress of industrialisation

The organisational change, though virtually complete by 1815, was recent, however. In 1715 there were not even intimations of such a transformation, though naturally the preconditions were there. But by mid-century technical changes in the textile industry enabled it to enlarge its scope to such an extent that other industries were drawn into the vortex of change. The iron industry expanded in response to the demand for material for smelting and to power the new steam engines invented by James Watt, and the Napoleonic Wars were also important in so far as they increased the pace of change, hastening the metamorphosis.

Industrialism was already creating its own momentum, and population was increasing to feed it in terms both of labour and consumption, but the war created an artificially high demand for textiles (for uniforms) and munitions and encouraged the spread of mechanisation still further.

The effects of industrialisation

Adverse developments

The newness and rapidity of industrialisation created problems. Economic conditions were created which no one had provided for or knew how to control. Thus many people were trapped by the pendulum swing of boom and slump, the latter condition giving rise to large-scale unemployment and to starvation and need. The advance of mechanisation also contributed to unemployment amongst workers who had formed an aristocracy in pre-industrial days. By 1832, a handloom weaver employed in the cotton industry was earning between 5s. 6d. and 6s. a week. In some areas the earnings were down to 1d. a day. Many others led squalid and despairing lives in the hastily-erected factory towns in which there were no adequate hygienic arrangements, or worked long hours, sometimes eighteen to twenty hours a day, women and children among them, in factories in which their capacity for production seemed of greater importance than their humanity. Thus the idea has arisen that life in early industrial Britain was dark and insanitary, so lacking in hope and dignity that the only escape was through the gin palace or the beer hall into oblivion.

To a certain extent this picture is valid. Unemployment did cause immense suffering. The fate of those workers like the handloom weavers and stockingers whose skills were superseded was tragic. Hours of work were interminable, protection in the course of work was inadequate and the quality of life in the new towns left much to be desired, but there is another side to the coin.

The argument in favour

The first thing to be understood is that although times were bad (1815–34, 1836–48 and 1876–95 were years of industrial difficulty with much attendant suffering), they were not always so, and when industry flourished many workpeople did too. (The music hall was the other side of the coin to the gin palace.) In many ways too the cycle of prosperity and hardship was not new. In pre-industrial society it had happened with probably greater

79

frequency, and the lower classes were vulnerable every time a harvest failed. Over all, the prosperity of the British lower classes increased in the nineteenth century. Not all categories of workers prospered at the same time, but the general pattern was of increased material prosperity. Disease and death certainly occurred, but population expanded rapidly in the nineteenth century in spite of large-scale emigration, and the death rate even at the height of the cholera epidemic of the 1830s was lower per head of population than in rural France at the same date, or in Britain seventy years earlier.

As for abuses in the factory system such as child labour, it should be remembered that the factories were merely applying a labour practice common in pre-industrial society. Nursery rhymes such as 'Little Bo-Peep' and 'Little Boy Blue' inform us that child labour was an ancient custom. This is not to argue that because child labour had always been in existence it was therefore justified, but it is important to establish that many practices thought to be peculiar to industrialism actually have an older history and that industrialism was often adaptive rather than innovative. It is after all as easy to fall into the trap of believing that industrialism initiated all the bad practices in respect of labour as it is to let the 'satanic mills' aspect of the Industrial Revolution predominate. Industrialisation brought many benefits and created many opportunities and that should not be forgotten. It did not replace a golden rural age in which innocence and prosperity were the order of the day. It replaced a hard and difficult way of life with one equally hard though perhaps more bewildering, since life close to nature however erratic does seem to have some kind of primitive meaning. But the new way of life was one which carried the seeds of reform within it. As one historian has remarked, it brought open drains and squalor but its technology provided the pipes for drains and the engineers to lay them. It brought degradation and toil but these had always existed and it brought also opportunity (George Stephenson was an illiterate but he became one of the greatest men of his age) and in the end education and greater equality. Interestingly, Devilsdust, a character in Disraeli's novel *Sybil* who was abandoned at the age of two to fend for himself, and was a living testament to some of the worst abuses attending industrialisation, pays tribute to the advantages it had brought in terms of education and opportunity.

The alternative to industrialism
It is certainly worth speculating what would have happened if

industrialisation had not taken place and population had continued to increase. To a certain extent population increase was a consequence of industrialism, but not entirely. In Ireland which had no industry the population increased as rapidly if not more so. When the potato harvest failed in 1845 large-scale famine ensued (a million died) and the British government had to intervene with supplies of cheap foreign corn. (This was the event which precipitated the repeal of the Corn Laws.) The point to note here is that a nation with an expanding population and no industrial resources is in a dangerous position. Industry and trade make possible a barter system: food for goods. The alternative is dependence upon charity in emergency. How ineffective this is is demonstrated by Ireland in 1845 and by Africa and India today. It invariably comes too late.

In conclusion it is worth reflecting on the final paragraph in T. S. Ashton's book *The Industrial Revolution*, though one could now exclude China from his pity:

'There are today on the plains of India and China men and women, plague-ridden and hungry, living lives little better in outward appearance than those of the cattle who toil with them by day and share their places of sleep by night. Such Asiatic standards and such unmechanised horrors are the lot of those who increase their numbers without passing through an industrial revolution.'

Conditions of work

Having said all this in defence of industrialism, it nevertheless remains true that the process of industrialisation was painful, and that conditions of employment up till the 1830s and '40s when the reform movement began to be effective makes grim reading. In the factories, mines and workshops of industrial Britain the work force was very much at a disadvantage; unprotected in respect of continued employment and without the right to compensation for any injuries suffered in the course of work. Labourers were forced to work in the absence of even basic safety precautions and were subject to various kinds of monetary injustice. **Essential equipment**, like the lamp which miners needed, had **to be hired**, at a rate which would have paid for it several times over in the course of the year. **Fines** were often imposed for breach of factory regulations. A man arriving late for his shift might forfeit as much as half a day's wage. Pay was not always rendered in money but often in 'tokens' which could be exchanged for food and basic items in the factory or 'truck' shop. (Sometimes it was called the Tommy shop.)

The **'truck' system** was a major cause of complaint and in his novel *Sybil*, Disraeli has a group of workmen attack and destroy the shop, enraged at having to buy rancid bacon and over-priced tea. Some historians have estimated that where the system was applied it could reduce the value of a wage by as much as 3*s*. in the pound, although it is important to realise that the system was not universal and that it began to decline noticeably after the 1831 **Truck Act** which was designed to check the worst abuses.

Hours of work in the mills, mines and workshops were long and sometimes eighteen hours at a stretch were worked by children as well as adults, especially in the textile industry during the so-called 'brisk times'.

The **organisation of labour** too had its unsatisfactory aspects. To the other inconveniences experienced by the factory worker in the 1820s and '30s was added the feeling of being an impersonal cog in a machine. Under the domestic system the master had often been a craftsman himself and was in direct charge of his labourers. In the new factory system where the scale of manufacture was larger, the factory owner might never know his workers individually, and might therefore be disinclined to take account of their humanity when making demands in respect of productivity. His relationship with them was entirely monetary and the 'butty man' or the factory foreman would act as a mediator between him and his workers. In the tailoring trade the more lurid nickname of 'sweater' was applied to the foreman or manager and it expresses of itself the resentment many felt at his role.

It is this impersonal system of organisation rather than the **size** of the work units which created the 'alienation' which has often been noted as an important feature of nineteenth-century industrialism.

Size of industry

The scale of industry increased rapidly after 1815. Output in the **iron industry** was 700,000 tons in 1830 and the amount of raw **cotton** processed had risen to 273 million tons. The **coal industry** by 1850 was producing some 50 million tons a year; by 1870 output had doubled yet again to over 200 million. But although the size and scope of the basic industries was increasing, the basic units of production were small. Though two Scottish cotton mills employed 1,000 workers in 1815, in forty-two mills investigated in the Manchester area at the same date the average workforce was only 300. Thereafter the size of the average cotton mill fell so that in 1830 it employed just over 150 workers. The **woollen mills** had need of even fewer and in 1839 the average figure employed was only 79. Coal mines, in spite of their impressive production record, were run on an even smaller scale. Eighty was considered a representative number in 1850. The **iron industry** had the largest units of production and 500 or 600 men employed in an iron works was not unusual.

Employers and workers

Though the size of work units was small by modern comparison, it was large compared to the domestic system. To be one of hundreds rather than one of five or ten, as had probably been the case a generation earlier, was perhaps bewildering – especially in the absence of personal contact with the factory or mine owner. The latter, by the end of the century, probably directed or was party to several enterprises. This point of the separation of the classes under the factory system has often been stressed. Many historians remark upon it and the novelists of the period of the 1840s, when the effects of it seemed most cruel, make it their central theme. Disraeli makes the point dramatically in *Sybil* with his image of two nations, rich and poor, but Mrs Gaskell makes it too in *North and South* and *Mary Barton*. Once the employers and workers meet as individuals in these novels and the sufferings of the latter begin to make an impression, the worst feelings of alienation, the sense of being flotsam and jetsam with no control over the current which cast them hither and thither in the new economic system, are abated. In real life, the outcome for many workers was less satisfactory and many factory owners never had the chance or the inclination to make contact with their workpeople. (It would be wrong to suppose that workpeople never had contact with the capitalists who owned the means of production however, and that they never acquired any personality in the eyes of their employers. In D. H. Lawrence's novel *Women in Love*, the miners go to Mr Crick, the mine owner, with their personal troubles and are known to him as individuals.)

In a subject of this nature it is very easy to distort the true picture and some very respectable historians have done this, drawing a contrast between the gentle rural world where everyone had a sense of identity and where the relationship between the different classes of society was personal, and the grim, dark world of industrialism in which exploitation was made even less bearable, for one had lost not only freedom but identity. How often the upper and lower classes made contact in rural England and how far personal contact with one's employer in any case was a mitigating factor in suffering: these points are difficult to assess. Flora Thompson indicates how little contact there was in a rural setting when she describes the Oxfordshire gentry in the late nineteenth century as kingfishers 'flitting' across the path of the lower orders whom she likened to sparrows. A sudden flash of brilliance and they had gone. As for the question of close relationships, as George Kitson Clark remarks in his book *The Making of Victorian England*, some of the worst abuses in respect of employment occurred in very small trades such as chimney sweeping where the master and employer were in close and direct contact.

So the possibility that the social relationship between worker and employer may not have changed as much as has sometimes been supposed must be considered, as also the point that an intimate and direct relationship was just as likely as the factory system to give rise to tyranny and exploitation.

Moreover the factory system did not always do this. What were perhaps disorientating features about industrial employment were the setting (the towns) and the uncertainty of employment. The frightening swing of boom and slump, in which both employer and employee were trapped, was merciless and brought extreme material suffering to the latter. Certainly the butty system had some unsatisfactory aspects but not all butty men were unscrupulous and not all factory owners were cast as ruthless villains in the mould of Dickens' famous Mr Bounderby (*Hard Times*).

Child labour

By 1815 the scale of child labour had actually been reduced, though of course some of the worst abuses of the system were by no means ended. But it was in the early years of the Industrial Revolution before the widespread adoption of steam power that the largest numbers were employed.

Before becoming dependent upon steam power, industry was located where water power was available, but where very often labour was not. Whilst the labour market adjusted, pauper children had been apprenticed to the mill owners who assumed responsibility for their upkeep. The system was widely abused but in **1802**, an **Act** of Parliament placed restrictions on the use of pauper child labour. Although it did not cease altogether (throughout the nineteenth century there were frequent complaints of pauper children being apprenticed against their will), the labour force became more mixed. Children were still an important part of it however, for they were cheap. Thus in 1833 the cotton mills employed some 84,000 children and young persons, a larger single category of labour than any other (60,000 men and 65,000 women were also employed) and they earned about 3s. 6d. a week, less than a fifth of the adult male wage. Children (about 35,000 of them) were also employed in the woollen industry, whilst the silk, lacemaking and coal industries also made demands upon their labour. Remuneration in the coal industry was higher than in textiles and a child could earn about 5s. a week.

Nature of employment
In the textile industry the nature of the work varied. Children wound bobbins, collected waste from under the machines, and pieced broken threads together. Some of the older children actually supervised machines.

The constant bending and stooping often resulted in deformity and the hours of work were interminable especially during busy periods, leaving the children in a state of exhaustion. One witness reporting to the **commission set up in 1831** under the leadership of **Michael Sadler** to enquire into labour conditions in the textile industries described how the children, the youngest only eight years old, worked from 3 a.m. until 10.30 p.m. ($19\frac{1}{2}$ hours) during the 'brisk times'. They were too tired he said to eat: 'Many times we have cried often when we have given them what little victualling we had to give them. We had to shake them, and they have fallen asleep with the victuals in their mouths many times.'

There were horror tales about child labour in the mines also. In some respects there the exploitation was worse since there were no restrictions upon the age of employment, as in the textile industry, until 1842. A **commission** appointed with **Lord Ashley** at its head, to enquire into the mining industry, found children of five, six and seven frequently employed, and one case of a three-year-old down the mines.

Children acted most commonly as trappers; that is, they operated the trapdoors which were essential to the proper functioning of the ventilation system in the mines. In this capacity they might find themselves alone in the dark for twelve hours at a time. Children were also engaged in pushing coal-filled carriages along passages, sometimes only 18 inches high, or in pumping water in the lower reaches of the mine, to do which they needed to stand all day in several inches of water. In some areas children were employed as enginemen and were in charge of lowering and raising the cages which took miners to and from the surface. As in the textile industry, disease and deformity resulted. Children in mines, denied sunlight, often suffered from vitamin D deficiency which manifests itself in rickets, and the constant stooping and crawling in narrow passages made them bent.

The employment of children in the textile industries and mines, and the abuses which resulted were well publicised by 1842, but there were many other trades and occupations in which children were employed in circumstances equally if not more horrifying. There were the boy chimney sweeps, who suffocated in narrow flues or died of cancer of the groin; the girls who worked long hours for a pittance as seamstresses, or who made and sold the matches which rotted their jaws; or the boys who sweated in the tailoring trade – these should all be remembered, as should the children employed in agriculture, perhaps as members of a gang:

> 'And well may children weep before you
> They are weary 'ere they run
> They have never seen the sunshine nor the glory
> Which is brighter than the sun.
> They know the grief of man without its wisdom
> They sink in man's despair without its calm.'

Gradually of course the worst abuses were eradicated. Elizabeth Barrett Browning's poem 'The Cry of the Children' (1842) is indicative of a growing awareness of the horrific consequences which made the employment of children intolerable. Not least of these was the realisation that a whole generation of children was growing up so committed to a life of toil that they had no knowledge of either God or man.

The **moral** and **spiritual effects** of industrialisation upon children made as important an imprint upon the consciousness of the Victorian reformers as stories of their physical suffering. The knowledge that many of these children did not know who Jesus

Christ was came as a great shock. Something would have to be done; though powerful arguments mainly to the effect that industry could not survive without child labour were advanced against reform, as we shall see.

Female labour

Female labour was also of immense importance to the development of industrialism. Over half a million women were employed in the textile industry alone by 1851, though the number employed in another basic industry, coal, had by then reduced considerably to about 3,000, the 1842 Coal Mines Act having been passed. As with children the main impetus to their employment was financial. The cost of employing female labour was one-third to a half that of employing a man.

The **social effects** of the employment of female employment in the new industrial setting are interesting. Under the domestic system it had been easier to combine the role of wife and mother with that of breadwinner. And it may be that much of the sense of alienation and confusion which was so uncomfortable a feature of industrial life derived from the absence of a settled home background. It is interesting that Mrs Gaskell in her novel *Mary Barton* has one of her male characters regret the absence of his wife at work. No 'bright fire in the grate' and his 'meals all hugger-mugger and comfortless' were circumstances, he said, liable to tempt a man to the gin shop and to invite the evil consequences of drink.

The practice of female employment also had an unfortunate effect upon very young children who were often put out to a child minder. She (usually an old woman past working herself), in consideration of about 3*d.* a week, would keep the babies from crying with doses of laudanum and feed them an indigestible bread and water pap. A conscientious mother would breast-feed her baby before leaving in the morning and upon her return at night, but not all were so scrupulous and many children did not survive. Some were abandoned and cast loose to fend for themselves (like Devilsdust in Disraeli's *Sybil*) from an early age. Infanticide was a common practice, for whilst children were welcome when old enough for employment, until then they were often regarded as encumbrances, especially if they stood in the way of a woman going out to work.

Thus the practice of employing women in industry had then (as now) a disruptive effect upon family life, and it is important to take this into account when assessing the quality of life in early industrial Britain. On the other hand it also gave some measure of freedom and independence, especially when wages were good and employment easy to find.

Towns

The idea that the growth of towns was entirely dependent upon industrialisation is being challenged nowadays, but there is no doubt that it did 'generate new energies of urban growth', and that many new towns grew up in industrial locations and for no other purpose than to serve industry. Middlesbrough (Cleveland) is a case in point, since it was entirely dependent for its creation upon iron-ore mining. There is no doubt too that many existing towns expanded simply because manufacturers arrived to exploit an existing labour force. This siting of industry thereafter drew more people into the area.

Certainly towns increased at a phenomenal rate in the nineteenth century. An urban population of $2\frac{1}{2}$ million in 1801 had increased to $19 \cdot 8$ million by 1891. The most intensive years of this expansion were 1820–30. The rate of growth in those years was unprecedented and has apparently never been surpassed.

Problems

Such rapid expansion gave rise to problems, both emotional and material. In 1851 less than half the population of London over twenty was born there and the same kind of pattern was repeated in other towns and cities. This meant that people were being drawn into an urban mode of life without having previous knowledge of it. The experience could be disorientating in so far as the established traditions and patterns of behaviour which had lent stability to country life were absent. Often they reasserted themselves and the small village community was repeated in 'neighbourhoods'. Here, individuality could be established and neighbourliness came into play. There was no need in such communities to feel faceless or friendless. But this kind of development was not universal nor was it usual in the very newest areas, nor it seems in those where the worst material conditions obtained. Of children in Glasgow in 1842 a police superintendent remarked, 'I should be able to find a thousand who have no name whatever or only nicknames like dogs.' This was a description of the rootless and impersonal society to which urban industrialism had given rise.

Living conditions

Any description of material conditions in the new towns soon develops into a catalogue of horror stories with the unifying theme of sewerage. Many of the buildings had been erected rapidly, in close proximity to the factory and with an eye to cheapness rather than comfort. Because the problems to which concentrated populations gave rise in respect of water supplies and sewerage had not been encountered before outside London, no proper thought was given to waste disposal. Systems which had sufficed without creating serious hazard in small communities were employed now with dreadful consequences. Cesspools and open conduits leading to the nearest stream or river were the main outlets for sewage, though the midden too was a common sight. Oozing noxious liquids and giving off foul vapours, it stood exposed to public view. Seepage was a common problem not only from the midden but from the unemptied cesspools which soaked into the underground cellars like the one which **Dr Lyon Playfair** described when making his report to the **Health of Towns Commission** in **1845**. 'I have known instances where the floor of a dwellinghouse has been constantly wet with foetid fluid which has filtered through from a midden and poisoned the air with its intolerable stench: and the family was never free from sickness during the six months they endured the nuisance.' In these conditions it was not surprising to hear that water supplies were tainted. The same commission heard how faecal matter was plainly observable in a water sample taken from a well used by an entire community for drinking and cooking.

The important point to grasp is that these were not isolated instances. They could be found in any industrial town and the sum total of their effect was as Mrs Gaskell described in *Mary Barton*. Mrs Gaskell lived in Manchester and drew this account of Bury Street from life:

'It was unpaved and down the middle a gutter forced its way, every now and then forming pools in the holes with which the street abounded. Never was the old Edinburgh saying of "Gardez l'eau" more necessary than in this street. As they passed, women from their doors tossed household slops of every description into the gutter; they ran into the next pool which overflowed and stagnated. Heaps of ashes were the stepping stones, on which the passer by, who cared in the least for cleanliness took care not to put his foot. Our friends were not dainty, but even they picked their way till they got to some steps leading down into a small area, where a person standing would have his head about one foot below the level of the street, and might at the same time without the least motion of his body, touch the window of the cellar and the damp muddy wall opposite. You went down one step even from the foul area into the cellar in which a family of human beings lived. It was very dark inside. The window panes of many of them were broken and stuffed with rags, which was reason enough for the dusky light that pervaded the place even at midday. After the account I have given of the state of the street no one can be surprised that on going into the cellar inhabited by Davenport, the smell was so foetid as almost to knock the two men down. Quickly recovering themselves, as those inured to such things do, they began to penetrate the thick darkness of the place and to see three or four little children rolling on the damp, nay wet brick floor, through which the stagnant, filthy moisture of the street oozed up; the fireplace was empty and black; the wife sat on her husband's chair and cried in the dark loneliness.'

How many lived this life it is difficult to say, but it is estimated that the cellar populations of Manchester and Liverpool in 1845 were 18,000. Cellar-dwellers were reckoned to comprise 6 per cent of Lancashire's population.

Another feature of these towns was the overcrowding. There are no national figures available but a report on overcrowding in Preston was compiled for the Health of Towns Commission which found that in 442 dwellings, 2,400 people slept in 825 beds. In 84 cases, four shared a bed, in 28 five, in 13 six, in 3 seven, and in 1 eight.

These were the very worst conditions and as can be seen the scale on which they were endured was disturbingly large, but they were not universal to the British working classes. The skilled workers often lived on a much more comfortable level. Mrs Gaskell, describing the Barton household in the 1840s (John was a skilled cotton operative), described a modest but pleasant house. There was well-scrubbed furniture, enough crockery for Mrs Barton to take pride in showing it off, a cheerful fire in the grate and a meal of ham and eggs in process of preparation. Even where comfort was found, however, it was precarious. Succeeding chapters in *Mary Barton* reveal the Barton household being slowly denuded as the slump strikes the cotton industry. Everything is sold or goes to the pawn shop as the family struggle to find enough to eat.

Disease

Disease followed inevitably in the wake of overcrowding and bad sanitation. Cholera, which first appeared on Wearside in 1831, took a very heavy toll. Fifteen hundred died in Liverpool alone in that year. In 1849, another bad year for cholera, there were over 53,000 reported cases in the country, and over 5,000 deaths in Liverpool. The problem was exacerbated by medical ignorance both in respect of cause and treatment. It was thought by many respectable medical men that cholera germs travelled through the air, and mustard compresses were applied in place of the saline injections which are given today to effect a cure. Typhus, a disease spread by rats which flourishes where there is malnutrition, was also a major killer, especially in the late 1830s and '40s. Its worst outbreak in fact coincided with the great depression. The fact that 10,000 people died of typhus in the north-west of England in 1847 gives some idea of its virulence. Typhoid fever was also common and no respecter of classes, since Prince Albert died of it. As with cholera its source is tainted water, and it manifests itself in much the same way occasioning great gastric upheavals. Interestingly smallpox outbreaks also occurred in spite of vaccination. The crowded conditions of urban Britain provided an ideal setting for this highly contagious disease.

Child mortality was also high in consequence both of poor sanitation and the factory system. Neither the babies left with child-minders nor the young children worn out and deformed in the factories had much resistance to disease. The death-toll was truly alarming and it is claimed that in some urban areas a quarter or more of those born died before their first birthday; 'respiratory and convulsive disorders, scarlatine, measles and whooping cough adding to the dangers already described'. On the other hand it is worth remarking that child mortality halved between 1750 and 1830 which indicates that although towns were unhealthy places in which to live and the industrial labour system took a heavy toll, conditions had been worse under the old domestic system and in a rural setting.

Work conditions also contributed to disease and death. Miners suffered from various pulmonary complaints consequent upon the poor ventilation in the mines, whilst the textile worker was affected by the dust of textile waste which gave rise to phthisis. Everywhere consumption was rife: again a disease often associated with poor living conditions, and certainly encouraged by over-exertion and poor diet.

Crime

The moral effects of the crowded and poverty-stricken lives of the lower-class inhabitants of industrial England, the resort to drink and crime and the nature of the latter, have been described elsewhere but they must be mentioned here if only in passing as they too are important indicators of the flavour, texture and quality of urban industrial life.

Conclusion

Finally, therefore, it must be said of industrialisation that it brought great distress. Living and working conditions were equally unsatisfactory and industrialism exaggerated many of the more reprehensible features of the pre-industrial age, such as child labour. The often impersonal character of life in the cities and the absence of tradition and the stabilising influence of family life led to feelings of alienation. Thus to the physical discomfort of life was added a sense of spiritual and emotional bewilderment. Further, squalor and hard labour were brutalising influences, and certainly the early and even middle years of industrialism were years in which people were degraded and dehumanised.

And yet having said this one comes back to the question: how different was the alternative? Rural slums existed, social relationships in the countryside could be equally impersonal, and the exploitation equally hard (a point which, ironically, Lord Ashley, famous in connection with factory reform, was forced to concede in respect of his father's Dorset estates). And the material circumstances were often worse. Margaret Hale, a character in Mrs Gaskell's novel *North and South*, remarks upon the greater hardship of the rural classes in conversation with northern industrial workers hit by the cotton slump.

The fact is that greater material prosperity did attend industrialisation and that many benefited from it. The confidence and poise of the model unions is a testament to this. Reform did come in the end and although it could not cure all social ills it did give the working classes wider access to the benefits of industrialism. Also by crowding them together in such close quarters it made the lower classes more aware of their numerical strength. The greater sense of political identity manifested by the Napoleonic War disturbances and the Chartist Movement owed everything to industrialism. It therefore carried within itself the political as well as technological means to its own reform.

Chapter 5
Communications

In 1815 the people of Britain heard the news of the battle of Waterloo which ended over twenty years of war in Europe. This news travelled slowly by sailing ship across the Channel and by stage-coach over land; from London it passed to the rest of the country, marked by the ringing of church bells. Remote areas may have waited for days before hearing it and for those interested in the details of the battles maybe as long as a week elapsed before they read them in their newspapers. At the end of this period in 1939 the descendants of those men and women who had been excited and relieved by the news of Waterloo heard of the outbreak of another war. They sat beside their wireless sets and heard of the war the moment it was declared and within hours read the details in newspapers carried by trains and motor vans to every corner of the nation and even further, for aeroplanes conveyed London papers to Paris. So in the space of four generations there had been an enormous acceleration in the pace of communications. Men, their ideas, and the products of their labour moved with an increasing rapidity and efficiency.

These changes in the means of communication fall into two distinct categories. The first involved the harnessing of steam power and took place between 1820 and 1860, and the second which relied upon the petrol-driven engine and radio waves was under way between 1880 and 1910.

Steam power

Railways
Railways had their origins in the bringing together of two forms of industrial technology which had been developed in the eighteenth century. The first was the use of horse-pulled trucks whose wheels ran on specially designed rails, and the second was the steam engine, a device commonly employed to power machinery such as pumps. In 1804 **Richard Trevithick**, a Cornish engineer, had devised a locomotive, driven by steam, which would pull trucks on rails. This was to all intents and purposes the first steam railway in the commonly accepted sense. Other inventions

followed, but like Trevithick's prototype they were confined to railway locomotives used in mines or other industrial sites.

The development of public railways conceived and built for the carriage of goods and passengers and relying on steam-driven engines began in **1825** with the opening of the **Stockton and Darlington Railway**. Behind this venture and many of its successors were two remarkable men, **George Stephenson** and his son **Robert**, whose combined vision and talents provided much of the impetus for the spread of railways. George Stephenson's greatest contribution was in the promotion of railways: he planned railways and his enthusiasm and persuasiveness convinced people of their potential and profitability. Although George had a considerable knowledge of the practical problems of building railways, his son Robert was the engineer who faced these difficulties in the field and overcame them.

The first Stephenson triumph was the **Liverpool and Manchester Railway** which was opened amidst great public jubilation by the Duke of Wellington in **1830**. It was a double track railway which ran for 31 miles with bridges, tunnels and viaducts. These had been designed by Robert Stephenson to overcome the seemingly impassable hindrances along its route. The wagons which went to and fro along this railway were drawn by steam locomotives based on the Rocket, a brainchild of the Stephensons which in 1829 had trounced its rivals at a series of trials at Rainhill in Lancashire. The track, layout and engines of the Liverpool and Manchester set the pattern for the future.

The success of the Liverpool and Manchester line was the signal for the formation of many other railway companies. In the 1830s and 1840s industrialists and investors quickly appreciated the advantages and value of this new form of transport. By 1840 1,400 miles of track had been laid. More followed with a fresh impetus in the mid-1840s when the country was convulsed by a heady enthusiasm for investment in railways known as '**Railway Mania**'. These years (1844–6) were a time of feverish building with a rush of reckless investment in frequently unsound enterprises. Still, there was a boom in industry and plenty of capital was available to the railway companies and by 1850 6,000 miles of track had been completed. After this date the excitement died down and with all the nation's major cities and towns joined together, the first great era of railway expansion came to a close. Yet although Britain had now built the backbone of her railway system there was still room for more lines, especially in country areas. So in the early 1860s there was another brief railway boom and investors were tempted to part with their money to finance further lines. The small branch lines constructed during this secondary boom were soon found to be unprofitable and this short spurt of building ended with bankruptcies. Thereafter until 1914 railway construction was on a small scale, limited to small rural branch lines.

Reasons for expansion

Why had there been such a great growth between 1830 and 1850? Most importantly, the men who founded the railway companies and the investors who backed them recognised the need for railways. In the first place the need was seen in terms of **cheap transport for raw materials and finished goods**. The railways were able to break the monopoly of the canal companies and force them to lower their charges. But once the railways had been built a new demand was created, that of the passengers anxious to take advantage of cheap and fast travel. To the surprise and delight of the railway companies, they found that more than half their revenues were coming from **passenger fares**. By the later part of the century takings from freight transport rose but passenger services still accounted for 40 per cent of all the railways' income.

The railways had revealed an enormous demand by men and women for quick and convenient transport. Before the railways the traveller had to rely upon either the stage-coach or the even slower carter's wagon. Stage coaches could only take eleven passengers and their luggage and the journey time was extended by the frequent changing of horses and overnight stops. In 1841 a man travelling by coach from London to Exeter spent 21 hours travelling and his journey cost him £3 – £3 10s. plus a further 15s. in tips. In 1846, after the completion of the Great Western Railway's line to Exeter, his time of travelling was only 6½ hours and his first-class fare cost him £2 4s. 6d. Moreover, more people could travel by train for the stage-coaches had never been sufficiently numerous to cope with the numbers who wished to undertake journeys. In the summer of 1835 the Leeds and Selby Railway was carrying an average of 3,500 passengers a week, whereas previously coaches between the two towns could only take a maximum of 400 each week.

The creation of the railways had thus revealed a public demand for cheap and speedy travel. They also served their original purpose for they carried the raw materials and products of industry at competitive rates. This was recognised by the corporations of towns and cities who did all they could to entice the railway companies to lay lines to their towns. The railway was the touchstone for future prosperity.

Construction

The process by which the railways were built was a simple one. First a company was formed which invited investors to back their venture with capital. Obviously the founders of the company had to demonstrate that there was a need for their particular railway and that once built it would be well used and therefore show a profit with which the investors would be rewarded. This was usually easy since such early companies as the Liverpool and Manchester paid out dividends of up to 20 per cent of the sums invested (later these spectacular returns fell to a steady 4 per cent). Once established, the company instructed surveyors to find the most convenient route for the line to follow and to find out what obstacles would need to be overcome. Then a bill authorising the railway was placed before Parliament, which invariably gave its approval.

When everything was ready for the engineers to begin work, the railways were constructed by gangs of labourers (known as 'navigators' or more commonly as '**navvies**') who worked with picks, shovels and gunpowder. Administration and the design of tunnels, bridges and viaducts lay in the hands of specialist engineers such as **Isambard Kingdom Brunel** who was employed by the Great Western Railway. As the lines were laid, masses of stone and earth would have to be moved by the navvies with their picks and shovels. Tunnels would be blasted through the rock, cuttings laboriously hacked out and great embankments piled up with earth dug by the navvies and moved, load by load, by horse-drawn carts. The prodigious scale of these operations amazed all who saw or heard of them. Nothing like this had ever been witnessed nor ever would be again for the only comparable modern enterprise, the motorways, are built by machinery and not muscle and sweat.

In 1845 at the height of railway mania, over 200,000 navvies were at work up and down Britain. As many as 20,000 were employed on the London to Birmingham railway in the previous decade at a time when few factories employed more than 200. For many, the navvies were men apart from civilised society. Their work was tough, hard and dangerous; it took a year to make a navvy out of the strongest farm labourer. The navvies were paid between 14s. and 22s. a week and they lived, sometimes with their wives and children, in shanty towns, always moving from place to place following the march of the new tracks. Their consumption of liquor and their work-hardened violence shocked contemporaries. Many were Irish and there were frequent bloody battles between them and the English and Scots. When the great era of railway building was over, many navvies followed the great contractors like Brassey or Morton Peto abroad and lent their muscles to the building of railways in Europe and America. Here as in England the great cuttings, embankments and tunnels are their monuments.

Impact of the railways

By 1850 it was possible to travel from London to any one of the major towns and cities of Britain. The railways had spread to every corner of the land, to Birmingham, Manchester, Liverpool, Leeds, Sheffield, York, Newcastle, Edinburgh, and Glasgow in the north, to Norwich and Lincoln in the east, and to Cardiff, Holyhead, Bristol and Exeter in the west. A man living in any one of these places might expect, if he used his timetable wisely, to reach another within a day or less. He would have travelled at 50 m.p.h. although many railway companies frowned on such an excessive pace since it aroused passengers' anxiety. Such mobility and such speed were undreamed of twenty years before.

Industry had benefited from the railways. Its raw materials and finished products travelled quickly and cheaply and new markets were opened up as a consequence. Welsh slates and Fletton bricks were carried to each corner of the country with the result that many local building materials were superseded. The railways were also consumers of iron and coal and so production in both these industries increased to meet the new demand. The railway companies also needed labour and so created new jobs at a time when they were badly needed (1830s and '40s). Masons and bricklayers were employed in great numbers to build stations, bridges and viaducts, and once established the railways needed men as engineers, drivers, guards and station staff. By 1850 they had become a new industry. Agriculture also found new markets through the railways which enabled fresh food to be brought daily to the hearts of the great cities. Milk from the farms of Somerset could be in the households of Londoners within a day and by 1848 70 tons of fresh fish from Yarmouth were delivered each week to London.

Society also changed as a consequence of the railways. Men and women found a new mobility for by the **1844 Railway Act** each company had to send at least one train a day along each of its main lines which stopped at every halt and station and on which a minimal cheap rate of 1*d.* a mile was chargeable. Even the humblest could now move where he or she wished. Since the Post Office had been quick to take advantage of the railways, personal letters and parcels travelled more rapidly. It was also possible for London newspapers to be distributed throughout the country within a day. By the 1890s the new popular newspapers of the day such as the *Daily Mail* were travelling to each and every town in Britain. Local papers, for long the staple reading of people in the provinces, dwindled in importance to be replaced by the national London press. Another way in which the railways extended the influence of London was through the imposition throughout the country of London (Greenwich Mean) Time. Before the 1840s there had been different times in different areas so that Reading time was 4 minutes after London time and further west Cirencester time was 17 minutes in advance of London. The need for national railway timetables made it necessary to abandon such local eccentricities and so they vanished, minor victims of a greater change.

Finally, whilst railways increased personal mobility, they tended to enforce existing social differences. Every company had first-, second-, third- and occasionally fourth-class carriages to suit the pockets of different users. Social differences were upheld and in the 1930s at least one passenger, indignant at having been shown to a third-class compartment when he possessed a first-class ticket, pulled the communication cord, stopped the train and walked to the right carriage! A consequence which followed the network of railways and stations around the larger cities was the creation of a class of commuters. These men, usually in clerical and administrative posts, were able to work in, say, London or Manchester and live in comparatively rural surroundings in Surrey or Cheshire. Every morning and evening they would travel by train to and from their work, whereas their fathers and grandfathers had lived in the cities near to their places of work. So from the 1850s onwards the suburbs grew, firstly for the wealthier and then by the turn of the century for the masses of clerical workers. At the same time, working men living in the towns could on special occasions afford the specially cheap excursion tickets which took them and their families away to the countryside or more usually the seaside. Margate and Southend and many other coastal resorts, easily reached by the railways, became centres for recreation and that popular institution 'the day by the seaside'.

Conclusion

To the people of the time the 1830s and 1840s were sometimes known as the 'Railway Age'. The railways stood for progress and symbolised the skills, enterprise and inventiveness of the industrial revolution. They provided the lifelines of industrial society and encouraged expansion. They brought prosperity, mobility and wider horizons for many and in subtle ways influenced the structure and outlook of society. Whilst many other features of the Industrial Revolution have vanished or been replaced, the railways even in a truncated form survive and their artefacts remain as a testament to the willpower and genius of their age.

Steamships

Ship design and propulsion underwent three major changes during this period: the replacement of sail power by the steam engine, the introduction of iron and steel as materials for ship-building, and lastly, at the turn of the century the adoption of oil turbine.

Steamships developed slowly. Whilst the first prototypes had appeared in the early 1800s, there were only 924 registered in 1847 and most of these of small tonnage and used for short voyages. These vessels were propelled by steam-driven paddles attached to the sides of their hulls and all required auxiliary sails for extra speed or use in an emergency. A new system of steam propulsion was under development at this time by which the steam engine drove propellers or 'screws' which were attached beneath the waterline at the stern of the ship. In 1845 the two types of propulsion were tested by the Royal Navy which organised a tug of war between a paddle steamer and one of the 'screw'-driven vessels. The 'screw' steamer won.

Screw propulsion gave greater speed and efficiency and within the next decade was adopted for nearly all new steamers. There was however a further problem for ship-builders, that of designing steamers with sufficient storage space for the coal needed to drive their engines. Sailing ships did not have this need and could therefore be built with larger holds and so carry larger cargoes. At least until the 1860s the sail-driven 'clipper' ships dominated the Far Eastern routes and it was to meet their challenge that **Brunel** designed his **Great Eastern** which was **launched in 1858**. It was an iron-hulled ship of 19,000 tons with sufficient room to store all the coal that would power its screws and paddles for the non-stop voyage to Australia. Relying on paddles, screws and auxiliary sail, this hybrid vessel proved difficult to handle in rough weather and so was unsatisfactory for its purpose.

The setbacks which Brunel tried to overcome were finally bypassed by other means. Once the technical problems of building **iron ships** had been removed, it was possible to build them to any size with room enough for cargo and coal. The abundance of British coal and the willingness of the ship owners to set up coaling stations at ports on major sea routes meant that the iron-built steamer was an economic proposition. Moreover its cargo capacity was far greater than any sailing vessel. By the 1870s the days of the sailing vessel were numbered and the major sea routes were increasingly dominated by steamers. Further innovations followed. By the early 1880s refrigeration plants were installed on ships, powered by auxiliary batteries which enabled vessels to carry frozen meat from New Zealand, Australia and Argentina to Britain. Larger and faster vessels also speeded up the cheap bulk transport of grain from America. Developments of marine technology were changing the diet of the people of Britain.

In the 1890s Sir Charles Parsons' oil-driven turbine increased the speed of ships. Whereas in 1838 the *Great Western* had crossed the Atlantic in fifteen days, the turbine-driven *Mauretania* took four and a half in 1909. Two years later the *Titanic* was expected to take even less time. This vessel was an embodiment of all the technical achievements of the past century; it was driven by turbines and steam engines, it possessed electric light and wireless, and its design was so advanced that many regarded it as unsinkable.

It was a floating symbol of the ability of the inventors of the nineteenth century to overcome all natural phenomena, of man's mastery of the elements and power to harness them for his own use. On its maiden voyage it struck an iceberg and sank. The disaster was a chastening experience to a generation which had come to have such faith in its own genius and inventiveness.

Electric telegraph

Parallel to the development of the railways came the expansion of the electric telegraph system. This worked by the sending of impulses along iron wires and had been first used in the 1840s when the Electric Telegraph Company had been formed. The wires ran alongside railway lines and the company's offices, open day and night for the sending of messages, were usually established at railway stations. In **1851** a **telegraph cable was laid under the Channel** and in **1857–58** another was laid under the **Atlantic**, linking Britain with the United States. The telegraph was convenient for short and urgent messages and it also revolutionised journalism. It enabled the reporter **W. H. Russell** to send his despatches from the Crimean War in a matter of one or two days and so news of the war reached British newspaper readers within less than a week. It was also important as an aid to the maintenance of public order, and was a factor in the containment of Chartism.

The internal combustion engine and wireless

Introduction
The last quarter of the nineteenth century saw a revolution in communications as far-reaching as that which had followed the harnessing of steam power to transport. The two major sources of change were the invention in 1876 of the internal combustion engine, which was followed, ten years later, by its use in the first motor car, and the discovery of wireless in the 1890s. Together the motor car and wireless had a profound effect on the lives of the people of Britain. At the same time two other important innovations appeared: electricity was being used to power tram cars and underground trains and Dunlop's pneumatic tyre and changes in design made the bicycle a cheap and convenient form of private transport.

Motor cars
The **first motor cars** appeared on the roads of Britain in the mid-**1890s**. For the next twenty years they remained the temperamental toys of the rich, although doctors were quick to appreciate their usefulness for carrying out visits to patients. In 1904 there were 8,500 private motor cars in Britain; by 1914 the number was 132,000.

The early motor cars were luxuries: a Rolls-Royce, the finest car then available, cost over £1,000 in 1913. Such vehicles were hand-built and their bodywork was constructed by men who had learnt their skills making the horse-drawn private coaches of the previous generation. By 1914 the British car market was being infiltrated by the mass-produced motors made in the United States in the factories of Henry Ford. These machines were put together on a conveyor belt and whilst they lacked the style, comfort and panache of many of their contemporaries, they were cheap. By 1910 **Ford** had established a factory in England which in 1914 was turning out 8,352 cars a year. An Englishman, **W. R. Morris**, had already taken up Ford's example and his factory at **Cowley** had been in production since 1912. Before the outbreak of war, the mass-produced cheap car was established in Britain.

The war was a temporary setback to the motor industry for the factories had to turn to production of war materials. By 1918 the motor companies returned to normal production and the opening rounds of a cut-price competitive war of their own. **Sir Herbert Austin** had predicted the closeness of an age of 'Motoring for the Millions' and he and his rivals set about producing inexpensive cars which would make this dream a reality. In 1922 his company's 'Austin Seven' was priced at £185, slightly more than Ford's famous 'Model T' or 'Tin Lizzie'. The competition soon became hotter: in 1932 the cheapest Ford cost £100 and its closest rival, the Morris Minor, was £118. In spite of the slump, car production was rapidly increasing, having risen from 71,000 cars a year in 1923 to 305,000 in 1939.

Why did so many people want to drive cars of their own? At the beginning of the century the motor had been a prestige symbol confined to the Edwardian upper-middle and middle classes. But Ford and his competitors had realised that a demand for cheap cars also existed and that if they could be made available, there would be no lack of buyers. Why? The simplest answer was the freedom which ownership of a car gave. Advertisements for motor cars of this period show the new owner of the latest model at the wheel, his wife beside him and his children in the back. They are heading along an open road and around them are fields, trees, villages and the wide, clear sky. The motor car combined the romance of the open road with the practicability of convenient travel without having to rely on railway timetables. The creation of new models by the companies also played on a concern for status. In an advertisement of 1932 the potential buyer of the latest Austin ponders on the fact that one in four cars on the road is an Austin – surely an indication of reliability. At the same time the 'new model' is said to possess a great many accessories, presumably unavailable to its predecessor.

Whilst the middle classes became entranced by the freedom of the motor car, the internal combustion engine was also altering the lives of the lower classes. In 1897 five **motor buses** appeared on the streets of London to challenge the seventy-year-old monopoly of the horse-drawn bus. By 1905 their number had risen to twenty and by 1913 3,000 buses plied the London streets and the horse buses vanished for ever. Another casualty of the advance of the motor bus was the electric tram. Trams, which had appeared in many towns and cities in the 1890s, required special rails and overhead wires. The motor buses were faster and more versatile and so gradually the trams disappeared from the streets, although some cities still had them in 1939. Another victim of the motor car was the horse-drawn hansom cab which by 1920 had been driven off the London streets by the faster motor taxis.

Motor buses were responsible for sweeping changes in the lives of country people during the 1920s and 1930s. With the arrival of buses, villages, far from railway stations, were for the first time brought into contact with the towns. Mobile shops and libraries followed the buses into remote rural areas bringing with them changes in recreation habits and diet. The traffic was not all one-way for the villages found themselves visited by townspeople either as motor tourists or day-trippers out for an excursion in a 'charabanc'. Just as the railways had joined together the separate parts of Britain in the 1830s, so a hundred years later the internal combustion engine drew together town and country. The greatest change made by the motor car was the gift of personal freedom and mobility to thousands of people, for by 1939 the dream of 'Motoring for the Millions' was well on its way to fruition.

Aviation
In **1903** the American **Wright brothers** made the first flight in an aeroplane powered by an internal combustion engine. The significance of their achievement and the potential of the aero-plane were quickly understood. In **1909** the Frenchman **Blériot** flew the Channel and already the Army and the Navy were developing aeroplanes. Whilst the use of the aeroplane for civil transport was anticipated by a flight from London to Windsor in 1911 which carried mail, early development was almost entirely for military uses.

During the First World War there were a large number of technical changes and advances which meant that by 1918 planes existed capable of long-range journeys carrying cargoes and passengers. In **1919 Alcock** and **Brown** flew the Atlantic in a twin-engined Vickers Vimy bomber, originally designed for raids on Berlin. By this time several commercial companies had been formed and regular flights to Paris and the Isle of Man were under way. The new commercial companies suffered various financial difficulties in the early 1920s and partly to overcome these and co-ordinate their efforts, **Imperial Airways** was formed in **1924**. This company was an amalgamation of several smaller firms and with the help of a million-pound subsidy from the government aimed at the exploitation of commercial air travel.

Britain at this time was still a great imperial power and one of the attractions of air transport was its use in linking various parts of the Empire. During the 1920s there were various experimental flights to Egypt, India, Australia and South Africa undertaken with the intention of establishing regular flights to these countries. At the same time there were scheduled services between various parts of the British Isles such as Belfast and Liverpool and to various continental capitals.

By the 1930s airliners could carry up to forty passengers and in 1938 a flight to India took $3\frac{1}{2}$ days and to Sydney, $9\frac{1}{2}$. Fares were expensive: in 1927 the $2\frac{1}{2}$-hour flight from London to Paris cost £9 return first class and £7 10s. second class. Still, flying had caught the popular imagination and the possibilities of air travel raised great excitement. During the inter-war years there were frequent flying displays at Hendon and Croydon and the pioneer flights of such aviators as Sir Alan Cobham and Amy Johnson aroused great interest and admiration.

Wireless
In the **1890s** an Italian, **Marconi**, was investigating the possibility of sending messages by electric impulse over the air. His results were promising and aroused the interest of the British government which was prepared to give him every assistance. A newspaperman who witnessed the sending of one of the first 'wireless' messages in 1896 remarked, 'The air is full of the promise of miracles.' At first these miracles were used by ships and the armed forces, for as with the aeroplane, it was the military and naval potential of wireless which was exploited first.

The First World War led to the widespread use of wireless and many new breakthroughs of which the most important was the discovery of the means to transmit the human voice. Hitherto the wireless, like the earlier telegraph, relied on the Morse Code, a system of variously-timed impulses which corresponded to the letters of the alphabet. By 1922 it was possible to transmit and receive the human voice and public broadcasting for entertainment and instruction was a possibility.

Public broadcasting already existed in the United States but there transmission was in the hands of various local companies who relied upon advertising revenue. The commercialism of the American radio stations had led to the proliferation of programmes of a poor or worthless quality. In order to avoid this and establish a national service, the government formed the British Broadcasting Company in 1922. This body had a monopoly of all broadcasting in the British Isles. It was independent of the government, non-profit-making, and financed by the 10s. licence fee paid by every wireless owner. The **chairman** of this new body was **J. C. W. Reith** and from the beginning he was determined that the corporation would uphold high moral and intellectual standards. He was also insistent on the B.B.C.'s independence when during the General Strike of 1926 the government wished to take over the news broadcasts.

The popularity of broadcasting was immediate and by 1939 many millions possessed wireless sets. A wide range of programmes including talks, variety and music opened up new worlds for the listeners. Home-made entertainments such as the musical evening in the parlour died, but their loss was to some extent offset by the quality of the programmes put out by the B.B.C.

Conclusion

The changes outlined above made a great impact on the lives of the people of Britain. Steam railways and steamships carried the raw materials and products of industrial society quickly and cheaply. The goods produced by the mass production techniques of the nineteenth and twentieth centuries were easily and widely distributed. Individual people benefited from the freedom and mobility of the railways and later buses and cars. There were less obvious benefits such as changes in diet brought on by the cheap movement of foodstuffs, and the advent of motor ambulances and fire engines. Personal mobility meant that families were often divided but at the same time the speeding up of mail services strengthened the links between individuals however distant. New forms of recreation were possible and older ones such as football and cricket could be enjoyed by larger audiences.

There was opposition to these changes, sometimes inspired by suspicion and sometimes by rational misgivings. In the 1840s there were those who feared that railways would destroy civilised society and fill the countryside with noise and smoke. The redoubtable M.P. for Lincoln, Colonel Sibthorp, fought a stormy rearguard action against railways throughout the 1840s, fearing the destruction of the old peaceful England and dreading the arrival of the new. Sailing ships had their champions and there were those believers in wooden vessels who were delighted whenever an iron vessel floundered and sank. Motor cars were regarded with deep horror in the 1890s and until 1896 they were obliged by law to proceed at 4 m.p.h. led by a man with a red flag. Their noise, their fumes, the dust they created and the mud they threw at bystanders were all features that were bitterly regretted. The changes in communication had also injured many, the stage-coach companies, the builders of sailing ships, the proprietors of horse buses, the purveyors of 'live' entertainment such as the music hall, all suffered from the innovations previously described and therefore did their best to resist them.

But for the most part the people of the country were entranced by the amazing novelties of the railways, steamships, motor cars, aeroplanes and wireless. They were exciting and seemed to reflect a spirit of adventure as well as the growing ability of modern man to overcome the hazards of the environment. Most importantly, they were welcomed because they brought, however vaguely, the promise of better things.

Chapter 6
Reform of Working Conditions

Attitudes to reform

People in authority became aware that some aspects of conditions of employment were unsatisfactory at quite an early date. Efforts were made to improve safety for instance, and in 1815 **Davy's safety lamp** was introduced into the mines. In **1802** a Bill was brought in by **Sir Robert Peel**, himself a manufacturer, to end the worst abuses in respect of pauper child labour. It became illegal to employ them for more than twelve hours a day, or at all at night in the cotton industry. In **1819** the protective power of the Act was extended to 'free' children; that is, those children placed in employment by their parents rather than the parish authorities. No child under nine was to be employed in the cotton industry and children between the ages of nine and thirteen were also confined to twelve hours' labour in any one day. (Sir Robert Peel and Robert Owen were responsible for this bill.)

Nevertheless there was strong **resistance** to reform, even when practical demonstration indicated that such long hours of labour were injurious to health. Respectable medical practitioners could be found to argue, to the contrary, that such strenuous work was actually beneficial. In any case even if physical drawbacks did attach to work, its **moral desirability** was strongly urged. The evangelical notion that work and endeavour were spiritually uplifting and that idleness was a precondition of vice enabled many manufacturers to assert that they were doing good to their employees in keeping them occupied and out of reach of the gin shop. **Economic impracticability** was also put forward as an argument against reform. The nation, it was suggested, simply could not afford to reduce the hours of work as the reformists wanted. The economic viability of manufacture would cease and the whole industrial edifice would collapse. Others opposed reform out of simple **ignorance**. They had no idea that conditions were so bad, and the reports which came to their notice opened their eyes. Finally, reformist legislation was opposed on the grounds that evidence presented to the commission was biased and inaccurate. This objection was levied at **Sadler's Factory Commission**, which met in 1831 to enquire into conditions in the textile industry, and at **Ashley's Mines Commission**, which presented its report in 1842. 'The trapper is generally cheerful and contented and to be found like other children of his age occupied with some childish amusement as cutting sticks, making models of windmills, wagons etc. and generally in drawing figures with chalk on his door, modelling figures of men and animals in clay,' asserted Lord Londonderry, a prominent coalmine owner, in opposing the **Coal Mines Bill**. Nevertheless, the reform movement pressed on its inexorable path, and by the end of the century much reform had been achieved, though not on the voluntary basis which Owen had hoped to see established.

Robert Owen

Robert Owen had been factory manager of cotton mills in **New Lanark** in Scotland, but with financial help from friends he became owner in 1800. He hoped that the lines along which the mills were run would prove an inspiration to other mill owners. Labourers worked for shorter hours in his mills than was usual elsewhere, and they were provided with recreational facilities, schools, shops, and good standard housing. All were paid for out of the firm's surplus profits. In spite of its welfare commitments, the firm still prospered. But Owen's example was not followed, mainly because as a socialist he was regarded as an enemy of capitalism.

Owen thought the system led to inhumanity and exploitation. The capitalist confined his interest to money and profit, and cash was the only bond between master and man. Since the capitalist did not share the life of the worker in any respect, he failed often to see him as a human being. Instead he became a production unit yielding, or not yielding, enough profit to justify his continued employment. Owen wanted to disband the whole capitalist system and replace it with a new **Co-operative Society** (see page 56) in which money, having little part to play, would be replaced by a system of barter. He was also instrumental, even inspirational, in the establishment of the first **National Trade Union** (page 133). Thus it was clear to many industrialists that whilst as a factory owner he was nominally 'one of them', he was spiritually on the side of the workers and committed to the destruction of the system that gave the factory owners their *raison d'être*. If they accepted Owen's leadership and followed his New Lanark example, where might it not lead them?

Owen's atheism was also a factor against his influence, for the nineteenth century was an extremely religious age. Thus few factory owners were prepared to follow his example although he had some very influential friends (Jeremy Bentham was one of his partners at New Lanark).

Ten Hours Movement

The failure of voluntarism led to the growing emphasis on the need for statutory reform. To this end the **Ten Hours Movement** under the leadership of **Michael Sadler**, a Tory Banker and M.P., was formed in 1831. The movement aimed specifically at the reduction of working hours in factories to ten hours, but it had a much broader general aim and was behind most of the factory reforms which took place until the **Ten Hours Act** was finally passed in **1847**.

Factors in success

The success of the movement owed much to the individual endeavour of philanthropists like **Robert Owen, Robert Fielden** and **Lord Ashley**, though these are only a few of the names associated with reform. These were the men, some of them (Owen and Fielden for instance) factory owners themselves, who gathered evidence, publicised the worst conditions and steered the reform Bills on their perilous path through Parliament. But the reform movement also depended for success upon changing economic practice and as the century progressed on the altered social and political balance. The **trade union movement** in all its stages of development and the **Parliamentary Reform Acts** form an important background to legislative reform affecting employment. In the earlier period **Chartism** too had an important part to play for there was much Chartist agitation on behalf of the Ten Hours Movement, and the politicising of the grievance was a warning light to some who would otherwise have opposed reform. **Novelists** and other writers also did much to rouse public concern. Their mode of 'propaganda' was especially effective because they could personalise suffering by placing it in a character setting, and some writers, like Disraeli, could be very specific about abuses in connection with employment, for they had drawn upon documentary material to write their books. Certainly the writers were important in creating a sympathetic climate for reform.

Legislation

The textile industry

The **1833 Factory Act** was the first significant piece of legislation in respect of employment in industry. Its scope was limited (the terms of the act applied only to the textile industry and even then silk workers were exempted from all clauses except those relating to factory schools and inspectors), but with the passing of the Act the reformers had got their foot in the door. It was only a matter of time before its provisions were extended to other industries. The Act was the result of the findings of two commissions, Sadler's which met in 1831 and Ashley's, which met the following year (Sadler lost his parliamentary seat in the 1832 general election and was therefore disqualified from leading the commission).

Terms of the Act

The Act forbade the employment of children under nine, limited the hours of 'children' under thirteen to eight, and those of 'young persons' (between thirteen and eighteen) to twelve. It required the provision of two hours' daily schooling for 'children' and stipulated that machinery was not to be cleaned whilst in motion.

Ashley was disappointed not to have achieved the ten-hour day for 'young persons' for which he had striven and the school scheme was not a success since the government neglected to make financial provision for it. Still, the inclusion of the clause testified to a growing concern about the ignorance of the lower classes, and overall the Act is important as evidence of a departure from strict adherence to *laissez faire*. The government, in allowing the passage of the Act, was admitting that labour relations could not be left to regulate themselves and politicians were beginning to recognise some of the governmental implications of industrial society.

Evasion of the Act

There was some evasion of the Act, by masters and workers. Children often went to great lengths to disguise their true ages and this deception was easily carried out since records of births were incomplete (registration was not compulsory till 1847). Even when avoidance was made more difficult (certificates of age had soon to be obtained from reputable surgeons), it was still practised. Elder brothers would stand in for younger to gain the certificates and there was a profitable line in forgeries. Reform may have appeared desirable to the Ten Hours Committee but it was not only the factory owners who felt they could not afford it.

Later reform
Another **Factory Act** passed in **1844** went some way towards meeting the shortcomings in the 1833 Act. **Education was extended and became compulsory**. Children now had to attend the factory school for half the day and inspectors were given additional powers. It became their job to supervise education and they could dismiss incompetent teachers. The hours worked by children and females were also affected by the Act. **Children were not to work more than six and a half hours or women more than twelve.**

The problem of evasion was partially overcome by an **increase in fines for non-observance** and by the new judicial practice of having **two J.P.s** in place of the former one, **to hear cases of alleged breach of the Act**. The fact that J.P.s were largely drawn from the factory-owning class in industrial areas led to abuse of the law, and hampered its impartial administration. Now one J.P. could act as check upon the other.

The **Ten Hours Act** for which reformers had campaigned since 1831 was finally passed in **1847**. Since it was steered through parliament by **Robert Fielden** it is sometimes known as Fielden's Act. Only women and young persons were affected by it but advocates of the Bill hoped that men would benefit as well. It would be difficult and uneconomic, since women and young persons comprised the bulk of the labour force, for factory owners to operate a different shift system for men. The act was not an immediate success however for factory owners were able to take advantage of a loophole in the law. The Act had not specifically stated that the ten hours were to be worked continuously, though this had been the understanding of exponents of the Act. A relay system was thus introduced and legally approved by Judge Baron Parks in a **test case** heard in **1850**. Workers were employed for only a few hours at a time and were laid off on the factory premises in the interim.

Acts passed in **1850** and **1853** clarified the law and fixed times of opening and closing in mills. This effectively brought about the ten-hour day for men as well as women and young persons, though the position of men was not formalised until **1874**. The reform was accomplished without the severe damage to the industrial edifice which factory owners had predicted.

The mining industry

The most important milestone of reform in the industry was the 1842 **Mines Act** which had a very similar background to the 1833 Factory Act. It too was based on the findings of a commission (again headed by **Lord Ashley**). This report had even greater impact on account of the drawings which illustrated it. Pictures of women working naked underground and of children pushing heavy trucks up a steep incline had a definite shock value.

The **effect** of the Act was to **prohibit children under ten and women from undertaking work underground**. It also placed **restrictions on the use of pauper child labour**. Such children could not be bound beyond the age of eighteen. Again **inspectors** were appointed as overseers but their powers were more restricted than in the factory sphere. They had no right to comment on physical conditions in the mines, such as the condition of machinery or state of the tunnels, so could do nothing to ensure safety. They had responsibility only for the state and condition of persons working in the mines. The Act placed no restrictions on hours of work and made no provision for education. These shortcomings, especially the one in respect of safety, were the result of amendments proposed by the mining 'interest' in the House of Lords. In **1850 inspectors gained the right to report on the state of mines and machinery** but they were unable to alter basic conditions. Mining remained an extremely dangerous occupation until the twentieth century.

Other industries

The textile and mining industries were the pacemakers of reform, and gradually the protection of the Acts was extended to other industries.

In **1860** trades and occupations allied to textiles such as dyeing and bleaching were included in the Acts already passed, at **Lord Shaftesbury's** instigation (Lord Ashley inherited the Shaftesbury title in 1851). At the same time he had recommended an enquiry to be made into conditions in other industries. As a result of reports, pottery and matchmaking were brought within the scope of the law in **1864**. Blast furnaces, iron, steel and copper mills, glass, tobacco, printing and most other trades followed in **1867**. Those who worked in the 'sweated trades' and in shops were the last to benefit. They were helped by the **Trade Boards Act** (1909; see page 66) and the **Shop Hours Act** (1912).

Other relevant legislation

The **Employers' and Workmen's Act** passed in 1875 which placed both parties on the same legal footing in the event of breach of contract (formerly the workman had been guilty of a criminal offence and was therefore liable to imprisonment) is also important to any study of reform of working conditions, for in ending the legal inferiority of the working man, it dignified his standing in the eyes both of himself and his employer and lessened the distance between them. They now had the same responsibility and were liable to the same punishment.

The **Workmen's Compensations Acts** (1897 and 1906; see page 66) should also be mentioned in this context, for in dealing with the vexed question of industrial injury they had a dual effect: they achieved monetary protection for the injured man and his family and in making owners liable, no doubt encouraged them to reduce dangers in the place of work.

Trade unionism

Nor must trade unions be forgotten, for changes within individual trades and industries were often the result of private agreement between the two parties involved rather than of statutory legislation. The dockers, for instance, were able in 1889 to achieve better pay and terms of employment on their own initiative and in doing so they were setting the trend for the future. As trade unionism gained strength there was less dependence upon state initiative in respect of working conditions. The trade unions acted as vigilantes.

The climbing boys

The climbing boys and the struggle to end their employment are worth special attention since the failure of reform until 1875 shows how hard the struggle to ameliorate conditions of employment could be. There have been several intimations of this point but it is nowhere as graphically illustrated as in the case of the boy sweeps.

The cause of the climbing boys was one of the first to be taken up, since it has its origins in the eighteenth century. **William Blake** wrote a touching poem about them and the **Prince Regent** was president of the first society established for their protection. And yet they were among the last to benefit from reform.

Reasons for opposition to reform

Formidable interests ranged themselves against the climbing boys. The opponents of factory or mine reform, or of reform in any other industry if it comes to that, were the directors and owners. They formed a very small percentage of the nation, but the 'interest' which opposed abolition of the climbing boys was the all-embracing domestic one. Everyone had a chimney which needed to be swept and the majority were convinced (unreasonably) that machinery could not do it as well as a human agency. (In fact adequate machinery existed from 1819.)

The question of the Englishman's liberty was also at stake. The attempts to reform chimney sweeping impinged upon the privacy of the nation. The state was presuming to enter a man's house and tell him how his chimney must be swept. Thus the conditions of employment of the boy sweeps was by no means the only issue at stake. Opposition to reform in this instance is only another facet of the same attitude of mind which opposed public health reform. The line of demarcation between the public good and the freedom of the individual was clearly drawn in favour of the latter in nineteenth-century Britain. This largely explains the ineffectiveness of legislation to abolish climbing boys. The failure to appoint inspectors to oversee the various acts of government legislation until 1875 is also important. Given a public attitude of mind which encouraged evasion, this act of omission was folly.

Legislation

A bill regulating the employment of boy sweeps had been proposed in **1819** but failed in the Lords' stage of the reading. Lord Lauderdale's belief that reform should be voluntary (and left entirely to 'the moral feelings of possibly the most moral people on earth') carried the day. But in **1834** some legislation was achieved. Then, an Act **prohibited the employment of any child under ten as a chimney sweep**. It also laid down that **any boy requiring apprenticeship to a sweep was to be examined by two magistrates**. (This was to overcome the pressure of parents and the master sweep himself, for children were frequently sold into the trade.) Lastly **building regulations** stipulated a minimum size of flue and prohibited the more acute angles. These last clauses were designed obviously to protect any child going up a chimney. Deaths from suffocation were frequent and this was known.

Although heavy fines lay in store for those who flouted the Act, many were able to do so with impunity. No authority existed to administer it and magistrates were often indifferent or hostile. In **1840** a more severe Act was brought in under the auspices of **Lord Ashley** who had embarked upon what was to be a lifetime's career in helping the climbing boys. This Act **prohibited anyone under twenty-one from climbing chimneys**, and made the **apprenticeship of children under sixteen illegal**. But this Act failed also and for the same reasons as the last. The fate of yet another Act in **1864** designed to **prevent sweeps from employing children under ten and forbidding children under sixteen from entering a house with any sweep** (sweeps had argued that such children came only to hold the tools, but once inside they were sent up the chimney) fared no better, in spite of the public furore occasioned by Charles Kingsley's recently published and pathetic tale about boy sweeps, *The Water Babies*. The horrific real-life cases of suffocation in hot chimneys, of raw knees and elbows and of intimidation and brutality, publicised by the **Climbing Boys' Society**, also went unheeded. And yet the society calculated that 4,000 boys were employed in the trade as late as 1858. The campaign finally bore fruit in **1875**, however. Then a **system of licences was introduced**. Sweeps had to renew them annually and the power of enforcement of earlier legislation was vested in the police.

Chapter 7
Public Health and Medicine

Between 1815 and 1939 there was an enormous improvement in the health of the British people. By 1939, children survived the diseases of infancy, men and women lived longer and when they were unwell could, without cost consult doctors. Cholera, typhoid, typhus and diphtheria, once fatal illnesses, could now be prevented and cured. These changes were the consequence of action by national and local authorities to eliminate the conditions which had bred disease, advances in medical treatment and curative surgery and the extension of adequate medical care to all classes.

Public health

The growth of industry and the expansion of towns and cities in the early nineteenth century had been followed by disease. The life of the urban poor has been described in detail elsewhere but it is worth remembering that contaminated water, airless and damp dwellings and the lack of any means to dispose of waste and sewage combined to produce conditions in which disease of all kinds flourished.

In spite of certain limited advances in midwifery during the eighteenth century the infant death rate, which had been falling, rose after 1815. Medical men and philanthropists noticed that the urban death rate amongst adults appeared to be rising and in 1850 the army authorities publicly admitted that the bulk of recruits from industrial areas were invariably sickly and debilitated. In 1842 the **Royal Commission** which conducted an inquiry into the sanitary conditions of the labouring population reported that in Liverpool the life expectancy of a labourer was fifteen years. **Typhoid** and **typhus**, diseases known to the Victorians as 'fevers', were endemic in towns and between 1861 and 1870 over 14,000 sufferers from these diseases were admitted to the London hospitals.

The enormity of the problem of public health and the pitiful inadequacy of the new industrial towns to cope with it was recognised by philanthropists and doctors. Yet it was one fearful disease which finally stirred the public, who in turn agitated for legislation. This was **Asiatic cholera** which first reached Britain in 1831 and carried off thousands, mainly from the poorer classes in the great cities. The fear of cholera and subsequent epidemics here and in Europe concentrated public opinion on the matter of health legislation.

Yet in spite of the immediacy of the problem, there was much opposition to any schemes for national and local health codes. Legislation to enforce sanitation, and control the supply of water, was regarded in some quarters as an affront to personal freedom. *The Times* argued that it was the right of every Britisher to have his dunghill if he so wished, and elsewhere supporters of the *laissez-faire* school of thought claimed that the government had no right to impose its will in such a personal matter as hygiene. In mockery of these views **Punch** cartoonists portrayed smoking cities over which hovered spectres labelled 'Cholera' and 'Typhus' and the Thames was shown as a stagnant pond on which floated swollen corpses of animals and other less identifiable but equally noxious matter.

Yet cholera and fevers were no respecters of private liberty and whilst the exact causes of these diseases were yet unknown to medical science, there was a general agreement that they were encouraged by unwholesome water. The force of such arguments, the extent of the problems and the voices of those calling for action could not be ignored. In **1848** Parliament approved the first **Public Health Act**, the first of a large number of measures designed to improve the health and living conditions of the nation. A **Central Board of Health** was set up and local authorities were encouraged but not compelled to set up their own boards and appoint sanitary inspectors who would be under the control of the national board. **Edwin Chadwick**, who had for long campaigned for such a measure, was the first **Secretary** of this board. Opposition to the Act was great and many local authorities ignored it completely. Newcastle, where there was a serious cholera epidemic in 1853, chose not to take action and it was left to the parliamentary commission to expose the local authority's indifference to the appalling problems on its doorstep.

The life of the Central Health Board came to an end in 1854 largely as a consequence of parliamentary opposition. In the meantime however, the government was growing aware of its responsibilities and during the 1850s a series of Acts was passed aimed at stamping out various abuses and anomalies. **Sanitary** and **nuisance inspectors** were empowered to enter and examine lodging houses and, where conditions made it necessary, obtain their closure. In London a specially created **Metropolitan Water Board** was placed in charge of the city's sewage and water supply, and Glasgow secured permission for the demolition of uninhabitable slums. In **1855 vaccination** against smallpox was made **compulsory**.

In **1872** and **1875** came two of the most important **Public Health Acts**, the latter being largely the work of **Sir Richard Cross**, Home Secretary in Disraeli's cabinet. These acts made it compulsory for municipal authorities to appoint sanitary inspectors, medical officers of health, and inspectors of nuisances. In the countryside the local Poor Law guardians were given similar power so that every part of the country had some form of organisation responsible for public health. At the same time each area had to provide at least one hospital. In **1875** another important piece of legislation was passed, the **Sale of Food and Drugs Act** which empowered local authorities to appoint analysts who were to investigate allegations of the adulteration of food. If the charges were found to be justifiable then the local authority was obliged to prosecute the offender. For many years the **Lancet** (a medical journal) had been campaigning against the tendency of food-sellers to add harmful substances to their products such as alum in bread and white and red lead in confectioneries. In **1860** an **Act** had attempted to halt such practices but local authorities were reluctant to enforce it. The publicity which faced the food adulterators and the knowledge that they would face prosecution slowly put an end to this distasteful abuse.

The **laws** passed between **1848 and 1875** provided the framework for action by local authorities. In spite of indifference in some areas, many corporations were more than willing to use the powers conferred on them by the government. There was in many cities such as Birmingham a growing local pride which expressed itself in ambitious schemes of public works. Here and elsewhere the engineering skills of the Victorians were harnessed to such problems as water supply and sewage disposal. The strict enforcement of laws controlling lodging houses and certain forms of industrial waste and the demolition of decayed houses by local authorities all contributed to the bettering of conditions within cities.

Perhaps the best measurement of the success of this legislation was the decline in deaths from such diseases as cholera and typhoid. In 1861–70 the death rate from fevers was 885 in every million and from 1871–80 it was 442, half what it had been in the previous period. The provision of pure water supplies and the efficient disposal of waste had eliminated cholera and typhoid. Public agitation, civic action and engineering had combined to eradicate two of the worst scourges of urban industrial society.

Public medicine

Great problems remained to be solved. The most important of these was the continued existence of slums where unhealthy conditions kept the infant mortality rate at a high level and sickness was still largely unchecked. Poor diet and poor housing produced men and women who were weak and liable to frequent illness. The poor physical condition of men from the slums was noted by the army recruiting department during the Boer War and later during the Great War. The facts discovered by army doctors supported the results of the detailed reports of Rowntree and social workers in slum areas. All this evidence was forthcoming at a time when medical science was making great leaps forward in the understanding and treatment of disease. The only answer to this problem was some form of state medical care by which those thousands who, for lack of money, could not or would not visit a doctor could receive free and effective treatment.

Medical treatment was, however, costly and so frequently beyond the reach of the poorer classes. Some doctors ran their own private insurance schemes by which poor patients paid 1*d.* a week, and the trade unions and friendly societies also managed similar services which provided members with medical fees and sick pay in return for a small weekly subscription. There also existed a number of hospitals which were supported by voluntary charities.

Yet these facilities were not comprehensive and so many went without medical care. Instead these people turned to the numerous patent medicines widely sold in nineteenth- and early twentieth-century Britain. Turn the page of any large circulation newspaper and there are columns of advertisements offering pills, potions and ointments which the makers claimed cured every kind of ailment from chilblains to cancer. These quack medicines were costly and worthless and in the first decades of the twentieth century were increasingly exposed by the medical profession as fraudulent.

The turning point in the provision of medical treatment for the masses came in 1911 with the **National Insurance Act**. This has been more fully described elsewhere, but it should be remembered that it entitled the contributor to sick pay and free treatment by a doctor. It did not however cover the expenses of hospital treatment nor convalescence in a nursing home, nor did its benefits extend to the family of the contributor. In 1919 the administration of this Act and of all medical and sanitation services came under the **new Ministry of Health**.

By this time the health of the poorer classes was being improved by other measures. In the **1860s** a few local authorities had been specially empowered by the Acts of Parliament to **demolish slums** and build new houses for working people. These powers were extended to all local authorities by Acts in **1875** and **1890** and slowly programmes of demolition and rebuilding began. The unnecessarily high infant mortality rate and the prevalence of undernourished children in slum areas had prompted the opening of the first milk dispensary in St Helen's, Lancashire, in 1899 and other local authorities and charities followed suit in the early years of the twentieth century. The milk dispensaries soon became the infant welfare clinics where the child received medical attention and the mother qualified advice on diet. In 1926 the government undertook the provision of milk and school dinners which for the poor were free, although such schemes had existed in various areas for twenty years.

Medicine and surgery

The development in public medicine came during a period when medical science was undergoing a revolution; in the struggle against sickness and disease the balance was swinging in favour of medical science.

In 1815 medical science was for the most part baffled by disease and the public was on the whole sceptical of the medical profession. The doctor was the 'quack', his remedies were bogus if not harmful, and the surgeon was the 'sawbones', a figure of terror whom few, however ill, would dare face. In the following hundred years men of medicine were able by their own efforts to destroy for ever these misconceptions and amply demonstrate their skills.

The first major advance in medical knowledge was in the field of **anaesthetics**. In the preceding centuries, surgeons and anatomists had made considerable advances in their knowledge of the human body and in their techniques. These were, however, worthless since they were forced to operate on fully conscious and terrified patients. In the 1820s and 1830s attempts had been made to use laughing gas (nitrous oxide) to render patients unconscious. In 1847 the Edinburgh surgeon **Sir James Simpson** used **chloroform** with great success. The patient was rendered unconscious and the operation was successfully performed. The use of chloroform quickly spread and gave surgeons the chance to show their skills; operations once dreaded were no longer feared.

In spite of chloroform, post-operational death was commonplace in the 1850s. The killer was sepsis, caused by bacteria and germs often carried on the surgeon's hand or instruments. The Frenchman **Louis Pasteur's** discoveries concerning germs and bacteria provided the inspiration for the surgeon **Lord Lister**. In 1864 he insisted that the instruments used at his hospital, the **Glasgow Infirmary**, were sterilised, as was the operating theatre. His methods worked and the number of post-operational deaths dropped dramatically. By destroying bacteria and germs within the operating theatre Lister had made an enormous breakthrough and with justification he observed at the end of his life, 'I may have been the means of reducing, in some degree, the sum of human misery.'

From 1865 until the end of this period, medical research advanced at a rapid pace. The work of Pasteur was followed in Britain, Europe and the United States by studies aimed at the identification of the sources of disease. Once the scientist could isolate the source of disease, then he and others would devise measures to fight it. So by discovering the bacteria which lay at the root of a disease it was possible to devise the antidote and even the means of immunisation. By 1900 the cause of cholera was known and in 1911, once the body louse was identified as the cause of typhus, it was possible to take effective measures to combat the disease and eradicate it. Vaccines were developed to render persons immune to such illnesses as diphtheria. One result of this research was the passing of various quarantine laws. By these, contagious diseases were notified to the local Medical Officer of Health who was then enpowered to take measures to halt the spread of infection. School-children were regularly inspected for lice and other disease carriers and schools were regularly fumigated.

As the powers available to fight disease increased, so the standing of the medical profession increased. In **1858** an **Act** was passed which made the registration of doctors compulsory and laid down codes for medical education. This was the death knell of the ill-qualified or ignorant 'quacks' who were now liable for punishment and **by 1900** the **eleven major medical schools** in Britain were regarded along with those of Germany as the finest in Europe. On her return from the Crimea, **Florence Nightingale** used her experience in the army hospitals to improve the professional basis of nursing. In **1858 St Thomas's Hospital School of Nursing** was set up under the direction of Miss Nightingale and supported by public subscriptions. She had made nursing a respectable and honourable profession, imbued with high standards of duty and conduct.

Conclusion

The most outstanding feature of developments in public health and medicine was the way in which scientific advances and public action in the area of health went hand in hand. First had come the belated intervention of government to eradicate the appalling hazards to health created by the Industrial Revolution and then the realisation that the health of all members of the community was the concern of the government. Yet without the advances in the understanding and treatment of disease these measures would not have succeeded.

Chapter 8
Crime and Punishment

The rapid growth of population and the concentration of the new masses of industrial society into towns and cities accelerated the crime rate in the late eighteenth and early nineteenth centuries. The reasons for this significant increase in crime are many and complex. Many of the inhabitants of the industrial towns had been cut adrift from close-knit village societies where the censure of neighbours and the watchful eyes of parson and squire provided a kind of discipline. As many middle-class reformers repeatedly pointed out, the industrial workers lacked any kind of religious and moral education which might have given them the strength to resist temptation. Temptation to commit crime existed in abundance and for some was unavoidable. Lay-offs and subsistence wages could leave men and women pitifully short of money with no alternative but petty crime. The unending monotonous and grinding routine of the mine, factory or mill contrasted poorly with the attractions of a life of full-time crime which at least offered excitement, easy reward and independence. All these explanations for urban crime are neatly rolled together in Charles Dickens' *Oliver Twist*. Oliver, the workhouse child, was condemned to a life of drudgery and ill-usage until he was discovered and enlisted into a gang of pickpockets, managed by a fence, Fagin. Here, in spite of the lack of morals of his fellows, Oliver is treated with kindness and enjoys good company for the first time in his life.

The countryside was not isolated from the crime wave produced by the Industrial Revolution. Large numbers of vagrants roamed from village to village, living by casual labour and robbery. The railway navvies, hardened by the brutality of their labour, provided a further hazard to country dwellers; several times in the 1830s masses of these workmen ran amok in remote areas and had to be controlled by hastily summoned troops. Navvies, vagrants and farm labourers all poached and would, if challenged, not hesitate to use their guns to resist arrest. So great had this problem become that in **1819** resisting a game-keeper became a hanging offence (**Ellenborough Law**) whilst poaching carried a sentence of up to fourteen years' transportation.

The crimes of this period fall into two main types: those committed for gain, which included the vast bulk of offences, such as begging, counterfeiting, picking pockets, pilfering and robbery; and those undertaken for less obvious personal motives, such as murder. In the last category came that offence which so aroused the indignation of social reformers, drunkenness. Long drinking hours, the abundance of drinking houses, especially after the **1830 Beer Act** had made licences easily obtainable, and the cheapness of beer (strong ale was $4\frac{1}{2}d.$ a quart in 1830) made drunkenness an epidemic especially amongst the labouring classes. Social factors also encouraged heavy drinking. Grim home surroundings made the men and women of the slums seek the conviviality of the beer house or pub and beer and gin were palatable alternatives to the unwholesome water supplied in so many towns and cities.

Drunkenness was regarded as the root of many social evils; it led to wife-beating, it destroyed the home, weakened moral standards and encouraged thriftlessness. To fight the evils of drink, the **Temperance Movement** came into existence. From its beginnings in 1828 it endeavoured through lectures, pamphlets, parades, songs and individual persuasion to turn the working man away from drink. 'Drink is the enemy of the Working Classes' was one of its slogans and it was only by 'signing the pledge' never again to drink that a man might be saved. The movement had some success. Drunkenness began to decline by the 1870s. The **Licensing Acts of 1872 and 1874** limited drinking hours (5 p.m. to 12.30 a.m. in London, 6 p.m. to 11 p.m. in other towns and 6 p.m. to 10 p.m. on Sundays), better housing conditions and the appearance of alternative recreations such as parks and libraries also helped to reduce drunkenness. Nevertheless old habits died hard, for in 1892 the trade union leader Ben Tillett claimed that working classes' addiction to drink 'killed their self-respect'.

The other crime which was very common at this period was **prostitution**. Prostitutes openly plied their trade in all large towns and especially London. They ranged from wealthy 'professionals' to wretched individuals like the many seamstresses who had to augment their woefully low wages by walking the streets. Whilst many individuals and charities attempted to reclaim women from their moral degradation, the question of prostitution was largely ignored and often the laws against it were half-heartedly enforced. The **Criminal Law Amendment Act of**

1885 which forbade prostitutes from publicly soliciting changed matters slightly for many were forced off the streets. The same Act also dealt heavily with brothel-keepers and those involved in child prostitution. Still, for most men and women the existence of prostitutes, or 'fallen women' as they were sometimes called, was an unavoidable fact about which little could be done.

Punishment

The growing numbers of criminals and the frightening expansion of crime alarmed public opinion and posed immense problems for the administration. Reactions to the problem differed; some wanted harsh penalties which would deter the criminal and protect life and property, whilst others questioned the effectiveness of such retribution and looked for ways in which to reform the criminal. It was left to successive governments in the nineteenth and twentieth centuries to find a workable balance between these two viewpoints.

Capital punishment

In the century before 1820 the government's answer to the crime wave had been to stem the flood of lawlessness by extending the death penalty to cover a vast number of offences. By **1820** over **200 crimes** including forgery, housebreaking and such bizarre and unlikely offences as breaking a river bank or impersonating a Chelsea Pensioner were **punishable by hanging**. When in 1812 the government had made machine-breaking a hanging offence Lord Byron protested, 'a new capital punishment must be devised, new snares of death must be spread for the wretched mechanic . . . Is there not blood enough upon your penal code?' His words were ignored; the government feared revolution and was willing to use any measures which might coerce the discontented.

Yet Byron's arguments and those of others who questioned the indiscriminate use of hanging had made their mark on **Sir Robert Peel** who became Home Secretary in 1822. During the next eight years Peel **simplified the complex legal code** and drastically reduced the number of hanging offences. He argued that the old system was both inhumane, unworkable and ineffective. Juries would ignore overwhelming evidence and acquit a man rather than see him hanged for a trivial offence. Judges were sometimes reluctant to pass the death sentence and even when they did, the Home Office preferred to remit the sentence to one of transportation. Thus, between 1818 and 1825, 7,770 death sentences were delivered but only 579 were carried out. More-over the removal of the death sentence from such offences as petty theft and forgery did not lead to an increase in these crimes. By 1833 only four crimes (treason, murder, piracy and attempted murder) carried the death sentence and after 1863 it no longer obtained for attempted murder.

Hangings were still public at this time and attracted large crowds; in 1856 special excursion trains carried the curious to see the hanging at Stafford of the celebrated poisoner Dr Palmer. These occasions were rowdy, drunken and brutal and so in **1868** an Act (**Capital Punishment Amendment Act**) was passed which ended public executions. Such spectacles were considered unworthy of a Christian and civilised nation.

Transportation

The gradual abandonment of the death penalty in the 1820s and 1830s made it necessary to replace it with other punishments. One existed already, **transportation**. Convicts were taken to moored hulks (old warships) from where they were periodically shipped to Australia. On arrival they were either detailed to perform hard labour on roads or harbours or else assigned to settlers as unpaid workers. A contemporary ballad describes their fate:

'The first day that we landed upon that fatal shore
The planters they came round us full twenty score or more,
They rank'd us up like horses, and sold us out of hand
Then yok'd us up unto ploughs, my boys, to plough
                                    Van Dieman's Land.'

The subsequent life of the convict was hard, for any breaches of the stern code of discipline were punished by flogging.

Whilst this system recommended itself to the British government the Australian settlers became increasingly resentful of their colony being used as a dumping ground for convicts. Their protests increased so that by the **1850s** the settlers finally had their way for with the refusal of further convicts by the govern-ment of Western Australia, **transportation ended**.

For the most part transportation had been a terrifying experience. A well-behaved convict might earn remission and a 'ticket of leave' which was a form of parole, although the authorities discouraged him from leaving Australia. For a brief time **Alexander Maconochie**, the governor of Norfolk Island, experimented with a form of self-help by which the convicts earned 'marks' for hard work. In his words they were encouraged to 'earn their freedom by the sweat of their brows' under a benevolent administration. This was exceptional and in spite of its success it was replaced by a fiercer regime where the stick and not the carrot ruled.

Prisons

Long before transportation had been abandoned, the government was looking for alternatives and therefore there was a reorganisation of prisons at home. In **1835** the **Prisons Act** brought all prisons under the control of the Home Secretary and subsequent legislation increased Home Office surveillance. At this time there was much rebuilding of prisons since many of the older buildings were totally inadequate for their purpose. Two rival types of prison system existed, the 'silent' in which the prisoners were forbidden any kind of communication, and the 'separate' in which convicts were kept completely apart from one another. **Pentonville**, which was completed in **1842**, was a model prison built on the 'separate' principle which depended on one prisoner to one cell. An example of such a prison, still in existence, is at Lincoln where the chapel is so constructed that every convict had a pew in which he could sit completely unseen by his fellows. The 'silent' system lost ground as it was impossible to uphold without recourse to a savage punishment if the rules were broken. Whilst in prison the convict was expected to perform various onerous and futile tasks such as operating the treadmill (a massive wheel turned by the treading of the convict's feet and often adjusted to force him to run continuously or face a dangerous fall) and the carrying of heavy shot. These exercises remained in use until the turn of the century.

Faced with the ending of transportation, the government passed the **Penal Servitude Act** of **1857** which replaced shipment to the colonies with a sentence of hard labour. This usually consisted of heavy work in quarries. With his shaved head, coarse clothing (marked with broad arrows) and sparse diet the convict faced a rigorous life in a world of stern discipline. Changes took place in the early years of the twentieth century. Many prison governors with the approval of the Home Office softened the regimes of their prisons and aimed, where possible, to introduce conditions which would help reform the criminal and prepare him for a future in the outside world. Wakefield prison was particularly associated with such ameliorating alterations in the prison code. In **1934** the Home Office opened the first '**open prison**' where restriction was minimal and where conditions were such as to encourage personal reform and preparation for release and new life.

The **Probation Service** (formally introduced with the **1908 Probation Act**) also had an effect on types of punishment meted out by the courts, especially to first offenders. An offender would be placed under the supervision of a probation officer who would be responsible for his conduct and who would assist him to find a new life and where possible to avoid a further brush with the law. Such a system kept many first offenders and petty criminals out of prison and so free from the dubious influence of hardened criminals.

Juvenile offenders were recognised as a special category of criminals by the **Parkhurst Act** of **1838** by which a special prison was built for them on the Isle of Wight. Here, and later, it was hoped that they could be kept away from contact with older and hardened criminals. In **1837** a **Reformatory Schools Act** set up training establishments for young criminals and vagrants, although conditions in such institutions were invariably harsh. In reaction to the starkness of the reform schools, an American, **Brice Ruggles**, introduced a new type of institution for young offenders at Borstal in Kent. His methods, which aimed at rehabilitation in an atmosphere of strict fairness, proved successful and in 1908 received Home Office approval. Similar institutions appeared elsewhere, all taking their name from the birthplace of the original.

Police

Perhaps the best guarantee of public order, the protection of life and property and most importantly, the prevention of crime, was the establishment of a professional police force. In **1815** law enforcement was a haphazard business in the hands of a few small independent police offices in London and the hapless parish constables in the provinces. The **Bow Street Runners**, in spite of their fame and public respect, largely confined themselves to the profitable business of recovering stolen goods rather than tackling murderers. Often troops had to be employed to handle large-scale disorders as during the unrest in 1818–19. The disorganisation and feebleness of the forces of law enforcement caused public disquiet and provided excellent arguments for a regular and organised police force.

It was this situation that prompted Sir Robert Peel (Home Secretary 1822–9) to found the **Metropolitan Police** in **1829**. The new force had its headquarters in a building overlooking Scotland Yard and its jurisdiction covered Westminster and its environs. In 1835 the **Municipal Corporations Act** included provisions for the new local authorities to set up their own forces. Many refused to do so and therefore in 1856 the **Police in Boroughs and Counties Act** made it the duty of each local authority to form a police force. Each force was locally run (usually by watch committees in the boroughs) and was liable to inspection by the Inspectorate of Constabulary. If the inspector's report was satisfactory a government grant was forthcoming to cover a quarter of the costs of clothing and wages.

Twenty-seven years elapsed between the establishment of Peel's force and the spread of police forces throughout the kingdom. Why? The plain answer was deep-rooted public suspicion of the police. The idea of a police force was for many alien and un-English; it reeked of continental despotism and one M.P. remarked that police were more suitable for 'Naples than for England'. (For most people Naples embodied all the evils of brutal foreign tyranny.)

Once set up, each force had its own chief constable who was usually an ex-army officer with, below him, superintendents (who supplied their own ponies and traps), inspectors, sergeants and constables. The constables were invariably either sturdy and sober labourers or ex-soldiers (many Waterloo men joined the original Metropolitan force) who after a month's training were paid 15s.–20s. a week.

In **1842** following public irritation over the slowness with which a murderer had been apprehended, the Home Secretary approved the formation of a small **detective branch** at Scotland Yard. This group grew and in 1878 was reorganised as the **C.I.D.** (Criminal Investigation Department) under a barrister, Howard Vincent. This new department faced many problems including a great deal of public criticism which in 1888 was justified by the incompetence of detectives seeking to catch the notorious White-chapel murderer (known then and since as Jack the Ripper). This case also highlighted another problem for the police, the inability of local forces to co-operate, for the murders involved the Metropolitan and City of London police who wasted much time in tripping over each other's boots. So it was that in the 1890s the fictional private detective such as Sherlock Holmes always appeared, one, two, or three jumps ahead of the bumbling C.I.D. officers who humbly sought his assistance.

By 1900 the methods of the police were advancing. Systems of classifying fingerprints and blood groups and the establishment of a comprehensive file of criminal records aided detectives.

Forensic laboratories were set up and sophisticated scientific methods were employed to beat crime. The patient detective work, careful collection and scientific assessment of evidence which led to the arrest of Kennedy and Brown for the Gutteridge murder in 1928 showed the new police methods at their best and won great public admiration.

Conclusion

The Industrial Revolution had seen an alarming increase in crime. By the end of the nineteenth century and the beginning of the twentieth the crime rate was falling. Why was this? Changes in living conditions, more widespread education and greater prosperity (all described elsewhere) played their parts in diminishing crime. Attitudes towards the criminal and his treatment also changed. It was discovered that life and property could be adequately protected without resort to vengeful, brutal and often unworkable penalties. So the indiscriminate use of the death penalty and the severities of transportation disappeared and were replaced by prison which in turn became an institution where rehabilitation became of importance. Here as in many other areas, Britain was becoming a more humane nation. Lastly and most importantly, the emergence of a professional police force played its part.

As their methods improved and they won public confidence, the police showed that they could not only detect crime but by their presence, they could prevent it.

Chapter 9
Trade Unions

In 1815 trade unions were illegal. Two Acts passed in 1799 and 1800, the **Combination Acts**, had made it illegal for workers to come together to improve wages, reduce hours of work and otherwise change their terms of employment. Strikes, meetings and the collection of funds were illegal. These Acts were passed in haste and out of fear that revolution such as had erupted in France in 1789 might occur here. Any lower-class organisation was to be regarded with suspicion since it might become a centre of disruption. Manifestations of working-class unrest, such as the Luddite riots, Peterloo, etc., caused this fear to be maintained until the 1820s. In **1824** the Acts were **repealed**. Two men working in conjunction were responsible: **Francis Place** and **Joseph Hume**. Place was a self-employed tailor, a radical speaker and writer. He had himself been a unionist, and had led a strike in the 1790s. Joseph Hume was an M.P. who because of his interest in trade union affairs was appointed to a parliamentary committee set up to enquire into the 'law of workman's combination'. This committee advised repeal, mainly on the grounds that the Acts were ignored anyway and were impossible to enforce.

Growth and collapse of unionism, 1824–34

Repeal was important because it brought trade unions into the open. Although unionism had continued surreptitiously whilst the Acts were in force, it could not prosper. The fact that they were against the law deterred many working men from joining unions. Now the numbers began to burgeon. The unsettled economic climate partly explains the expansion. Fluctuating markets and unstable prices engendered anxiety. But the effectiveness of the movement was hampered in so far as it was fragmented. It consisted of separate groups of men, defending the interests of their particular trade. What was needed was some form of **national organisation**. In 1830 the **National Association for the Protection of Labour** was formed under the auspices of **John Doherty**, a spinner. Membership of this union was 100,000 by the end of the year and twenty different trades were represented. This early attempt at national organisation foundered however, and by 1831 the N.A.P.L. was defunct.

Robert Owen: the G.N.C.T.U.

In 1834, **Robert Owen**, a visionary factory owner, founded the **Grand National Consolidated Trades Union**. Owen saw his union as the instrument whereby existing social and economic organisation might be changed. His aims went beyond the mere improvement of working conditions and the increase of wages which unionists hitherto had sought; he saw the huge membership (reputedly one million by the end of the year) as a means by which workers could take control of industry and dominate society. A **general strike** would be called which would precipitate a collapse of the existing system. The future of the union looked promising. The enthusiasm of working men was undoubted, and their need was particularly great since Owen's union arose at a moment of acute economic crisis, evidenced by severe disturbances in both rural and industrial areas. (Swing riots in the south and east; strikes and riots in coalmining areas of Northumberland and Durham.) And, Owen's leadership was purposeful. But the projected strike never occurred and by the end of the year the union had disintegrated. The action of employers, the inadequacy of union funds and the incidence of the Tolpuddle ruling were the main factors behind the failure.

Factory owners required workers to sign a pledge renouncing union membership and they staged lockouts of union men, employing blackleg labour in their place. The funds of the union were insufficient to meet the demands made by members thrown out of work or striking on their own initiative. But perhaps the most severe blow to the union was dealt by the legal ruling on the **Tolpuddle Martyrs**, the six Dorset labourers who, faced with a reduction in their wages ($8s. - 7s.$ a week), formed a branch of the G.N.C.T.U. and were prosecuted by local magistrates, unnerved by rural unrest. They could not proceed against the labourers on the grounds that trade unionism was illegal, but a law of 1797 which prohibited the taking of illegal oaths was applied. It was held that the oath they had taken upon joining the union was illegal and they were sentenced to transportation to Australia for seven years. The importance of this incident to the trade union movement was that working men became fearful of it. Too many risks were attached to membership and the benefits were not yet proven.

Model unions

Trade unionism continued to exist after 1834 but not as a powerful and coherent movement. The working classes preferred to support Chartism in the hope of changing their situation through political action, but in 1851 the **Amalgamated Society of Engineers** was formed. This was a new type of union. Its members eschewed the image projected by Owen of an organisation bent on radical social upheaval. This union aimed at peaceful negotiation between employers and paid union officials, to achieve improved conditions of work and pay. Strikes as a means of persuasion were not ruled out, but they were regarded as a last resort, one unionist commenting, 'strikes are like wars in the political world: both are crimes unless justified by absolute necessity'. The union also acted as a friendly society providing unemployment and sickness benefit and superannuation. Other trades followed the example of the engineers and established unions along the same lines. But the new model unions, as they were called, were subscribed to by **skilled** workers such as carpenters, bricklayers and boilermakers only. The unskilled could not afford the high membership rates (c. 1s. 6d. per week).

The Junta

By the 1860s these new unions were dominated by a small group of five leading officials centred on London, the most prominent of whom was **Robert Applegarth**, Secretary of the Carpenters' Union. The self-imposed function of this 'Junta' was to direct the activities of the unions. The influence they brought to bear was moderate and they sought to endow unions with an image of respectability.

The Sheffield outrages

The attempt of the Junta to remove the association in the public mind of trade unionism and violence received a setback when in **1866** gunpowder attacks were made on employers and non-union members by file grinders striking in Sheffield. Two men were killed during these disturbances.

The Trades Union Congress

The need for a national organisation was apparent by 1868. The publicity surrounding the Sheffield outrages had helped to create a climate of hostility towards unionism. A flagging economy also contributed to their unpopularity since any movement designed to increase wages and therefore the cost of production now seemed unpatriotic. It was also likely that greater influence could be brought to bear upon extremists if a more formal and representative organisation than the Junta existed to represent unionism as whole. Finally, the legal ruling in the action brought by the boilermakers against their secretary for withholding £24 of union money underlined the insecurity of the trade union movement. The judge held that the union could not recover its funds since trade unions were illegal and therefore had no rights at law. If this was so, trade unions were in a very weak position and stood in need of a firm and united base from which to urge reform. In **1868** the first **Trades Union Congress** was called. The authority of leaders democratically elected by the thirty-seven delegates representing 118,000 members and attending this conference was at first disputed by the Junta, but by 1871 the leaders of the Congress had established themselves as the spokes-men of the trade union movement and maintained a close watch over legislation affecting working men.

Trade Union Act, 1871

A parliamentary commission had been set up in 1867, following the 'Outrages', to enquire into trade unions, which had recom-mended the granting of legal status to trade unions. The **Trade Union Act** of 1871 achieved this, thus safeguarding union funds, but in the same year the **Criminal Law Amendment Act** was passed which, whilst recognising the right of unionists to strike, forbade picketing. Thus whilst the union movement was strengthened in one respect, its power was curtailed in another. Members agitated for the repeal of the Act, which was achieved in **1875**. The movement now stood firm and strong, respectable and united, possessed now of the means to take effective action against employers should the negotiating principle fail.

The unskilled unions

Some prominent unionists however were worried by the exclu-siveness of the movement. The Trades Union Congress repre-sented the skilled workers only. The unskilled remained outside the movement, deterred from joining the new models by the high subscriptions and the discouraging attitude of some members. Helped by prominent model unionists such as **Thomas Mann** and **John Burns** (members of the Amalgamated Society of Engineers) to form their own organisations and encouraged by the success of the matchgirls and dockers in their respective strikes, unskilled men joined the movement, bringing a more aggressive tone to the Trades Union Congress.

The matchgirls' strike

In 1888, encouraged by **Mrs Annie Besant**, a socialist worker, the matchgirls at Bryant and May's East End factory struck for better wages. The publicity surrounding their case won them considerable sympathy and they were successful.

The dockers' strike

Led by **Ben Tillett**, this strike took place the next year and was an important landmark in the development of trade unionism, not only because the dockers achieved their aim of a basic rate of 6*d*. and 8*d*. for overtime and minimum employment of four hours, but because prominent public figures such as Cardinal Manning and the Bishop of London supported the strike and because members of the general public contributed funds. Public sympathy, as more recent events have shown (miners' strikes 1973, 1974, firemen's strike 1978) can be the most important weapon in the armoury of any organisation.

The Taff Vale judgement

In 1901 the **Taff Vale Railway Company** brought an action for damages against the **Amalgamated Society of Railway Servants**, following a strike. The courts found in favour of the company and the engineers were ordered to pay **£23,000**. The implications of this case were serious for it rendered the strike weapon useless. Unions could not afford to strike if in addition to paying members during a strike they were obliged to compensate employers afterwards. In 1906 a **Trade Disputes Act** was passed in response to pressure from trade unionists, which nullified the Taff Vale decision and removed the threat. But one hurdle had been overcome for the unions to be faced by another. In 1909 the judgement delivered in the **Osborne Case** jeopardised their position once more.

By 1909, the Labour Party had become important to the trade union movement for it gave the unions a parliamentary voice. But the Labour Party depended upon trade union funds to pay M.P.s' salaries and to finance campaigns. **William Osborne**, a member of the Amalgamated Society of Railway Servants and a Liberal, objected to the political levy; the proportion of each subscription which went to support the Labour Party. He prosecuted his union and the House of Lords judged the practice illegal. The **Trade Union Act** of **1913** amended this decision, allowing the union to make the levy if the **majority of members** agreed. Individual members who objected could opt out of the payment.

The Taff Vale and Osborne rulings are important in demonstrating a growing hostility towards trade unions which had become powerful and aggressive (many strikes 1900–14). By 1913 4½ million workers were union members, many faced with a decline in living standards. Strength allied to a sense of grievance partially explains the aggressiveness of the unions, but another important contributory factor was **syndicalism**, an influential idea which aimed at the destruction of private ownership and the establishment of workers' control of industry. The concerted action of the most powerful unions was envisaged as the means to this end, as was the emphasis upon strike rather than negotiation in disputes. In 1913 the **Triple Alliance** was formed: the Miners' Federation, National Union of Railwaymen, and National Transport Federation agreed to strike in unison, but there was no chance to test the friendship until the war was over.

The war

The war was prejudicial to syndicalism. Militancy seemed unpatriotic and the full employment which ensued removed the most acute distress felt by many workers. The unions agreed to submit all disputes to arbitration for its duration. After 1916 discontent did reappear, especially on the Clyde where shop stewards activated strikes, but their removal or imprisonment prevented the spread of militancy and the industrial boom of the early post-war years rendered it unnecessary. But by 1921, an economic crisis was apparent. The situation seemed propitious for syndicalism.

Black Friday

In April 1921, it was suggested that miners employed in the coal industry, which had recently reverted to private ownership, should take a cut in wages (in some cases up to 50 per cent). Demand for coal had slackened and the industry was in difficulty. The miners responded by calling a strike and by turning to their allies for support. It was agreed that a general embargo should be put on the movement of coal, to take effect from Saturday 16 April, but on Friday 15 April the N.U.R. and N.T.F. reneged on the agreement and the miners were left to fight alone. After three months, they were forced to capitulate. Wage cuts followed in all industries during 1921. The **significance** of this incident is therefore **immense**. The Triple Alliance, having been put to the test, had failed to bring about the collapse of capitalism, even at a moment of its extreme weakness. The reason was the fear of the other two unions that they would be committed to a long and expensive strike. They were not prepared to make the sacrifice. The particularist outlook of the unions was too strong for the syndicalist idea to succeed. This fact was demonstrated also by the failure of the General Strike.

The General Strike

In 1925 miners faced another crisis. The industry had not revived, and the mine owners therefore suggested another wage cut or alternatively an agreement by the miners to work eight instead of the statutory seven hours each day. When the miners objected, the government intervened with an offer to subsidise the industry for a year whilst an independent commission looked into it. The **Samuel Commission** made its report in **March 1926** and agreed with the mine owners that wage cuts or longer hours were necessary. The miners went on strike at the end of April and this time the other unions prepared to follow. The general wage cuts which had followed Black Friday had shown unions that the mining industry was a yardstick. If employers prevailed against the miners, then a precedent would be set which would affect them all. Other workers could expect to have to take wage cuts too. But if the unions stood together and brought industry to a total halt, the government and employers would have to think of some other way out of the crisis than worker sacrifice.

The syndicalist dawn was at hand. On 3 May a **general strike was called**, but it lasted a mere ten days. The **failure** is largely explained by the preparedness of the government. The unions had depended upon a total disruption of all services, but the government had laid contingency plans and were able to keep food supplies going. This threatened to lengthen the strike and it was doubtful if unions could afford that. A large sector of public opinion, too, was on the side of the employers and government, and volunteers ran many essential services. Thus, the worst effects of the strike were not felt. Another factor in the failure of the strike is the fear of the unionists of the consequences of success if the government were brought down and worker control established. How would they solve the economic problem? The English working classes were on the whole 'conservative' in their social outlook. Many were not certain that they wanted to destroy the system utterly. They wanted a chance to share the prosperity of the upper and middle classes, not to displace them. Thus the revolutionary potential of the strike worried them. Union leaders were also concerned about the legal consequences of their action since lawyers were suggesting the illegality of a general strike. Prosecutions and imprisonment could follow. On

12 May the strike was called off, though the miners remained out until December.

The aftermath

In **1927**, the **Trade Disputes Act** was passed which established the principle of the illegality of general strikes. It also affected the power of the unions by altering the earlier ruling on the question of the political levy. Now unions could only collect the levy from members who specifically agreed to pay it. This was a minor attempt to undermine the political power of the unions. But in fact statutory limitations upon trade unions were unnecessary. The failure of the strike had been salutary, and the economic climate until 1939 was not conducive to activism. Workers were glad to have any job at all, and trade union leaders such as **Ernest Bevin** and **Walter Citrine** placed faith in the negotiating principle once more, and gave support to the joint consultative committee of labour and management over which **Sir Alfred Mond** of Imperial Chemical Industries Ltd presided. This desire of management to conciliate is an important consequence of the General Strike, sometimes overlooked. The failure of the strike may have checked the more revolutionary elements in the trade union movement but its near success also acted as a warning to industrialists. Unionism had been powerful and its potential remained, as also the reason behind its existence: the need of working men to protect themselves in respect of their employment.

Chapter 10
The Changing Status of Women

Social attitudes
The ideal woman
The ideal woman in the nineteenth century was cast in a domestic role. She was a gentle and loving mentor to her children and a soothing and admiring presence to her husband. She was capable of creating an ordered and harmonious background to life, and marriage was the most honourable and desirable occupation open to her. Home was a 'place of peace' and shelter; 'a rock' in the midst of the swirling stream of industrial life to which one could cling for safety and sanity. These images of the home (John Ruskin's) explain a good deal about nineteenth-century attitudes towards women and the role in which they were cast. The world women could create was in direct contrast to the hurly-burly and brutality of industry, and whatever their status in society, women were thought to have an important part to play.

'Confined to their cage with nothing to do but to plume themselves and stalk with mock majesty from cage to cage' was the life to which **Mary Wollstonecraft** thought women were committed when they conformed to this ideal. But if men did seek to confine women, the cage was gilded and the perch in the nature of a pedestal. Degradation and humiliation may have been the effect produced upon many women by their role but it was men's intention to dignify and enshrine them. Pictures of the period reveal this very clearly. The aura of light, the image of sweetness, delicacy, purity and charm, of dependability and loyalty is projected in many of them. Even the consciously bad and unsympathetic treatment of women can often be related to this conception, for the prostitutes and adulteresses, in shattering the dream and sullying the ideal, deserved to become social outcasts.

The domestic experience
Some women undoubtedly found fulfilment in the domestic role, and plenty to occupy their time. The task of ordering the average middle- and upper-class household was no mean one. The planning of meals, the governance of servants, the supervision of the younger children, the direction of a social life, the giving of

tea- and dinner-parties and the paying and receiving of calls: all these activities fell within her scope. A glance at Mrs Beeton's *Book of Household Management* will dispel any illusion that it was a life totally without challenge.

But certainly it was not intellectually taxing. Florence Nightingale complained for instance in 1852 that 'a woman cannot live in the light of intellect. Society forbids it.' The most she could do was to live through her husband. She had to achieve her ambitions vicariously if at all. 'A woman devotes herself to the vocation of her husband. She fills up and performs the subordinate parts of it. But if she has any destiny, any vocation of her own, she must renounce it nine times out of ten.' There is other evidence to suggest that intellect was considered incompatible with femininity, even a defiance of nature:

> 'Man for the field and woman for the hearth,
> Man for the sword and for the needle she;
> Man with the head and woman with the heart
> Man to command and woman to obey
> All else confusion.'
>
> (Tennyson: 'Princess Ida')

Certainly, the education required to fit women for this domestic role was limited. Some anecdotal history, a little French, drawing, singing and the pianoforte: these filled up her time. The only serious incursion was a little arithmetic which might come in useful for household accounts.

The alternatives to the domestic role
Few occupations were available for upper-class women. Those unsuccessful in the bid for a husband and without a sufficiency to maintain themselves were obliged (like Jane Austen) to become dependants in the homes of relations, in which case they suffered the shackles of domestic life without the compensation of respect accorded to the mistress of the house. The only other respectable outlet was to become a **governess**, a dreaded fate since the ambiguity of status which attended the position – 'did one belong in the dining-room or servants' hall?' – was humiliating, as Charlotte Brontë, drawing on her own experience, made clear in *Jane Eyre*.

Writing provided another avenue of escape, but the topics treated by the female writers of the age and the manner of publication only serve to underline the limitations placed upon women in nineteenth-century Britain. Several of them felt unable to command a following purely on their own merits and adopted male pseudonyms. (Currer, Ellis and Acton Bell were the names adopted by Charlotte, Emily and Anne Brontë.)

The extent to which women were confined by their sex is nowhere more evident however than in the writings of **George Eliot** (Marianne Evans). Two of her most prominent heroines, Dorothea (*Middlemarch*) and Gwendolen (*Daniel Deronda*), although accomplished and clever, tie themselves to men and marriage, solely to realise their ambitions. (They thus bear out Miss Nightingale's assertions.) Dorothea's moral and intellectual drive to reform the world and Gwendolen's smaller ambition to make her mark socially must be achieved through Casaubon and Grandcourt, their respective husbands. The emotional price paid for this sacrifice to ambition (which is not realised in either case) is a major theme in both novels.

Jane Austen's writings show women in pursuit of marriage, and even the cleverest and most independent of Miss Austen's heroines, Emma (she has a fortune of her own), is glad to marry and to have found in Mr Knightley not her equal, but her superior. The question of Emma's financial independence brings one to another observation: that even when the chance of independence existed, the social pressure to marry was strong. A woman on her own was regarded as incomplete.

The fact that women were tied to marriage did not mean that their preoccupations need be wholly domestic however, nor that they were altogether out of the mainstream of political and intellectual life. Lady Holland, a great political hostess in the early nineteenth century, is an example of a woman who was able to use her domestic and wifely position to her own advantage to become an important political patron. Glencora Palliser, Duchess of Omnium, a character in Anthony Trollope's political novels, is her fictional equivalent. But of course these women were exceptional and owed a good deal of their freedom and scope to their rank and wealth.

Working-class women

Most of what has been said applies to middle- and upper-class women. The image of the domestic woman encompassed working-class women as well, but industrialisation gave them a chance to diversify and establish an independence. John Barton, a character in Mrs Gaskell's *Mary Barton*, conceded this, though he did not remark upon it with approval. Sometimes during early industrialisation, especially when female labour was employed in preference to male, the two roles were reversed and man undertook domestic tasks: 'There sat poor Jack by the fire and what think you? Why he sat, and mended his wife's stockings with a bodkin.' This real-life scene was described by a Yorkshire woollen worker. His friend Jack was an unemployed handloom weaver.

Most working-class women however had to combine employment and their domestic obligations, and the freedom which their middle-class counterparts envied was largely submerged by drudgery.

Legal restrictions

Since society assumed that marriage was the proper occupation of women, and since the marriage service bonded the two parties into 'one flesh', it is not surprising to find the law assuming that their interests were identical. This presumption, and the belief in the mental inferiority of women which rendered them incapable of managing their own affairs, gave rise to a legal code which deprived women of control over their property or their children, and made it very difficult for them to break the marital bond.

John Stuart Mill, a prominent social commentator and philosoper, described the female position in 1869 thus:
'The wife is the actual bond servant of her husband and she can do no act without his permission, at least tacit. She can acquire no property but for him; the instant it becomes hers even by inheritance it becomes *ipso facto* his.' As for children – 'They are by law his children. He alone has any legal right over them', and in the event of separation, she can be denied access to them, unless proved to have an 'unblemished character'. (This last concession was the result of a fairly recent legal ruling: 1839.) Nor could she divorce her husband on equal terms. Whilst he could obtain divorce on the grounds of adultery alone, women had to prove cruelty as well.

Change affecting women

Background
Change was bound to come sooner or later but several circumstances helped it on its way. Impetus was provided by the

increase in the female population, for instance. By 1851 women far outnumbered men: $2\frac{3}{4}$ million spinsters over the age of fifteen were discovered when a census was taken in 1851, and by 1871 the number had increased to $3\frac{1}{4}$ million. The belief that marriage was the only proper occupation for women became nonsensical when for so many it was beyond the bounds of possibility.

The **reduction in the size of families** was another contributory factor to change. Between 1870 and 1924, the average number of children per family dropped from $5 \cdot 5$ to $2 \cdot 5$, partly as a result of improved knowledge of contraceptive techniques. The **development of various mechanical aids** in the home such as carpet sweepers and washing machines and the advances in electricity which provided a clean form of lighting and heating might also be mentioned here, for their invention, like contraception, left women free to expend their talents in other directions.

The **decline of religious belief**, apparent by the 1870s, may also have affected the way in which women were regarded and the amount of opportunity open to them. The Church had been very much influenced by St Paul's conception of domestic duty. Church teaching had thus underpinned (in fact to a large extent it had given rise to) the idea that woman's place was in the home and that within it she occupied an inferior position to her husband, to whom she owed obedience.

Probably the most influential contributory factor to change, however, was the determination of individual women to achieve emancipation. The example of women like **Josephine Butler** (who dedicated her life to helping prostitutes, forcing society both to take cognisance of them and to accept some responsibility for their situation), of **Florence Nightingale** (who established nursing as a respectable profession) and **Sophia Jex Blake** (who became one of the first women doctors), was an inspiration to many. In refusing to conform to the domestic image and in pursuing the careers they did, these women indicated alternative ways in which the female sex could benefit society.

Determination and example were not enough however. In order to play a full part in society women had to be allowed to establish their separate identity in law and be educated to the same level as men. Several reforms and developments helped to bring this about.

Legal reform

Children

Reforms establishing the rights of women at law in respect of their **children** began in **1839** with the **Custody of Infants Act** which gave mothers of good character limited access to their children. The **1857 Matrimonial Causes Act** extended this right of access and an Act passed in **1873** removed the ban on women of 'bad character': adulterers and the like. In **1886 the Guardianship of Infants Act** allowed a woman to be sole guardian in the event of her husband's death. This Act thus recognised that children were the property of the mother as well. Subsequent Acts actually began to turn the tide in favour of the mother and it was the husband who had to prove suitability before being given custody of the children in the event of separation. Several Acts and legal rulings (**1891**, **1925** and **1933**) allowed the husband custody only if he was proved to be the most desirable influence. He no longer had the earlier automatic and prior right to them.

Property

At the same time women were acquiring control over their **property**, though again the process was gradual. It began when the first **Matrimonial Causes Act** allowed women to retain property acquired during a judicial as opposed to informal separation. Women who had been awarded a protection order on the grounds of their husband's desertion also had a right to property gained after the order had been given. Thus the law was providing for the protection of property to be accorded to those women who had lost the protection of a husband. Women still joined to their husbands did not benefit until **1870** when the first **Married Women's Property Act** allowed them to retain up to £200 of their own earnings. In **1882**, however, men lost the automatic right to their wives' property, and in **1884** the right which a man had had over his wife's person was also removed. She was no longer his chattel, but a person in her own right. An Act passed in **1925** underlined this fact when it required husband and wife to be treated as separate individuals in any property transaction.

Divorce

Divorce reform in favour of women was achieved more slowly. Several Acts from 1866 improved their position in regard to maintenance, but women could not sue for divorce on identical grounds to men until **1925** and even then the opprobrium which attached to a divorced woman was slow to dissipate.

Education

Schools

Educational opportunities also improved. Though the establishment of the first girls' public schools and university colleges has claimed more attention, the **1870 Education Act** is an important starting-point in a study of this nature for it provided an elementary education for girls and boys equally, enabling women of all classes to take advantage of expanding opportunities. Undoubtedly, however, the social and professional prominence of women did depend upon the provision of education at a higher level, and this is why the girls' schools and colleges are important. **Cheltenham Ladies' College** (established 1854) and the **North London Collegiate School** (1850) were the first schools to provide girls with an education comparable to that of boys. Classics, history and mathematics were taught there to a high level. The names of **Frances Mary Buss** (1827–94) and **Dorothea Beale** (1831–1906) are associated with these schools and undoubtedly their influence on education was strong. The **Girls' Public Day Schools Company**, set up in the 1870s, established day schools, taking Miss Buss's North London Collegiate school as their model. (Manchester High School for Girls, founded 1874, was an early example.) Miss Beale's important contribution was to boarding-school education. She was appointed headmistress of Cheltenham in 1854.

University colleges

London University was the first to admit women to degrees (Queen's College, 1848) but they were excluded from Oxford and Cambridge until the last quarter of the nineteenth century. In **1872**, **Girton College** (originally Hitchin College) was established in **Cambridge** with Emily Davies, its founder, as its mistress. **Newnham College** had been founded a year earlier but Girton has pride of place in antiquity as the Hitchin establishment had been set up in 1868. Women's colleges in Oxford began in 1879 with the opening of **Somerville** and **Lady Margaret Hall**. By 1900, **St Hugh's** and **St Hilda's** had joined them. But although women were able to sit the university examinations and were placed in class lists, often achieving real distinction (e.g. Agnete Ramsay who achieved the best performance in the classical Tripos at Cambridge in 1887), they were debarred from taking their degrees until after the First World War.

Female employment

The professions
Teaching and **nursing** were the first professions to become available to women (Miss Nightingale founded St Thomas's Hospital School of Nursing in 1858). **Medicine** followed, more slowly. **Elizabeth Garrett** was the first woman doctor in this country but she was forced to qualify abroad. The same was true of her successors like Sophia Jex Blake, until **1872** when the **London School of Medicine** for women was founded. Then in **1876** an Act of Parliament gave medical schools the power to examine women students. Their success and that of their more academic colleagues in the universities encouraged some to believe that women would soon enter all the professions. George Bernard Shaw wrote an amusing play in 1890, *Mrs Warren's Profession*, in which he contrasted the opportunities available to Mrs Warren (she had become a prostitute and then the director of a chain of brothels) and her daughter, who had just come top of the class list in the Mathematical Tripos at Cambridge and was about to embark upon a career as an actuary (having turned down a proposal of marriage). Shaw was drawing the moral that whereas Mrs Warren had had to rely entirely upon exclusively female attributes to earn a living, her daughter was not so circumscribed. In fact, many barriers remained and few openings existed even as late as 1915. In that year it was remarked: 'A woman may not sit for the English and Civil Service Examinations. She cannot enter the Church. She cannot become a barrister or solicitor. She cannot enter parliament. She is forced to consider the great profession of teaching from an entirely different standpoint to that from which it may be regarded by a man. It cannot be so much a question with her of her special vocation as it is of gaining a living. There are so few other openings.' It was not until 1919 that most of the professions were opened to women. Then the **Sex Disqualification (Removal) Act** made it illegal to debar women from employment in the professions on the grounds of their sex. The Church was (and is) an important exception.

Other employment
New occupations, alternative to the traditional openings in industry and domestic service, were also becoming available. The

inventions of the typewriter and telephone were important in widening the scope of female employment and women readily adapted to this kind of work. In 1901 9,000 women office workers were in employment. By 1911 the figure was more than 179,000.

The impact of the First World War
The war was important to the cause of female emancipation since it required women to undertake all kinds of tasks which had hitherto been regarded as part of the male preserve and it encouraged women who had not contemplated a career to take one up. The level of competence achieved by women in these occupations encouraged both sexes to regard women in a new light. Not all women stuck to their new employment, but after the war was over the number of women employed in 1920 in basic industries and occupations was greater than it had been in 1914 (though not as great as it had been in the final year of the war). For instance the number of women employed in finance and commerce was 40 per cent in 1920 whereas in 1914 it had been only 27 per cent. The differential in other occupations was less spectacular but significant all the same. Overall, females comprised 28 per cent of the total labour force in 1920, an increase of 4 per cent over 1914. (During the war the percentage had been 37 per cent.)

Female suffrage

The move towards political emancipation was thoroughly consonant with the desire of women to participate more actively in society, but whereas legal and educational reform were accepted fairly readily, the struggle for political equality was bitter, protracted and violent.

Attitudes
Society still clung to a romantic notion of femininity. This idea was not seriously undermined by the extension of education and the admission of women into the professions, for as we have seen the professions open to them, teaching, medicine and nursing, employed the 'female' talent for nurture and compassion. It was another matter to admit them to the hard, thrusting, ambitious world of politics.

It was not only men who felt this. Several prominent women, among them Mrs Humphry Ward, the novelist, Lady Randolph

Churchill and Mrs Leslie Stephen (mother of Virginia Woolf) put their signatures in June 1889 to an article opposing women's suffrage.

Nevertheless women did participate in politics in the nineteenth century: Josephine Butler's followers involved themselves actively and directly when in their fight to achieve repeal of the Contagious Diseases Act (which regulated prostitutes) they canvassed at elections against supporters of the Act. 'By their exertions', said the nineteenth-century historian G. M. Young, 'a government candidate was defeated at one by-election and a Cabinet Minister nearly defeated at another.'

Furthermore, women found respectable support for their political claims. **John Stuart Mill**, in his *Subjection of Women* published in **1869**, regarded the extension of the franchise to women as a logical step in the progress towards true democracy: 'To have a voice in choosing those by whom one is governed is a means of self-protection due to everyone.' There was sufficient support for his opinion among men for a parliamentary bill outlining female suffrage to be presented to parliament every year after 1869. In 1884 98 Conservatives actually voted in favour of it.

There was much opposition however, and the opinion against the female vote, when not rationally defended, took refuge in ridicule. Anthony Trollope included a suffragist group in one of his novels, *Is He Popenjoy?* The ludicrous names of the suffragists, Lady Selina Protest, Baroness Banmann and Dr Fleabody, form part of the mockery which his physical description completes.

The Baroness is dressed in dark and mannish clothes. She has a moustache and double chin beneath which a 'virile collar' buds over her enormous bust. Her very imperfect grasp of English adds the final touch to comedy.

In satirising the Rights of Women Institute to which these characters belong, Trollope was pouring scorn on the societies which were beginning to emerge during the 1870s and which were finally drawn together into Lydia Beck's **National Union of Women's Suffrage Societies**.

The suffragettes

The National Union was a pacific organisation. **Lydia Beck** and her friend **Millicent Fawcett** hoped by their calm reasonableness to persuade the government to concede the vote. They were not against gestures of defiance. Members of the union were prepared to withhold their taxes for instance, to pressure the government, but they were against specific acts of violence. Followers of the movement were thus called **suffragists** to distinguish them from the more disruptive members of the **Women's Social and Political Union** founded in 1903 by **Mrs Pankhurst**. It was Mrs Pankhurst's followers who became known as the suffragettes.

Campaign of violence

Mrs Emmeline Pankhurst (the widow of a Manchester doctor), who with her daughters **Christabel** and **Sylvia** dominated the movement, was convinced that the mild tactics of the N.U.W.S.S. would achieve nothing. The Trollopian idea of politics as indecorous and unfeminine was, she believed, too firmly entrenched. Nor was the idea of female political emancipation to the forefront of the national consciousness. Shock tactics would put it there.

Everyone must know of the methods the suffragettes employed to draw attention to themselves. The dogging and heckling of prominent politicians like Mr Churchill and Mr Asquith, the desecration of works of art, the processions to Downing Street, even the bombardment of London with suffragette pamphlets from a balloon: these are just a few of the tactics deployed by Mrs Pankhurst's followers. **Emily Davison**, who once said 'the movement needs a martyr', was even prepared to sacrifice her life to the cause. In June 1913 she threw herself in front of the King's horse at the Derby and died three days later. After 1909 the hunger strike was deployed as a tactic by suffragettes in prison; most effectively since the government was terrified that one of the suffragettes would die on its hands.

It is often said that Mrs Pankhurst's campaign was ineffective since it alienated many influential people. But in fact the suffragettes became such a nuisance that political groups were only too anxious to conciliate. The fact that no statute was on the book when war broke out was due to intransigence of the W.S.P.U. who wanted reform entirely on their own terms. **From 1910** the government indicated its willingness to consider the question of the votes for women and Asquith as leader of the government undertook not to oppose any Bill bringing in female suffrage. But the government planned to incorporate female suffrage into a general Bill whose prime purpose was the extension of the franchise to those males who had been excluded from the 1884 Representation Act. Mrs Pankhurst was adamant in her demand for a separate Bill for women. She was not prepared to see women in the rearguard.

Reform

Reform came in 1918 with an Act, the **Representation of the People Act**, which allowed women of thirty and over, married to a property owner, or property owners themselves, to vote in elections. Thus female suffrage had been achieved, although true equality was not conceded since women did not have the vote on the same terms as men.

Historians disagree on what was the decisive factor behind this reform. The war and the chance it gave women to show their worth is always contended for. And certainly Mr Asquith in 1916 did raise the question of political emancipation in the context of war work, but on the other hand the suffragettes must take some of the credit for it was they who first raised the issue in forceful terms.

Full equality did not come until **1928**. Then all women over twenty-one were given the vote. The last vestiges of opposition to women had rested on the numerical imbalance: women out-numbered men by about 1½ million in the 1920s and some were fearful that the female and domestic 'interest' would cause the larger national issues to be lost sight of. In fact the complexion of politics changed very little, though the format of election propaganda did alter slightly. Posters, etc., often made a direct appeal to women.

Women in Parliament

Women had a legal right to sit in Parliament after 1918 and the first to do so was **Lady Astor** who contended her husband's seat (he had become a peer) in 1919. **Miss Margaret Bondfield** was the first woman cabinet minister. She served as Minister of Labour in the second Labour Government (1929–31).

Conclusion

By 1939, all the facilities for female equality existed. Women were legally and politically emancipated but many were reluctant (and still are) to take advantage of the opportunities available.

Chapter 11
Education

There were reckoned to be some $2\frac{1}{2}$ million children in England and Wales in 1819 and of these only just over half a million were attending school. Eighty per cent then had no access at all to education and would grow up illiterate and ignorant: a danger to themselves. The mines' commissioners were horrified to find in 1842 children who had no conception of God and therefore in the Victorian view no chance of spiritual salvation. They were a danger to the nation too, for as industrialism progressed the demand for technological expertise became greater, and the demand for unskilled labour less. The nation became unable to sustain such a large burden of ignorance.

The story of education in the nineteenth century is therefore one of steady expansion in which the state, of necessity, became involved but which depended a great deal upon the voluntary efforts of religious organisations.

Educational facilities in 1815

Elementary education was provided by the following.

Dame schools
These were small informal establishments often, as their name suggests, run by a female teacher (usually unqualified) and very often in a domestic setting. In George Eliot's *Middlemarch* Mrs Garth runs just such a school, though with a greater degree of competence than was often the case. Dame schools were not always run by women, however. The term encompasses all schools for the very young run on the free-enterprise principle and not under the auspices of any specific religious or other organisation. In 1819, 53,000 children were educated in these schools, often in extremely unsatisfactory conditions. Pupils paid about 3*d.* a week to attend.

Industrial schools
These existed for pauper children only, and had been founded with the idea of teaching them a trade, but they existed on a very small scale. A survey taken in 1806 found that of 195,000 children, only 21,600 were being educated in these schools.

William Pitt, when Prime Minister in 1796, had proposed extending the system to all children working in industry but this idea was not put into practice until the passing of the 1833 Factory Act.

British and Foreign Schools Society

This was one of the most influential educational organisations. It had been founded in 1814 and grew out of the theories and practice of **Thomas Lancaster**, a Quaker, who founded a number of schools in the eighteenth century. Their **distinguishing mark** was the use of child pupils as **monitors**. Following instructions from one master they could help him educate many pupils at once ('a thousand or many more' was a contemporary calculation) cheaply (the cost worked out at about 5s. per head). The chalk and slates system in operation in his schools was also economical, for the slates could be reused.

Although Lancaster was himself a member of a religious sect the religious teaching in his schools was 'non-sectarian'. Bible-reading was undertaken, but officially no particular slant or interpretation was placed upon the text. Though a clever innovator, Lancaster was a poor businessman and his financial ineptitude lost him the support of his backers who in 1814 ousted him, founding the British and Foreign Schools Society in which only his ideas were implemented.

The National Society

This was founded in 1811. The full title was 'The National Society for the Education of the Poor, in accordance with the Principles of the Established Church', and it is worth quoting because the aims and impetus of the movement are largely explained by it. It was an **Anglican organisation** set up to rival the Lancaster schools which were disliked on religious grounds. Though the British and Foreign schools did not undertake any obvious religious instruction, the very emphasis on bible-reading smacked of sectarianism to many Anglican churchmen. The National Society also employed the monitorial system (in fact it was first the idea of an Anglican clergyman, Dr Bell, who became prominent in the society. Lancaster had merely adopted it). But though the organisation of both institutions was similar, the strong Anglican character of the National Society differentiated the two. Only children who were regular churchgoers could attend National schools, whereas no religious barrier stood in the way of acceptance into British and Foreign schools.

Between them these two voluntary organisations provided the bulk of education in the early nineteenth century. 150,000 children attended them and they were the base upon which the state system of education was erected.

Sunday schools

These were also important vehicles of education. They were Anglican but imbued with a strong evangelical flavour. The emphasis was not upon the achievement of any mechanical proficiency but of a basic moral standard. Their object was 'the sanctification of the Lord's Day and the salvation of souls'. They were influential however, since in 1819 about half a million children were thought to attend these schools, and because they established what became an important and distinctive feature of Victorian education and child nurture: the moral lesson couched in story form. The tales of Mrs Sherwood, who was the most successful exponent of this method, were famous and the Sunday School movement left its stamp upon the whole educational scene, in believing that character-building and the development of a moral sense were just as important in the field of education as basic mechanical instruction.

Secondary schools

As for secondary education, the facilities were even more meagre. There existed the old **grammar schools**, some dating back to the Middle Ages. They had been endowed with private gifts, the terms of which were often very restrictive, specifying the subject matter to be taught as well as the sort of pupil for whom provision of education was envisaged.

The **public schools** had a very similar background, but by the nineteenth century were distinguished by the social origins of their pupils who were exclusively upper-class. In many cases the original intention of the founder was disregarded. It had been Henry VI's intention for instance to provide education for poor scholars at Eton when the college was founded in the fifteenth century, but by 1800, no pupil there would have qualified for that description.

The **tone** of the public schools often left a great deal to be desired. Debauchery and drunkenness were common features and since discipline was organised by the elder boys, with little supervision from above, a great deal of bullying and depravity resulted. The spirit of independence ran to the point of rebellion and the great **Harrow Mutiny** of **1808** in which boys rose up against masters was only one of many in public schools before 1830. In 1815 when the boys of Eton rose in rebellion the guards regiment from Windsor briefly besieged the school.

The **subject matter** in these schools was almost exclusively geared to the study of classics, and 'modern' subjects like mathematics and geography were neglected. So were any literary studies other than classical, or artistic ones like music. It was the purpose of a public school education to turn out the nation's governors, and the understanding of government and the freedoms which it was designed to protect could, in the contemporary view, be derived from no better a source than Greece and Rome where they had been first developed.

As for the grammar schools, their subject matter was very similar but corruption manifested itself in a rather different guise with masters pocketing the founder's money but neglecting to provide any education at all. It was a fairly common practice to hire someone at a nominal fee to teach on one's behalf, and in some rare cases, especially in the more rural areas where the demand for secondary education was slight, and where the trustees were slack, the situation arose of more masters than pupils. Thame Grammar School (Oxfordshire) was a case in point.

Dissenting academics
These must also be mentioned since they too provided education at a secondary level. The Dissenting Academics (like Bootham School, York, which was run by Quakers) had grown up since the seventeenth century and existed to provide education for children of nonconformists. Since nonconformists were barred from any posts in the universities and in local and central government, as also in the armed forces, until the nineteenth century the emphasis veered much more towards practical instruction than was the case in the grammar and public schools. This perhaps explains why so many entrepreneurs and inventors were nonconformists. But these schools were not numerous.

Scotland
Scottish education was infinitely superior to English in the nineteenth century. The nonconformist tradition always fosters education, since the emphasis in all nonconformist belief is upon man's individual responsibility for salvation. Knowledge of God must be his own discovery and the bible is the key to it. Thus literacy was not regarded as just a practical accomplishment; it

156

was a spiritual necessity and Scotland boasted a free and universal system of education by 1815.

England and Wales however were far behind. An explanation of how the situation changed is what follows.

Development of state education

Change got under way slowly in England on account of the fear of social revolution. It was felt by many that an educated lower class would be discontented with the *status quo*, and throughout the early and middle period of the nineteenth century there was enough political activity on the part of the lower classes to underline this fear (Chartists, etc.). Influential pressure was gradually brought to bear upon the educational scene, however, for the reasons outlined in the introduction to this chapter and it bore some fruit when the provision of education for children working in the textile industry became a requirement of the **1833 Factory Act**.

In the same year the first **government grant** was made to education. £20,000 was shared between the British and Foreign Schools and National Societies. In 1839 the grant to the same two organisations increased to £30,000 and government inspectors were appointed to supervise education in those schools benefiting from the grant. The government subsidy increased thereafter, at regular intervals, and by 1859 it had risen to £750,000. The pattern of the state working in conjunction with the two main voluntary organisations was thus well established by mid-century.

Payment by results
The manner in which the grant was distributed had some unfortunate aspects to it. The method of payment by results was put into general effect after 1858 on the recommendation of the **Newcastle Commission** which met in that year to survey the state of elementary education. The size of the grant to which each school was entitled depended upon the performance of pupils who had five grades to aim at. An examination conducted by the local schools inspector was held each year. Children were rehearsed mercilessly so that they would make a good showing on the crucial day, for each failure meant a reduction of the school grant. Drill and repetition thus became the hallmarks of the nineteenth-century educational scene. The monitorial system also contributed to the trend towards rote-learning, since the pupil

157

teachers were not in a position to teach, only to hear lessons and carry out simple tasks like dictation. Interestingly, the character of education at an elementary level did not change until the end of the century for the 'payment by results' system was not abandoned until then, and the monitorial system too survived Forster's great educational reform.

Forster's Education Act, 1870

Background

Concern about the facilities available for education grew as the century progressed. The state grant had become substantial but the **distribution of schools was very uneven** and total dependence upon the British and Foreign and National Society was being questioned. Over half the nation's children were still without access to education. By 1870 the conviction that national, political, and economic survival depended upon an educated working class was also widespread.

Economically Britain was entering a difficult period. Both Germany and the United States had come to challenge British supremacy in world trade and it was felt that Germany's rapid expansion had been possible largely on account of her educational system. Free state education had recently been introduced into Prussia. If Britain was to hold her own she would have to educate her working class.

The **political impetus** to the 1870 Education Act came from the parliamentary reform Act of 1867 which had enfranchised the urban working class. The working classes were thus endowed with political power. Education could help them use it wisely and prevent the mob element from dominating the political scene. Thus the contemporary observation 'we must educate our masters' sums up an important motive behind the 1870 Act.

Terms of the Education Act

The Act, which was named after W. E. Forster, the minister responsible for its passage through Parliament, stipulated the **continuation of grants** to the two voluntary religious organisations. But in areas where no voluntary schools existed or where they were insufficient to meet the needs of the community, the rate-payers were to erect a school board which had responsibility for the setting up of new state schools. These were known as **board schools**. There had been serious disagreement about the mode of religious education in all schools and these had prevented reform from taking place earlier. Many were worried by the possibility of children finding themselves in schools where the religious teaching was out of line with the convictions of their parents. In 1870, however, this difficulty was overcome by the inclusion of a **conscience clause** giving parents the right to withdraw their children from religious instruction classes, and in the new state schools religious instruction took the form of bible-reading, without commentary.

Importance of the Education Act

The act has been described as a milestone in the history of education. It was certainly no mean feat on Forster's part to have overcome the religious obstacles in the way of using the voluntary schools. The division of opinion over religion was fierce and bitter to a degree which we must find hard to understand.

The act did have many **shortcomings**, almost inevitably, since it was pioneering the way. Attendance at school was not made compulsory, for instance. Some local authorities had the power to enforce attendance, but not all, and in any case they were under no obligation to do so. Nor was education free. A small payment of a few pence a week was required, although the school boards had power to waive it. Both these omissions were unfortunate, however, for they discouraged many working-class parents from allowing their children to take advantage of the Act.

Another weakness of the Act was the continuation of the monitorial system. The number of pupil teachers rose substantially in the years immediately after the Act. There were 29,000 in 1875 and 32,000 in 1880. Thereafter the increasing numbers of training colleges and universities reduced dependence upon them. Nevertheless the Act, by increasing the number of schools, made an extremely important contribution to educational advance.

In **1876 Sandon's Education Act** was passed. This gave school boards and in areas where there were none, **school attendance committees**, the power to enforce attendance. The act specified the attendance at school of every child between the ages of five and ten. A certificate of **educational proficiency** or alternatively of **minimum attendance** (for those who did not reach the requisite standard) was necessary for the employment of children between the ages of ten and fourteen to be legal. **Mundella's Act**, passed in 1880, endorsed these powers of compulsion.

Evasion continued nonetheless. The **Log Book** kept by successive schoolmistresses in Akenfield, the village upon which Ronald Blythe based his recent book, shows how hard a fight it was to secure attendance. In **1889** the teacher wrote, 'There is now a night school for children who must work in the day time. Attendance bad. Picking stones ended and weeding in the fields continues. The school has been open 30 times this month (June) and Frederick Walls has attended half a day. Twenty boys hardly ever attend and are seen working. The law is broken here with impunity.'

The position in 1900

By 1900 education in Britain was free and the **beneficial effects** of the Act were beginning to show. The **literacy rates** had increased considerably and between 1873 and 1893 the percentage of men unable to sign the marriage register had fallen from 18·8 to 5 per cent. Female illiteracy fell to 5·7 per cent from 25·4, so that progress had been made in spite of high absenteeism in some areas. But there were some **unsatisfactory aspects** to the educational scene.

Although school boards had the power to provide education until thirteen, the **Factory Acts were still in force** legalising the employment of children of eleven. They had access to education on the half-time system and the certificate of educational proficiency also gave them educational protection, but the system was unsatisfactory. One contemporary educated on the half-time system recalls many of the children being too tired for work.

By 1900 also, **local government reform** called the continued powers of the school boards into question. Many felt that the newly formed councils should assume responsibility for education.

Then the question of secondary education had to be resolved. In some areas (London and Liverpool for instance) 'pupil teacher centres' had been set up and had acquired the character of schools. Legal opinion, however, held that the boards were acting illegally in establishing secondary schools since their brief was only for primary education. Yet undoubtedly there was a very urgent need for secondary education. The grammar and public schools were providing what there was, but geographical distribution and in the case of public schools their social composition, prevented wide access to them. This difficulty did not obtain in

Wales since the **Intermediate Schools Act** of **1889** had empowered authorities to establish secondary schools.

Another problem concerned the **voluntary schools**. They were considerably in debt by 1900 and consequently the standard in many of them had fallen drastically following staff cuts.

Balfour's Act, 1902

The time was thus ripe for another Education Act which this time took its name from the Conservative Prime Minister, Mr Balfour. This Act did much to rationalise the educational system. It also attempted to extend it.

Terms of Balfour's Act

The school boards were abolished and education brought under the control of the **counties** and **county boroughs. Local Education Committees**, (L.E.A.s) were established to run education on their behalf. The L.E.A.s were given the power to provide '**education other than elementary**' but they were under no obligation to do so. The **voluntary schools** were **aided** with an increased subsidy.

The **main significance** of the Act rests on the plan of reorganisation, but the clause relating to secondary education was also important. The Act has been criticised on the grounds that the government made no funds available and left development so entirely to the discretion of L.E.A.s that it resulted in a very uneven provision of education at the secondary level. But it did lay a foundation upon which to build, and in the years up to the outbreak of war in 1914 development and expansion did take place.

That it did so was largely as a result of **Robert Morant's** influence. He was responsible for the **Regulations for Secondary Schools** laid down in **1904** in which the provision of free places was recommended. In **1907** a **free place** scheme was actually implemented, and it became easier for children of poor parents to attend school. The main concern of the Liberal government centred, however, on the health of children.

Fisher's Act, 1918

Fisher's Act (named after the historian H. A. L. Fisher) was an expression of all the optimism and vision of the post-war age. People hoped that a new era would dawn and trusted education to bring it about. Fisher said of the docker trade unionists whom he met during the passage of the Bill, 'They expected from an education Bill what no bill on education or anything else can give – a new heaven and a new earth.' Certainly the Act outlined proposals of a very expansive nature and it bade farewell to the nineteenth century and its acceptance of child labour in no uncertain terms. The school-leaving age was set at fourteen, and L.E.A.s were given the power to raise it to fifteen. The half-time system in industry was ended and the employment of children under twelve was prohibited. A two-hour limit was placed on the employment of children between twelve and fourteen and no child of school age was to be employed at all in a factory or mine.

Fees in state schools were abolished (many secondary schools had continued to be fee-paying) and L.E.A.s were encouraged to increase the number of scholarships available. They also had discretionary power to establish nursery schools for children under five. Finally, teachers' salaries were raised substantially and an elaborate scheme for **continuation classes** after school-leaving was outlined.

This Act has often been dismissed as a dead letter. Certainly the post-war depression did intervene to prevent the full implementation of the Act. The nursery-school scheme is still incomplete. The school-leaving age did not rise to fifteen. The number of scholarships available did not increase substantially. Teachers' salaries did increase but they were diminished by the **Geddes Axe** and the **May Report**. The continuation scheme also came to nothing. But the act was **important** in revealing a very changed attitude to education and child employment. It did end the Victorian uncertainty of mind in respect of both. The state finally made the choice in favour of education.

The hopes which working men placed in the Act are interesting and contrast with the early indifference of many working-class parents in the years immediately after Forster's Act.

Hadow Report
The last major educational proposal before 1939 was the Hadow Report which was published in 1926. In this the division of schools into primary and secondary was recommended. The age for transferral from one to the other was to be eleven. The term 'elementary' education was dropped in favour of primary, and it was suggested that different kinds of schools should be provided at a secondary level, some with an academic emphasis, some with a more technical bent. Again, the raising of the school-leaving age

to fifteen was mooted. But since this would have necessitated 350,000 extra school places and 12,000 more teachers, the proposal was abandoned. An **Education Act** passed in **1936** did in fact make the statutory leaving age fifteen, but the rubric was not enforced until 1944.

Conclusion

Thus by 1939 comprehensive facilities existed for state primary education and every child was able to benefit from it. On the secondary-school front the system was only just beginning to take shape. The Hadow proposals were put into effect but very gradually. The Depression frustrated many good intentions and the secondary-school equivalent of Forster's Act did not come until 1944 with the passing of Butler's Act.

Grammar and public schools reform

It is interesting to speculate on how differently state education would have developed had the recommendations of the **Taunton Commission**, which made the report on the endowed schools in 1867, been fully implemented. The grammar schools might then have fitted more easily into a description of the development of state education up to 1939. Some grammar schools did come under the jurisdiction of the L.E.A.s after Balfour's Act but many remained independent. The only important incident of state intervention was the **Endowed Schools Act** passed in 1869 on the advice of the **Taunton Commission**. In it the government attempted to regularise the position of endowed schools and to correct some of the administrative corruption found there. An attempt was also made to amend some of the more ancient school statutes and charters, enabling new subjects to be taught and some of the outmoded ones, like rhetoric, to be abandoned.

Some schools had been founded exclusively for the teaching of Latin and Greek and no other subject could be taught there. The **Grammar School Act** of 1840 had given the Court of Chancery the power to alter the original statutes but the system was laborious and many endowed schools were in a perilous state.

The Taunton Commission was prepared to go further, however, and recommended the virtual reconstruction of secondary education under a **National Board of Education**. According to their recommendations a government minister should be put in charge of the board, which would take over the running of the endowed schools. These would lose their special status and character. A national and uniform policy would be put into effect. Curriculum and entry qualification would all be specified and the schools graded according to the standard they could provide. The National Board would be represented in the localities by **provincial authorities** based on the counties and large towns. It is interesting to note, and important to remember, that these sweeping and radical proposals, which might cause alarm even today (consider the present-day controversy over independent schools), were being outlined in 1867.

They were, however, too sweeping for the government of the day, which rejected the opportunity to establish state control. Only the worst administrative abuses were ironed out.

The public schools

The administration and curricula of many schools now accepted as public schools were also affected by the Endowed Schools Act but special consideration was given to the nine oldest, and a separate Act, the **Public Schools Act** of 1868, was passed to deal with aspects of their administration and to adapt some of the original charters. The **Clarendon Commission** which compiled the information which led to the Act considered Eton, Harrow, Winchester, Shrewsbury, Westminster, St Paul's, Merchant Taylors, Charterhouse, and Rugby. These schools are sometimes known as the **Clarendon Schools**.

These schools met with the approval of the commission who gave their governors credit for their pupils' capacity 'to govern others and control themselves'. It also admired 'their aptitude for combining freedom with order, their public spirit, their vigour and manliness of character, their strong but not slavish respect for public opinion, their love of healthy sports and exercise'.

Thomas Arnold

By mid-century the public schools had ceased to be the dens of vice depicted at the beginning of this chapter, and were set in their course as the educators of English Christian gentlemen.

Thomas Arnold, the headmaster of Rugby, has often been held responsible for this change. Certainly he did set an example at Rugby during the 1830s and his work is immortalised in Thomas Hughes' book *Tom Brown's Schooldays*. His influence spread to other schools as his old pupils went off to teach there. **C. J.**

Vaughan, for instance, became headmaster of Harrow in 1844 and **Pears** became headmaster of Repton in 1842 with Messiter, another old Rugbean, as one of his assistants.

Arnold must not take all the credit for public school reform, however. **E. W. Thring**, headmaster of **Uppingham**, was also in the vanguard and in any case these men were merely responding to society's need for a system of education which would reflect the changed social balance. The immoral and decadent character of the public schools before Arnold was totally at variance with the moral outlook of the middle classes who wanted their sons to be educated as the leaders of society, alongside the traditional upper class.

The emphasis in the public schools thus came to be placed upon character-building and the installation of the virtues of independence, self-reliance and self-denial. The deprecation of physical comfort was another important feature. The **chapel** was central to the whole educational process for it gave boys a respect for the weak and dependent. This was important, for elsewhere the emphasis was upon strength and manliness, and contempt for the weak could easily have crept in.

The number of public schools increased rapidly in the nineteenth century. Cheltenham, Marlborough, Rossall and Radley were founded between 1840 and 1850. Wellington, Clifton, Malvern and Haileybury followed before the century was out.

The **social importance** of these schools lies in the way they reflected the ambitions of the new middle classes, for the demand by them for more public schools is indicative of the challenge they were making for the upper-class strongholds of power. Education was after all the key to dominance, especially after the reforms in the 1860s of the Army and Civil Service, which ended the old system of patronage, replacing it with a more meritocratic system of competitive examination. The curricula of public schools and universities were geared to meet the requirements of these examinations.

In fact the curriculum in public schools did not change as a result of Arnold's reform. The emphasis upon classics remained; so too did the system of school discipline. The older boys still controlled discipline but their powers were moderated now by the new ethos in the schools. The idea of responsibility now matched that of privilege. And intervention from above, though not frequent, was decisive. This point is made very clear in *Tom Brown's Schooldays*. Dr Arnold is a remote and godlike figure in the book. He rarely descends to put himself in direct contact with the boys. They see him at a distance and on high (in the pulpit of the school chapel) but his influence in true godlike fashion permeates everywhere.

Chapter 12
Local Government

In the centuries before the Industrial Revolution, the central government in London had always relied on the local authorities for administration. The changes and problems created by the growth of industry and population made it necessary to change and adapt these existing local institutions so that they could take new and wider responsibilities. As successive governments made new laws and codes to cope with the new problems and needs of society, the burden of carrying out these laws fell upon locally elected authorities. So, during the nineteenth and twentieth centuries, local government underwent several stages of reorganisation.

Local government in 1815

Local government in Britain in 1815 was confused and chaotic. The **counties** were administered by the **Justices of the Peace** who would meet four times a year at the quarter sessions in the county town and there order administrative matters for their area. It was the justices' duty to maintain roads and bridges and generally attend to the well-being of their counties. They were, however, first and foremost magistrates, empowered to keep the peace and punish petty offenders. They were responsible to the High Court and were chosen by the Lord Chancellor from the clergy and gentry of the county. Often their appointment was political so that until 1830 most were Tory whilst under the Whig administrations of the 1830s, Whig or Liberal sympathisers were chosen.

The administration of the towns and villages varied. There were over 200 chartered boroughs which were towns and cities which possessed royal charters of incorporation. The charters gave each town the right to govern itself through a mayor and aldermen known collectively as the corporation. Sometimes the mayor and corporation were elected by the property-owning townsmen, but in many towns the mayor and corporation held their offices for their lifetimes. If there was a vacancy, then the corporation would themselves select someone to fill the place.

In some of the smaller corporations, the mayor and the handful of aldermen alone could elect the M.P. and so were in the position to sell their votes to the highest bidder. Many corporations dabbled in national politics. Northampton Corporation used the town's money to back the Tory candidate in 1826 and in Coventry the mayor and corporation, ignoring their duty to keep the peace, encouraged the local weavers to riot on behalf of the candidate who promised his support for the corporation. Such blatant if colourful corruption naturally invited criticism.

In villages and towns without charters, local administration lay in the hands of the **churchwardens** of the parish church who were often called '**the vestry**'. They, in their turn, were under the supervision of the local J.P.s. Birmingham and Manchester, in spite of their size, were governed in this manner.

Changes in the organisation, 1835–1933

The system or systems of local government which existed in 1815 tended to produce authorities which were either corrupt or incompetent and sometimes both. The old methods of local government were part of a wider political system and when this was drastically changed by the 1832 Reform Bill, it was inevitable that local administration would have to be changed as well. The Whig government, having reformed parliamentary representation, turned its attention to urban local government and passed two **Municipal Corporation Acts**, one in **1833** to cover Scotland and another in **1835** which applied to England and Wales.

These two Acts created borough and city councils which were elected by all adult male ratepayers of all religious denominations (previously only Anglicans could legally take part in local government). These new authorities replaced many of the older corporations and were empowered to impose local taxes on property (rates) and undertake such duties as the provision of lighting, pavements, drainage and the upkeep of roads.

The next major step in the reorganisation of local government was the **Local Government Act** of **1888**. All towns with over 50,000 inhabitants were made into county boroughs with their own elected councils. The old counties were also given councils, elected by their inhabitants and with responsibility for the duties which had previously been undertaken by the magistrates. In **1894** areas outside towns were placed under elected **urban or rural district councils**. Finally, in **1933** a further Local Government Act stipulated the types of local government, county councils, county borough councils, borough councils, urban and rural district councils and parish councils, and defined their powers and spheres of activity.

Responsibilities of local government

During the nineteenth century various Acts of Parliament imposed **new responsibilities** on local government. Yet whilst the central government was anxious that local authorities took action on such matters as **public health** and **police**, there was seldom compulsion. In some areas the elected authorities were careless of their duties either through laziness or an unwillingness to spend the ratepayers' money on projects which they considered unnecessary or trivial. So the justices of the wapentake of Kesteven (Lincolnshire) refused to form a local police force on the grounds that it injured 'good neighbourliness' and the municipal authorities of Newcastle refused to appoint a sanitary inspector. Many local authorities ignored the Adulteration of Foods Act of 1860 and refused to prosecute those who broke this law so that in 1875 a further Act was needed to compel all local councils to take the required action.

Against this picture of lethargy must be set one of amazing endeavour. Many cities, especially those which had grown in the years of industrial expansion, felt a strong local pride. This may still be seen in the splendid, solid and substantial town halls in many northern towns and cities. The men who inspired these grandiose expressions of civic pride and who dominated the town government were usually businessmen. Their local patriotism was usually mingled with radicalism and both qualities expressed themselves in the planning of building of museums, libraries, hospitals and other civic enterprises. **Birmingham**, confident and bustling with industrial energy, led the way under the radical ex-nail manufacturer **Joseph Chamberlain**. In the 1870s Birmingham could boast a municipal bank, gasworks, waterworks, sewerage farms and a free library and art gallery.

As municipal enterprise went ahead so governments placed greater powers in the hands of local authorities. During the 1840s many local authorities had been empowered to take over privately run gas and water companies. In **1881** the **Electric Lighting Bill**, warmly supported by Chamberlain (then Secretary of the Board of Trade in Gladstone's second ministry), gave local authorities the right to supply electricity. As well as taking over essential services in their localities, local governments were widening their spheres of administrative authority. In 1856 they

169

were placed in charge of the police and by the **Housing Acts** of **1875** and **1890** were given the right to condemn and demolish slum property and build their own houses which were to be rented to working men and their families.

Slowly local authorities took over the responsibilities of the other local bodies which had grown up in the nineteenth century. In **1902** the elected school boards were abolished and **education became the responsibility of the county borough and county councils**. The duties of the old **Poor Law guardians** were similarly taken by the local authorities by the **Local Government Act** of **1929**. From then on all welfare and health matters which had hitherto been the responsibility of the Poor Law guardians came under the authority of the county and county borough councils.

By the time of the **1933 Act**, local government had taken on a wide range of responsibilities. The **county and county borough councils** looked after **education, police, planning, highways, health, fire services, children** and **welfare**. The **borough, urban and rural districts** were responsible for **housing, water supplies, sewerage, refuse collection** and the **levying of rates**. In country areas the **parish council** – the survivor of the vestry – concerned itself with small local matters such as **footpaths, village greens** and **allotments.**

Conclusion

The story of local government during this period is one of reorganisation and growing responsibilities. The government in London, always conscious of a tradition which pre-dated the Industrial Revolution by hundreds of years, was prepared to allow local authorities to take the burden of carrying out the mass of legislation passed to deal with the problems of the age. The locally elected authorities were themselves inspired by local pride and concern and for the most part fulfilled their duties admirably. As in Birmingham, local affairs became the stamping ground for radicals who found that local government gave them every opportunity to carry out their cherished schemes of public improvements.

Chapter 13
1939-1945 The Second World War

The common experience of war

The Second World War was rightly called the people's War –
not just because until 1942 civilian casualties were greater than
those sustained by the military, but also because the sharp
division which had existed in the First World War between
soldiers and civilians, combatants and non-combatants was by
no means so clear in 1939–1945. Few people could escape the
experience of war or detach themselves from the **'war effort'**,
the drive to repair and rebuild, keep necessary services going
and produce essential goods. Most of those people not con-
scripted into the armed forces joined the Home Guard, the
Women's Voluntary Service or the Land Army, or worked in
munitions factories and other essential industries. Hardly anyone
could claim exemption from war work, save children, the old
(over 64) and disabled and those with dependants. Even
conscientious objectors, who refused on principle to fight,
usually worked in hospitals, on farms etc. Sleepy towns were
shaken up by the arrival of new people and the setting up of
new industry. The dales town of Sedbergh, for example,
became the home of Hawker Siddley aircraft manufacture after
Coventry had been seriously bombed, and 'prefabs' were hastily
built to accommodate the work force. Time-honoured patterns
of existence in such places were disrupted for ever. The war
brought town and country into closer contact than had ever
been effected by the rambling associations and the motor cars
referred to on page 37.

Many children found their lives dramatically changed. At the
beginning of the war those growing up in urban areas such as
the industrial heartlands of the Midlands and London's dock
areas found themselves separated from their families (although
sometimes their mothers went with them) and **evacuated** with
their schools to live with strangers in the country – out of
range of German bombs. Many returned before the end of 1939
as the expected bombs did not materialise (this period was
called the 'Phony War'). However, there was another wave of
evacuation when the bombs did eventually fall, not just on
London during the famous Blitz (September 1940–June 1941
was the period of most intense bombing) but on the south

coast towns like Portsmouth, Southampton and Plymouth, and on the great midland and northern towns of Birmingham, Coventry, Manchester and Liverpool. In Scotland, Glasgow was badly hit and even the Orkneys, an unlikely target, experienced bombing right at the beginning of the war. Along the east coast of England too, the inhabitants suffered, not only from direct bombing but from the machine gun fire of German planes which had crossed the North Sea from Germany and Holland. When the siren blew, giving warning of an imminent air raid, people rushed to the air raid shelters for refuge. These were the Anderson shelters, made from corrugated iron for use in the garden, or the Morrison shelters which resembled a substantial rabbit hutch and were for use indoors. There were also public shelters and, in London, the Tube (underground railway) stations were used. To make it more difficult for enemy bombers to find their targets, a blackout was imposed – no lights could be shown at night. Everyone was issued with a gas mask in case the Germans dropped canisters of mustard gas (although this never happened).

Government restrictions

Apart from the physical danger from bombs and the blackout (for in the absence of street lighting accidents were liable to occur), the freedom of movement of British citizens was severely restricted and many of the comforts of life were circumscribed by government rules. From January 1940, fuel, clothes and essential foodstuffs were rationed – each person received a ration book and was entitled to 8 ounces of meat, 4 ounces of bacon, 2 ounces of butter, 1 egg and 1 ounce of cheese a week. As can be seen, the amounts were very small, though bread was unlimited and many people, where they could, supplemented their diet from vegetables grown on allotments or in gardens. Some people kept a pig. Even here, however, the individual rights of the citizen were limited. Only half the pig could be kept for the owner's consumption, the other half becoming the property of the state. Anyone who attempted to flout this regulation incurred penalties, as did those who disobeyed other government regulations (by looting bombed buildings for example), or failed to perform mandatory duties such as civil defence.

Great Britain during the Second World War has been described as the most governed country in the world, after the Soviet Union. The authorities required everyone to carry identity cards, and told them where to go and what to do. For example, posters enjoined people not to travel merely for the sake of it. 'Is your Journey Really Necessary?' the hoarding asked sternly. People were required, again by means of posters, to be careful of what they said in public – 'Careless Talk Costs Lives'. (The suspicion that spies might be in their midst was very much in people's minds in the early years of the war.) The fear of spies and invaders led to the blotting out or removal of all signposts during this period. How deep a bath you could take (5 inches) and how best to make use of frugal food supplies were also subjects on which the government gave advice. (The famous Woolton Pie, a vegetable concoction named after the Minister of Food was an example of a government recipe.) What pictures you could see, both the still and the moving variety, what books you might read, what programmes to listen to also came within government jurisdiction and a special department, the Ministry of Information, was set up to deal with censorship. The B.B.C. and the film industry were brought under its control and, as well as providing entertainment to keep up morale, were required to project specific ideas and values. Government-sponsored films like *In Which We Serve*, *The Way Ahead* and *The Way to the Stars*, which documented the activities of the Navy, Army and Air Force respectively, put forward the idea of the social web, of all groups in society being united by the need to fight the enemy, and by the common experience of fear and grief. Heroism was not confined to one social class but was common to them all. Film was also used to promote a general understanding of the issues at stake in the war – odd snippets of advice or reminders were slipped into scripts, even of light-hearted comedy films like those starring George Formby, in much the same way as information about farming is wedged in amongst the gossip and trivia of village life in the present-day radio programme *The Archers*.

Strictly speaking these forms of propaganda do not amount to restriction, but they do indicate the increasing degree of government intervention in people's lives which was so much a feature of the war.

Economic policy – industry and the economy

That stringent economic controls were exercised during this time will come as no surprise. Given the expense of a war which was being fought world wide and the need for Britain to supply for herself the goods which had formerly been imported, it was necessary to control the means of production and to increase the supply of money available to the government. As far as supplies were concerned the government, by means of the Emergency Powers Act (1940) took command of industry. The Ministry of Labour and National Service, headed by Ernest Bevin had broad powers to deploy labour as and when it was needed. Industries in need of assistance were bolstered up and those of no value to the war effort were run down. In some industries state-appointed controllers were put in for the duration of the war.

Essential monies were raised by various means. Much of that required to buy war commodities (tanks etc.) was provided by an American scheme called **Lend Lease**, whereby the USA supplied essential goods as they were needed, to be paid for later. Although vast sums were raised (three months after Lend Lease was agreed to in March 1941, 4,000,000,000 dollars worth of goods had been marked for Britain's use) they still did not cover all the nation's needs. The rest had to be raised by means of **increased income tax** (the standard rate rose from 7/6d. (37$\frac{1}{2}$p) to 10/– (50p) in the £), by the **extension of purchase tax** to all goods save essential foodstuffs and by means of voluntary and what might justly be termed 'forced' loans. **Voluntary loans** were in the form of **War Bonds** and **National Savings** on which there was a 3 per cent rate of interest. The 'forced loans' or as they were more properly called, **compulsory savings**, were deducted from salaries at source, rather in the manner of income tax today. No interest was paid on these 'savings' and the repayment term was extremely long for some since the government returned the money only as the donors reached retirement age.

Politics – national and local government

War also imposed political constraints. At the outbreak of war the Conservative Party led by Neville Chamberlain was in power. However, Chamberlain's credibility had been irreparably harmed by Hitler's invasion of Poland. Chamberlain's foreign policy had been one of appeasement, of conciliating Hitler as far as he could in order to prevent a general war. He had therefore agreed to Hitler's acquisition in 1938 of the German-speaking part of Czechoslovakia, the Sudetenland, on the understanding that the rest of Czechoslovakia would be untouched and that Poland would not be invaded. Hitler broke both these agreements and Great Britain was morally bound to go to war, to protect the interests of Poland as she had promised. Chamberlain's government lasted into 1940, but when Norway fell to Germany in that year the *coup de grace* was delivered to his reputation and it was clear that a more vigorous leadership was needed. **Winston Churchill** therefore came to power as **Prime Minister in 1940** and gathered around himself a cabinet drawn from his own Conservative Party and the Labour Party, with some Liberals and Liberal Nationals. The government was therefore a coalition. In normal times such political shufflings would have been referred to the nation and an election called. These were not normal times however and there was no general election until 1945 at the war's end. There were by-elections held as seats became vacant on account of death, or through elevation to the peerage of existing members, so the democratic principle was kept alive but public opinion expressed by means of press and radio was otherwise the only means by which popular feeling could be vented. Representative local government too was curtailed during this time, emergency committees and regional controllers replacing the local councils and mayoralty of peace time.

Other features of the war

The picture was, however, not wholly bleak. In spite of the casualties, hardships and constraints of the war there are those who remember these years as a time of liberation, challenge and comradeship. Certainly they were for some a time of opportunity and the position of some members of the community, women and the working class for instance improved as a result of it. One must beware of romanticising the war of course, although it can be difficult for people to do so in the face of present-day uncertainty. Some take comfort from reflection upon a time when society had objectives, and was cemented by a common aim, and when physical danger lent drama and *frisson* to personal relationships. For this reason there are many plays and television series which recall in 'soft focus' the war years and their aftermath. In these re-creations the thematic emphasis is upon love and death, with incidental detail about the land army, rationing and the 'black market', that unofficial and undercover economy which ran throughout the war, supplying at inflated prices the goods which people wanted and could not legally acquire. Naturally enough, such films do not deal with the more mundane but important features of the war such as **high employment** (the two million out of work in 1939 disappeared almost overnight) and **increased welfare benefits** (school meals for children and health boosts in the form of free orange juice, milk and cod liver oil were supplied throughout the war and continued after).

Increased opportunities for women

Many women were drawn into employment, often in industries where formerly their presence had been minimal. In the engineering and vehicle building industries for example, the proportion of women employed rose from 9 per cent to 34 per cent. Agriculture and clerical services, like post and censorship, also depended heavily upon female labour as did the munitions factories. The forces accounted for at least half a million women. For those unable, on account of family commitments, to work full time scope for action existed in the Women's Voluntary Service (WVS) or the Home Guard, though without the advantage of pay. The advance of the 'women's cause' was limited perhaps in so far as women did not yet receive equal pay but the idea that they should was at least mooted in 1944. In that year they took another step forward when the Education Act prohibited the dismissal of women from teaching posts on the grounds of their marriage. Over and above this, women gained during the war years experience and confidence in occupations for which they were previously considered unsuited. There is no doubt that this war (like the last) altered the attitudes of women to work, and this time in a permanent fashion. In post-war years the number of married women in employment went up and up.

Some observers have suggested that not only attitudes to work were affected but that something of the present day sexual emancipation of women began in these war years. Such assertions are rather harder to substantiate than those to do with the numbers of women in employment which can be statistically verified. There is greater mobility in wartime and the disapproval of conventional society is less easily felt. The prospect either of death or parting establishes abnormal pressures. It is true that the illegitimacy rate went up between 1939–1945. So much fuss was made about the emergence of the permissive society of the late 1960s and '70s however, that one must suppose the interim period from 1945 to have been restrained as far as sexual behaviour is concerned. Certainly women's magazines of the 1940s and '50s saw sex and marriage as inextricably linked and did not encourage any other point of view. Thus the sexual aspect of female freedom during the war must have been shortlived.

Social reform

The war years were not a time when social development stood still. Perhaps the advancement of women was an unintended by-product of war, but attempts at reform in other areas were conscious and planned. Although resources were limited, there was a feeling that public morale depended upon the assurance that the society being fought for was worthy of sacrifice. It is true that some fought simply to combat the evil doctrines of Hitler. Others, however, recognised the need for something more to fight for and the vision of a new and juster future was held up by them for public view. If any reminder of the poverty and hopelessness of pre-war Britain was needed it was provided by the sight of the bombed areas into which an educated and often conscious-stricken volunteer force now entered. Arthur Marwick in his excellent book, *The Home Front*, quotes the reactions of one such volunteer, involved in a project to set up a play centre in Paddington, who visited a family there. 'I was asked into their room . . . In front of me stood a big bed, dirty and not yet made. Between the bed and myself, just opposite anybody who happened to enter the room stood an enormous chamber pot half filled with human excrement. One could not fail to see it . . . The rest of the room was littered with household things; laundry clean and dirty covered the floor, the few bits of furniture were buried under heaps of stuff and the impression of disorder of many years standing was bewildering and produced a feeling of hopelessness.'

Increasingly there was a sense that this sort of scene which would compare with the worst of Mrs Gaskell's descriptions of Manchester a century earlier (see pages 89–90) was inappropriate to the mid twentieth century. Nor could such poverty be regarded as an isolated case. The dirty vermin-ridden and 'unhousetrained' children evacuated from the slums of London and other cities proved that. 'Their clothing was in a deplorable condition, some of the children being literally sewn into their ragged little garments. Except for a small number, the children were filthy and in this district we have never seen so many verminous children, lacking any knowledge of clean and hygienic habits.'

'What kind of a world will come out of this war?' asked the novelist J. B. Priestley, in one of his regular broadcasts. 'A society in which all have the right to work, in which government controls the economy and takes responsibility for 'social organisations', in which equality is conceived in the broadest terms'. That was the gist of an editorial in *The Times*, July 1940, which articulated the thoughts of many.

Reconstruction

That the government soon responded to these feelings of concern is all the more remarkable when one remembers the desperate state of the war in 1940 and 1941. Britain was fighting alone. France was defeated and occupied and the USA and USSR had not yet weighed in on Britain's side. In January 1941 however, a government department was set up under the leadership of Arthur Greenwood. He was given the task of planning the 'reconstruction' of society after the war. Following this brief he set up many committees and commissions to enquire into questions like land purchase for public use such as housing and recreation, the resiting of industry and redevelopment of labour. Many reports were issued on all these topics but by far and away the most famous and influential was the **Beveridge Report**.

Sir William Beveridge was a onetime journalist and civil servant who had risen to prominence in academic circles. He had been director of the London School of Economics and Master of University College, Oxford. His life-long concern (he was in his sixties at the time of the Report) had been with social questions and when a committee was needed to deal with the question of 'Social Insurance and allied services' his qualities as civil servant and social observer made him an obvious choice. What needed to be investigated was the way in which the various insurance schemes, health and unemployment etc. operated and could be improved. Beveridge went far beyond this narrow brief however, and what emerged was a comprehensive scheme to reorder society and to slay what he saw as the **'Five Giant Evils'** which he listed as **Want** (by which was meant poverty), **Disease**, **Ignorance**, **Squalor** (such as the shocked voluntary worker had described) and **Idleness** (by which he meant unemployment). In this plan Beveridge suggested remedies in the form of housing schemes (to end squalor) a free national health service (to reduce disease) and an improved educational system (to combat ignorance). Want would be banished by full employment and by a family allowance scheme. The expense of such an ambitious plan would be partly borne by the new National Insurance scheme in which **all** were required to participate. Health facilities, sick pay and unemployment benefit would be financed from this common source. The provision of employment and housing was to be the responsibility of the state which was required by Beveridge to assume a much broader social responsibility than it had recognised pre-war. Then, the government had not acknowledged a **right** to work. Beveridge was now asking them to do just that.

Beveridge's plan was enthusiastically received by the press and public. His report was sold out within days and provoked a great deal of discussion. It was not in fact implemented *in toto* during the war, though some suggestions, such as the need to improve education and for family allowances were taken up then. **Butler's Education Act** (see below) was passed in 1944 and the idea of the **family allowance** was agreed to in that year also, although it did not come into practice until 1945. **The Town and Country Planning Act**, passed in 1943, which established a Ministry to deal with matters of land purchase, for housing and other purposes, may also be regarded as a 'spin off' of the Beveridge report, though since another committee under Mr Justice Uthwatt had reported specifically on this topic in 1941 *before* Beveridge it is unfair to give him sole credit for the Act. Indeed it would be a mistake to suppose that all his other ideas were original. The Labour Party had for instance been at work on a National Insurance Scheme in the pre-war period.

As for Beveridge's plan in respect of National Insurance and a health service, these had to wait until the war was over, the government having voted against the adoption of the plan until then.

All parties pledged themselves however, to implement the report with the arrival of peace although the Conservatives, worried about the expense, showed rather less enthusiasm than the other parties. **The importance of the Beveridge Plan** is therefore evident. What Beveridge had done was to provide the blue-print for reconstruction or post-war reform, that the government and people of Britain had been seeking. He had sounded the knell to the old order and had blown a blast on his trumpet to herald a brave new world!

Education Act

This piece of legislation, brought in under the auspices of Mr R. A. Butler, President of the Board of Education, was of immense importance. The Act established the three main stages of education – primary, secondary and further – and rationalised the system of secondary education in England and Wales. (A separate and much less sweeping Act was brought in in 1945 to 'amend' the Scottish educational system.) Butler's Act promised **free secondary education for all up to the age of 15**. (A school leaving age of 16 had been aimed at but such very great problems existed in the form of wrecked schools and a shortage of teachers in 1944 that it was deemed impractical. In fact, the raising of the age to 15 was delayed until 1947.) **The type of education to be supplied** was also discussed and was to be **'according to aptitude'**. This phrase laid the way open for the development of a tri-partite system of education at secondary level, **grammar schools** for those with an academic bent, **secondary modern schools** for those (the majority) for whom a more practical and vocational education was thought appropriate and **technical schools** (of which there were only a few) which displayed characteristics of both. Selection for these schools was made at 11 and determined by a special examination, the 11+ (which was still operating in some areas in the 1980s). Mr Butler emphasised in his autobiography however that this tripartite division was not an essential feature of his bill and said that the comprehensive system of education could have developed just as easily from his Act and that indeed he would have favoured it.

Other provisions in the Act dealt with the funding and administration of schools. Some of the old L.E.A.s, those which since 1901 had had powers in respect of elementary education only, were dissolved and a **system of Dual Control was established**. By this system a newly formed Ministry of Education (replacing the old Board), worked in partnership with the L.E.A.s sharing the expenses and responsibilities of education in the various localities. The bill provided for the funding of education by means of **government grant** and a **levy upon the rates**. The size of the government grant could be adapted to meet an area's special need. **The terms of employment of teachers** (remuneration to be the basis of recommendations made by the Burnham Committee on salaries, women teachers to have the right to continue in employment upon marriage), **the optimum size of classes, the physical and mental health of the school population, nursery schools, facilities for provision for boarding within the state system**, and **religious instruction** (it was to be non-denominational and parents had the right to withdraw their children from the newly instituted morning assemblies and from religious education classes); all these were topics of concern, issues raised and dealt with in a very wide-ranging Act which was a major event in the history of the development of state education. For despite the intentions of the Balfour (1902) and Fisher (1918) Acts, only 10 per cent of the nation's children had been able to avail themselves of secondary education before 1944.

Criticisms of the Act

In subsequent years, several criticisms of the Act were made. It was thought to have established an educational system which was too 'elitist'. Too many children (the majority) were put into the non-academic category and selection was made on grounds that were felt to be arbitrary and unfair. The chances of attending grammar schools (soon regarded as the 'best' schools) in Wales were twice as good as in Surrey simply because more grammar schools existed per head of population in Wales. Another criticism made at the time of its creation (and increasingly made today) was that Butler avoided the thorny question of the public or private fee-paying schools. It was felt their existence would inhibit the development of a good state system of secondary education since because of their exclusiveness they would always be assumed to be better. Pupils coming out of the independent system would consider themselves superior and the old divisions in society, the old assumptions of social and intellectual superiority and inferiority would continue. To this Mr Butler replied at the time 'Education cannot by itself create the social structure of a country . . . I have to take the world as I find it . . . One of the fundamental principles on which this bill has been built is that there should be a variety of schools.' Debate on both these issues still rages. The issue of the grammar schools has lessened in importance because since the comprehensive system swept the country in the late 1960s there are few of them left. But the issue of the public schools has intensified and the educational and political worlds are split between those who want to defend and perpetuate them and those who want to sweep them away, to effect the kind of social change which Butler felt was an issue apart from the question of education. How Butler's Act is regarded and evaluated therefore, depends to some extent on your social and political outlook.

What is not in dispute are the **benefits of his Act**. Whatever shortcomings it may have had it was a broad-minded piece of legislation which widened opportunities for many. Today many people in the 30–50 age group from economically poor backgrounds who have prospered in many professions and occupations ascribe their success to the educational facilities provided by the bill.

Social and economic significance of the war

It is said that the thought of death concentrates the mind wonderfully and the remark could apply equally to war. Certainly war is a powerful agent of change. New experiences, the breaking loose from the traditional structure of the family and from an habitual environment, all these things lead to the questioning of assumptions and a break in the chain of continuity. A strong jolt is administered to the system. So it was in the years 1939–1945. Things did not go on as before. People contemplated the prospect of death, surveyed their damaged houses, entered as evacuees into homes of strangers, took up new occupations and responsibilities, embarked upon adventures which had no certain outcome, and fought or worked side by side with others of quite different backgrounds from their own. After such experiences, few wanted to go back to the old order, to the pinched existence of the inter war years, with its glaring contrasts between poverty and wealth. Even those who seemed to wish to, the writer Evelyn Waugh, for instance, who wrote an elegaic novel *Brideshead Revisited* which lamented the demise of an aristocratic world of beauty and elegance, knew that it *was* over. That is why he sounds his regret. Thus when it comes down to it, the most important legacy of the war was a changed attitude of mind, a will to reform the order of things. What the war had done also was to provide not just the theory but the practical foundations of change. In the spheres of education, female emancipation, local government and the economy and welfare (a public assistance board had been set up during the war to help those who were bombed or otherwise debilitated by the war and we have already remarked on the provision of school meals and family allowances), steps had been taken towards a more equitable society which intended to see that everyone had the comforts and opportunities so far experienced by only a few. The development of technology and medicine and the Arts (the Council for the Encouragement of Music and the Arts, established in 1939, later became the Arts Council) also improved the quality of life. The nylon and plastics developed during 1939–1945 transformed society in ways just as radical as the bringing in of Education Acts and the like, as did the discovery of penicillin. Life is unthinkable to us now without both the ideas and the material benefits which were set in motion during the years of the Second World War.

Chapter 14
Brave New World 1945–1951

By May 1945, the war in Europe was over. Hitler was dead and his successor, Admiral Doenitz prepared to acknowledge defeat. By July Britain had gone to the polls in the first General Election since 1936. The result was a victory for the Labour Party which received 47·8 per cent of the votes, giving it 393 seats (a majority of 154). Although at the time this result astonished many people, the decision of the electorate ought not to be surprising, for we have seen before in this book how war has tended to foster a desire for change. In 1815, 1918 and now in 1945 the 'people' made a bid to wrest power from the traditional ruling classes. In the period after 1815, and after 1918, the attempts of the people's parties failed. In 1815, there was a lack of unity and cohesion amongst the various political groups who opposed the nation's rulers. In 1924 (Labour's first spell of office) the newly formed Labour Government lacked experience, but in 1945, that same Labour Party boasted experienced men who had served successfully in the wartime coalition, including Clement Attlee, who became Prime Minister, Ernest Bevin and Stafford Cripps. So it may be said that Labour triumphed on the wave of a desire to see the social transformations anticipated in wartime actually take place. It is true that Anthony Eden had pledged the Tories to implement the Beveridge Report after the war was over, but the party leader, Churchill, had been publicly cautious about the country's ability to bear the expense of such a programme in the immediate aftermath of the war. As one historian has nicely observed, the Tories could be expected to meander, rather than gallop towards social reform!

The changes about to take place were neatly symbolised by the arrival at Buckingham Palace in the course of 26 July of Mr Attlee in a small Standard 10 motor car, driven by his wife, Mr Churchill having left in a chauffeur-driven Rolls Royce. It seemed as if the age of the common man had arrived at last. Not that Mr Attlee himself altogether qualified for that description. The son of a solicitor and an ex-public school boy, his background was impeccably middle class, but in Parliament and even the Cabinet, there were several 'sons of honest toil'. 'Gracious' remarked one Tory M.P. as the new colleagues took their places, 'They look just like our constituents.'

The new government faced a huge task. **The economic problem** was perhaps the most daunting since Britain's debt was huge. War damage was estimated at £3 billion, £1 billion's worth of overseas investment had been lost and the nation owed £3.3 billion abroad. Added to this, Britain was committed to the maintenance of an occupation force in Europe which was to cost in the region of £700 million yearly. Moreover, sections of industry had been badly damaged by the war, and many of those not directly useful to the war effort had been run down. In those industries which had been kept going, the equipment was often worn or out-of-date. The constant exhortation in war had been 'to make do and mend'.

We must be careful not to exaggerate the difficulties. There are those who point out that some of the important pre-war industries which had been allowed to decline, like textiles, were doomed anyway. They say that the war positively encouraged the development of new commodities which would play a very important part in any post-war reconstruction. Chemicals, plastics, the electrical and electronic industries had all developed during these years, and agriculture too had reversed its long decline. But nevertheless there were great problems. How to build up markets abroad with a severely depleted merchant marine force was one. Half of Britain's merchant ships had been destroyed in the war. How to reinvest in old industries and new when there was no spare cash was another. American withdrawal of the Lend Lease facilities immediately the war ended was a severe blow.

There were immense social problems too – a critical shortage of housing for instance. Two out of seven homes had been affected by war damage, 200,000 having been destroyed, another 250,000 rendered unusable.

How was Britain to recover, let alone reform? There were plenty of excuses for ducking the issue and for postponing the advent of the 'Brave New World', but Labour did not flinch. Led by the self-effacing Mr Attlee the party set out to accomplish the national metamorphosis they knew was desired.

The economy

The problem of the economy was tackled in various ways, by raising of foreign loans, by the fixing of low interest rates (2 per cent) to encourage the borrowing of money for industrial expansion and to keep prices down, and by the tight control on the supply of consumer goods. A strict and highly moral attitude to the question of living beyond one's means was developed, as economic recovery was seen to lie in the creation of a favourable balance of payments, that is, exports must exceed imports. Unless this happened Britain would go 'bust'. Several foreign observers waited upon this event and who could blame them? The prognosis could not be thought good whilst imports exceeded exports by 80 per cent as was the case in 1945. So, those consumer goods produced in Britain which could have been used to improve the quality of life for the British people were sent abroad instead. On the same principle the import of foreign foodstuffs was restricted and the system of rationing extended. Bananas and oranges remained a rare sight, pineapples rarer still and butter and sweets were luxuries. Even bread which had been freely available in wartime was rationed for a short time (between 1946 and 1948). Public outcry ended this measure, but it did show the levels of self-denial expected of the nation.

Loans

The foreign loans referred to came chiefly from the USA and Canada. John Maynard Keynes, the Cambridge economist, by now **Lord Keynes**, was despatched to the USA in 1945 to secure the necessary money. The eventual **agreement concluded in 1946** was for $3,750 million (£930 million) to be borrowed at 2 per cent and repaid over 50 years. The first repayment was to be delayed, however, until 1951 by which time it was expected that the British economy would be able to bear the burden of clearing the debt. In 1948, the USA volunteered further loans by means of the **Marshall Aid Plan** (named after the American general whose idea it was) to help European economic recovery. By that year it was apparent that not only Great Britain but many other European countries were struggling to make ends meet. The Americans, who feared the spread of Communism, believed that continued economic 'straits' would encourage its growth. The plan was also designed to help a flagging US economy, since by giving the Europeans money to buy American goods that country could boost its own depressed industries. Hence Britain received £681 million via the Marshall Plan to add to the original £930 million which by 1948 was in any case virtually exhausted.

Canada also gave support and in 1945 agreed to lend $1,250 million. This agreement, like that with the USA, was negotiated on Britain's behalf by Lord Keynes.

The purpose of these loans was to give Great Britain a breathing space and to provide the money needed for capital investment in industry and for subsidies like those paid to aid agriculture which benefited to the tune of £500 million a year. The loans played a vital part in ending the long agriculture decline which had been going on since the 1870s. They also made possible the purchase of vitally needed foreign goods such as oil and foodstuffs and of course provided for the implementation of an ambitious social services programme which began immediately.

1947 – year of crisis

Britain's economic recovery was touch and go and 1947 saw the nation at the nadir of despair. An incredibly harsh winter (the freeze lasted from mid-January to the end of March and the temperatures were the worst recorded since the 1880s), was followed by a summer of floods. The coal industry whose parlous state in wartime had scarcely improved in peace was unable to meet the extra demand for fuel, and industries were forced to close down putting $2\frac{1}{2}$ million people out of work. The halting of production meant exports were lost and the balance of payments placed in jeopardy. Such a situation bred panic in the hearts of currency dealers and there was a run on the pound in the money markets. More critical was what came to be known as the **Convertibility Crisis**. The right of American creditors to be paid in dollars rather than sterling had been built into the loan scheme negotiated by Keynes. What also had been agreed in 1945 was that the exchange rate, the value of sterling against the dollar was to be set at 4.05 dollars to the pound. This very high rate of exchange meant that Britain lost heavily when goods assessed in pounds were then settled for in dollars. In one month alone Britain was forced to pay out $700 million, at a time when the social reforms by which Labour set such store had already eaten deeply into the nation's financial reserves. There were other contributory factors to the crisis. It must be said that the government had not always been wise in its use of money. Mistakes had been made, such as the foolish and ambitious Groundnut Scheme. This scheme, which required heavy capital investment in the African colony of Tanganyika (now Tanzania) was thought up in a spirit of good intent. It was calculated that groundnuts would help to solve the goods crisis at home. The aim was for the scheme to provide for one-third of Great Britain's fat requirement as well as providing Tanganyika with a valuable agricultural asset. Between £9–25 million were poured uselessly into the colony between 1946 and 1949, but the ground never yielded the crop in anything like the quantities anticipated, the wrong implements having been sent to break the ground, the weather refusing to co-operate and parasites having wrought havoc. Here was a spectacular example, not typical, but indicative nevertheless of money wasted. Another cause of the crisis was the fact that prices of goods purchased abroad, especially in the USA had gone up faster than anticipated and Britain's most vital industry, coal, had not responded to the demands placed upon it for fuel. Why it had not done so is a long story. Suffice it to say that the industry was disorganised and demoralised and had been for some time. Labour relations were appalling and the productivity levels had been falling even during the war when the utmost pressures had been brought to bear. The need to maintain an expensive military establishment was yet another factor to be taken into account. Thus by various means, Britain had arrived at a situation where the balance of payments deficit was £600 million and the loan barrel was empty. She was spent-up and on the brink of bankruptcy and disaster.

Recovery

The medicine was unpleasant. Higher taxation, some direct (for example a capital levy tax) and more indirect (for example of tobacco) was imposed. The social services programme was cut, as also were food subsidies, and there was an insistence upon wage restraint. Eventually in 1949 came devaluation of the pound, a device to make British exports cheaper. (After it the pound was worth only $2.80.) In short the policy was one of belts in, the notches even tighter than they had been in the war. 'We won the war, what happened to the peace?' one wit enquired. Even the entertainment industry was hit as American films were denied import licences, in order to protect the balance of payments.

Success

But the miracle was accomplished, the economy did begin to recover. A balance of payments surplus had been secured by 1950 to the tune of £300 million and exports were up 175 per cent on the 1938 level.

The architect of the recovery was **Sir Stafford Cripps** who succeeded Labour's first Chancellor of the Exchequer, Hugh Dalton in 1947. There was perhaps no one better suited to ask self-denial of the nation at such a time. An austere man with what seemed an almost messianic zeal for economy, stringency and discomfort, he prescribed the bitter medicine, successfully convincing the nation that the nastier it tasted the more efficacious it could be presumed to be. It is perhaps ironic that some have seen Cripps as the foundation layer to the boom economy of the late '50s and early '60s, when Harold Macmillan declared that the country 'had never had it so good'. Of course, Cripps' policies could never have succeeded without the Marshall Plan. But it can also be said that his moral outlook suffused society. People were to some extent prepared to accept his precept that a nation cannot live beyond its means, though once those means were safeguarded they rejected not only the medicine but the doctor by failing to support the government at the polls. By 1951 Labour had been voted out of office.

Social reform

It is important to have established the financial character of the post-war years before going on to discuss what was accomplished in terms of social reform. There are people who look back upon the period 1945–51 as years of betrayal. Here was a chance they say to reform society radically, and yet the tale is one of missed opportunities and deficient will. Yes, the Labour M.P.s sang the *Red Flag*, the socialist revolutionary song, as they took their seats in the newly formed House of Commons (the Labour Party sings it still at its annual party conference) but many of them could be seen to mumble and quite clearly did not know the words. That they did not could be revealing for it suggests that their commitment was not to *radical* socialist reorganisation. Many people say that all they set out to do was to effect some cosmetic and superficial changes to the face of society. Nationalisation was only partially and half-heartedly implemented. Compromises very soon began to be made in the pursuit of ideals like a free National Health system for all and the banishment of poverty and social inequality.

When judging the Labour M.P.s it is necessary to bear in mind the extent to which economic considerations bred caution and limited action. What *was* achieved through legislation was impressive. Remember also, that in any case few of the Labour leaders were interested in revolutionary socialism. Socialism in Great Britain was of a gradualist character, which is to say that most members of the Labour movement wanted society to change in an orderly and slow manner, without recourse to violent revolution. What was aimed at was for a greater share of the economic wealth of the country to be had by the majority of its inhabitants. But that aim had to be achieved by constitutional and democratic means. Change was to be effected through legislation, not through violence.

'We are the masters at the moment,' said Sir Hartley Shawcross, Solicitor General, in the new Labour administration, clearly anticipating that another political party, representing another point of view, would eventually come to power. This brings us to an important point – because Labour was a democratic party its government could not go further than the will of the people allowed. Great support was given at the outset for Labour policies but that support began to dwindle as the price of socialism in economic and other costs was felt. In 1950, the Party only just managed to gain a majority in the General Election and in 1951 they lost it altogether. The electorate which voted in a Tory government was presumably not giving the Labour government its marching orders because its policies were not extreme enough. The decision to vote Labour out can be interpreted rather as a signal that the British electorate had gone as far as it wanted to go for the moment. How far was that?

The Welfare State
The growing trend throughout the twentieth century had been towards the growth of a welfare state, a society in which government provided for the basic social and economic needs of the population. The Depression which followed the First World War had halted the progress of the ideal but it had remained in the minds of many and as we have seen the war years had heightened their determination to see it accomplished.

In **1946** the first of the great cornerstones of the Welfare State was laid with the passage of a **National Insurance Act** which owed a great deal but by no means everything to Beveridge (interestingly Beveridge had failed to get into parliament in 1945, having been defeated as Liberal candidate for Berwick). By means of this Act most of the contingencies and circumstances which might lead to poverty were covered. The Act provided for the eventualities of **unemployment**, **old age**, **ill health**, **widowhood**, and **maternity**. Previously, separate arrangements had existed for each category of need, and not everyone was covered. Now the flat rate contribution was made by virtually all employees who bore 20 per cent of the cost. Only school children, the unemployed or married women in part-time employment were exempt. The employer too, made a contribution to the scheme, as had been the case with the 1911 National Insurance Act, this time to the tune of 30 per cent, whilst the state paid the remaining 50 per cent.

It was intended that this Act should embrace all needs but of course it did not and in **1948** back-up was needed in the form of the **National Assistance Act**. This Act set up **area offices** in the larger towns throughout the country which offered extra benefit for 'those who could show need' and had somehow slipped through the net of the Insurance Act. These included deserted wives with or without dependent children or certain categories of the old who even in receipt of what they were allowed by the 1946 Act were still without sufficient means. (Pensions soon lost value in the face of inflation.) Another important aspect of the National Assistance Act was that it abolished workhouses, doing away at a stroke with the old Poor Law whose progress has been charted in this book (pages 49–55 and 62–64; see also page 76).

How effective were these two pieces of legislation in coping with the question of need? Certainly the improvement was substantial. The Rowntree Survey, carried out by Seebohn Rowntree in 1950 found only 3 per cent living below the poverty line whereas the 1898 and 1936 figures had been 33 per cent. Another achievement of these Acts was to bring to an end the invidious treatment of the poor which had been in evidence since the passing of the 1834 Poor Law Amendment Act. The workhouses and the implication that those who stood in need of relief were not merely unfortunate but somehow guilty had caused resentment. The Means Test of the 1930s had been read in the same way. The stringent enquiries establishing the justice of claims seemed to the poor to imply that they were trying to cheat and get something to which they were not entitled. Having to prove need and supplicate for help had connotations of inferiority, failure and moral turpitude and people bitterly resented this. The intention of the National Insurance and National Assistance Acts was that the poor should get what they needed *as of right*.

But though the situation of the poor was vastly improved, these Acts did **not banish poverty**, as the amounts specified as reasonable to deal with the various categories of need were simply not enough. Also the complexity of the system was such that people were not always aware of their rights and through ignorance or out of pride failed to claim their due. Finally no one could suppose or intend that social legislation of this order could abolish poverty. The only way to do that was by way of a radical rearrangement of the economy. All that the Acts could and were intended to do was to soften the effects of poverty, the material hardship and the humiliation which had often been attached to it. In respect of these two aims, they succeeded fairly well. The fact that everyone was entitled to the benefits of the National Insurance Act reduced the conspicuousness of poverty and salved the pride of those genuinely needing the social benefits which were now available.

National Health Service

This was the second cornerstone of the Welfare State. Again Beveridge had anticipated such a scheme but the inspiration went back further than 1942. The deficiencies of existing health cover were glaring and in 1939 only half of the nation was covered by insurance for medical treatment. Even then it was only cover for the services of a doctor. Anything over and above the basic cover – medicine, hospital treatment, etc. – had to be paid for. The 50 per cent without insurance had done without medical services, or had relied upon the informal philanthropy of those doctors who neglected to present bills. The **National Health Act** finally passed in **1948** ended all that, for it made **all forms of medical treatment**, **optical** and **dental included**, **freely** (in every sense of the word) **available to the entire populace**. Doctors were to be paid a salary based upon the number of patients on their books (usually not more than 3,000) and were allowed to retain some private patients as well. In the event only 3–5 per cent of the nation availed themselves of these private facilities, the rest opting gladly 'to go on the National Health'.

Hospital organisation was rationalised at the same time. Fourteen regional hospital groups were set up to control the hospital service in the various regions so that effectively hospitals were nationalised, brought under the control of the state and funded by it, just as the G.P.s were.

This Act was several years in the making. First put forward in 1946, its progress was halted by the opposition from the British Medical Association (B.M.A.), which for a mixture of motives put up a stiff resistance. Probably the most strongly felt objection was the loss of independence. Doctors did not like the idea of being servants of the state. However, a series of plebiscites (polls) taken among members of the medical profession saw them coming slowly round to the idea. By the summer of 1948 when Aneurin Bevan, as Minister of Health had made some concessions (such as allowing the continuation of some general private practice and the right to pay beds in hospitals), two out of every three doctors were prepared to co-operate with the state.

What did the Act mean to people at the time? If statistics are anything to go by a good deal. The **infant mortality** rate for instance, a key indicator to the state of the nation's health, **dropped** substantially. In 1936 it had been 56 per 1,000 of all live births. In 1950 the figure was 29 and by 1966 only 11.

The system did not however operate quite as its creator Bevan would have wished. The cost (to be borne out of taxation) was enormous (£208 million being spent in the first year, £358 million in the second) and this pressure was too great at a time when Great Britain found herself having to step up her military expenditure (the Korean war began in 1950). So compromises were made and in 1950 charges were brought in for spectacles and dental treatment and prescriptions which then cost 1/– (5p). The charges amounted to only a very small proportion of the cost. Nevertheless they made a mockery of the principle of a free health service. Aneurin Bevan resigned in protest at what he considered to be a breach of honour.

Housing

This was another important area of welfare, for, as has been pointed out, the housing shortage in 1945 was critical. Estimates of the number of houses needed varied from one to six million and as soon as the war was over people in desperation began to take matters into their own hands. Many became **squatters**, moving into empty houses or R.A.F. buildings on abandoned airfields and refusing to budge until offered an alternative. Sometimes the reaction of authority was to formalise the situation and 'prefabs' were built on airfields and bomb sites to provide temporary shelter. **Prefabs** were light structures, one-storied, constructed from wood and glass-fibre. They had come into widespread use during the war and 124,000 were built in the immediate post-war period. Aneurin Bevan, who, as Minister of Health, was responsible for housing, disliked prefabs and was determined to regard them as a temporary stop-gap (though in fact some of them lasted on into the 1960s). Accordingly he diverted all his energies (when not battling with the B.M.A.) into the construction of cheap good-quality housing.

The task was daunting, not merely because so many houses were needed but because supplies were so haphazardly obtained. It turned out that though Bevan bore responsibility for Housing, the Ministry of Works was responsible for basic building materials and the Minister of Supply for fitments such as baths and nuts and bolts. In such a situation many supplies easily got mislaid (or were purloined – there was a flourishing black market for any goods) or orders failed to coincide.

The great financial crises of 1947 also struck a blow. The need for cutbacks and restrictions upon imports meant that the country had to do without £10 million worth of timber which could have been imported from abroad. It is scarcely surprising then that the quarter of a million annual target was never met. By 1949 however 558,261 new houses had been built in addition to the prefabs already mentioned and a further 140,000 homes had been repaired and made habitable.

Thus though the Labour Government did not solve the housing problem it can be said that it went far on the way and that the important decisions it made to do with housing had impact later. For instance in **1946** it decided in the **New Towns Act** to build 20 New Towns both in the London area (e.g. Stevenage and Crawley) and as far afield as Glenrothes in Fife and Peterlee in Co. Durham.

Other social areas in which government intervened were **education** (where Butler's Act was interpreted and implemented) and **child welfare**. It was the Labour Government which actually put the **family allowance** system into operation and saw that each child (excluding the first) was entitled to 5/– (25p) per week. Labour helped children further by bringing in a **Children's Act in 1945** which gave local authorities wider powers to take into care children considered to be at risk from brutality and neglect, and the government involved itself in the area of penal reform again with the young in mind when it saw through the **Criminal Justice Act in 1947**. This Act abolished hard labour and penal servitude and raised the minimum prison age to 15. An attempt was made at the same time to abolish the death penalty, a move which was frustrated by the House of Lords. (The death penalty was not in fact abolished until 1964.) Finally, in 1948, Labour made a move to make legal remedies more easily accessible to the less wealthy members of society by taking the first steps towards a **system of legal aid**. This was an important innovation and part of the process of making the institutions and benefits of society more widely available. It was thought wrong that the benefits of law should be denied to those with only small financial means.

Trade unions

It would have been surprising had Labour neglected the trade unions. The close association between the Labour Party and the Trade Union Movement had been longstanding and mutually beneficial. But when Labour came to power in **1945 the Trades Disputes Act**, passed in the wake of the 1926 General Strike, was still on the statute book. It will be recalled that this Act passed in 1927 required union members *to opt* for the payment of part of their union subscription into Labour Party funds. This Act was designed to weaken the links between the two pillars of the Labour movement – the Labour Party and the Trade Union Movement. As many people did not bother to opt to pay into Party funds, the financial base of the Labour Party was weakened. When the Trades Disputes Act was rescinded in 1946, the situation of 1913 was reverted to, whereby a proportion of the union subscription went to the Labour Party unless a member contracted out, that is, made the effort to object.

Not that the relationship between the trades unions and the Labour Government was altogether rosy. Many union members disliked the years of economic austerity which followed upon Labour's return to power, and disliked the disciplines imposed in the way of wage restraints. There were strikes, more than there had been in the 1930s, in spite of the declaration at the 1946 Trades Union Congress that Labour (by which was meant union members) would subordinate their interests to those of the state. The Labour Party found in the 1940s, as it has done since, that the special relationship between the party and the T.U.C. is no guarantee of co-operation when the interests of government and the governed clash.

Nationalisation

Labour had come to power not only to achieve a more humane society by means of reforms like those already discussed in this chapter, but to achieve a society which was more just (and of course an economy which was more efficient). It was this conception of justice, of what was fair and right, which led the government along the road to nationalisation. The important assets of the country should be harnessed for the good of the nation as a whole. There was also the practical point that some large industries were in such a mess (the mining industry and the railways were cases in point) that their continued malfunction or dereliction endangered the wealth of the nation and the livelihood of its members. Thus nationalisation was also seen as an essential part of the scheme of economic recovery upon which everything else depended – a salvage operation in fact.

So between 1945 and 1950, Acts were passed to nationalise several major industries and institutions, beginning with the Bank of England in 1945 and ending with the Iron and Steel industries in 1949. Coal, Transport, Gas and Electricity were taken in along the way.

How did it work?

In appearance those industries taken over changed very little. They became public corporations responsible to the government instead of to the shareholders, who were given compensation as the state took over. But as the management often remained the same and the structure of the organisation intact, the old divisions between management and workers were exactly as they had been before. This did not go unremarked by those socialists who had hoped for something more radical, possibly along the lines of Robert Owen's co-operatives (page 56). And it was a source of amusement to some of the Tories – Quintin Hogg remarked for instance on Labour's nationalisation programme, saying that 'it was an elaborate game of make believe'.

Very little seemed changed, but in fact the take over by the State did alter things. For a start, it allowed for greater rationalisation.

Take the **mining industry** which prior to nationalisation had comprised 850 private companies. In 1947 all pits came under the control of one single authority, the National Coal Board. In the case of electricity, 500 organisations were replaced by 14 area boards. The State was also able, on account of the capital reserves, to inject much needed money into collapsed industries like the railways. However weak in financial terms the government might be, in being able to call upon national resources it was far better placed than a private company could hope to be.

List of nationalised industries

1945   **Bank of England**

1946–8   **Transport**   Road, rail and canals were nationalised together as part of a unitary plan. All came under the control of the British Transport Commission.

1947   **Coal**

1948   **Gas**

1948   **Electricity**

1949   **British Overseas Airways Corporation** (B.O.A.C.)

1949   **Iron and Steel**   In fact this Act was not implemented. Opposition from the iron and steel owners, aided by the House of Lords was too great. In 1953 the Act was rescinded by the Conservative Party and steel was not finally nationalised until 1967.

The results of nationalisation

In fact although it received a great deal of publicity nationalisation affected only a minority of working people, 80 per cent of whom continued to be employed in private enterprise. As had been expected, greater rationalisation was a consequence of the transfer to public ownership in some cases but the problems which had faced many of the industries taken over, did not disappear overnight. The decline of canals continued for instance, and though output in the mines went up by 10 per cent, within a year the miners were on strike, complaining this time, not about harsh and unsympathetic owners but about the inflexibility of the Coal Board. 'It has turned out to be little more than another government department' was a complaint made when the Coal Board frowned upon the unorthodox practices of the Grimethorpe (Yorkshire) miners who were in the habit of knocking off as soon as their target for the day was achieved, even though this point might be reached in mid-shift. Strikes in the mining industry actually increased in the first year of nationalisation, rising from 1,329 to 1,635, and absenteeism doubled. It was too much perhaps to expect the attitude of the workforce to change overnight. The mining industry after all had been plagued with bad labour relations for fifty years at least.

The railways too were slow to rally to a state of efficiency. Some would say that they are still struggling to this goal.

As the 1940s progressed less and less enthusiasm attached to the idea of nationalisation so that in 1949 when the **Iron and Steel Act** was passed it was against a background of opposition in which arguments revolved round a free as opposed to a wholly planned and state controlled economy.

Labour falls from power

An election was due in 1950 and Labour was returned once again but with a very much reduced majority. A year later confidence had slipped to such a degree (assisted by the Korean war and a financial crisis) that when Mr Attlee went to the polls again he found that the nation preferred the Tories. A remarkable era had come to a close.

What had been achieved?

The short answer is a great deal. The Welfare State begun in the early part of the twentieth century had been brought to fruition, epic financial crises had been weathered, and national bankruptcy avoided. The planned society had come into being and it was accepted that the state should control and regulate the economy more completely than had been the case pre-war (though of course the foundations for the assumption of state responsibility had been laid pre-war, and had been intensified during it). But for the moment appetites were sated. People wanted a breathing space and many of them a return to the old grooves and certainties. One has only to observe the subject matter of plays, films and novels of the early 1950s to be certain of this point. There is a cosy traditionalism in the domestic films of that period, in which the central characters are middle class, speak in refined accents and are shown against a background which is suburban or country market town. In the theatre also the focus was upon the antics of the middle class in their habitual settings (*The Browning Version* by Terence Rattigan was set in a public school), or plays concerning the moral dilemmas facing the middle class as in another play by Rattigan, *The Winslow Boy*, in which a young naval cadet is accused of stealing a postal order. People had wanted to look forward in 1945, and a cartoon of the period by David Low portrayed a giant common man striding towards the socialist era, knocking pigmy faint hearts dressed in the 'Tory' uniform of black coats and pin-striped trousers out of the way. But there was too much pain and difficulty involved in getting there. The title, 'Age of Austerity' has been applied to this period and with reason. There was too much drabness and self-denial. Of course this was not the fault of Labour, it was largely the consequence of an economy crippled by war but all too often people do not analyse the cause of their distress. They merely feel the discomfort and blame what is nearest to hand. In any case the Labour leaders themselves seemed to have run out of steam. Most of the Cabinet were in their 60s when they took office, and two at least, Bevan and Cripps, were on the verge of death (both died in 1951). The Conservatives on the other hand were regaining energy and purpose. They had been shocked by their defeat in 1945 and had been dazed by the speed with which legislation passed through the Houses of Parliament in the next five years. (Mr Attlee spoke the truth when he remarked in 1946 that in the space of nine months Labour had enacted more legislation than had been dealt with previously in an entire parliamentary session.) Perhaps for this reason among others they had not put up much opposition to the early nationalisations or to the welfare reforms. The sticking point came with steel however, an industry which was already centralised and controlled by a powerful owner's association, the British Iron and Steel Federation. The determination of the owners to resist a state take-over got the backing of the Conservatives and in the process of defending the industry against take-over the Tories rediscovered their will and came also by way of a principle which became the platform of their appeal to the electorate – the principle of individualism and of private enterprise. The steel nationalisation bill enabled them to sound the warning about the dangers of a society and economy too strongly state-controlled. H. A. Hayek, in his influential book, *The Road to Serfdom* published in the 1940s, a book which pointed out the inevitable losses of freedom in a socialist state, was a useful aid to fan fears.

So out Labour went and back the Tories came, to enjoy what is known as an Indian Summer. Fashions were ladylike and elegant, social behaviour formal. The emphasis was upon respectability and correctness. Society which had seemed to be loosening up, began to stratify and to stultify once again. It was as if the tide had come in, to wash over, flatten and eradicate a sand castle carefully built by a child. But in fact that comparison is not apt, for the castle Labour had built in those years was laid not upon sand but upon rock and its foundations went very deep.

1815–1951. Summary and Comment

If one were to compare 1815 with 1951 what essential changes could be seen? It is worth looking again at some of the topics which have been raised in this book to reach some kind of conclusion.

The role of government in social and economic policy

There is no doubt that the transformation in this sphere amounted to a metamorphosis. If an M.P. of 1815 and his counterpart of 1951 were to be placed side by side and asked to comment on the duty of the government, their answers would be very different. The M.P. of 1815 would be reluctant to concede that the role of government extended beyond the necessity of maintaining law and order, regulating trade and defending the realm against foreign invasion. The government had intervened in matters remote to these three concerns, in so far as parliamentary acts had by 1815 dealt with topics like river navigation, enclosure and the regulation of wages, but such interventions were exceptional and considered undesirable. It was thought right that the role of government should be limited to avoid the curtailment of individual freedom. It was in defence of this vaunted principle that the reactionary M.P. for Lincoln, Charles Sibthorpe, as late as 1851, opposed the Public Health Act, asserting that the right of each individual to his own 'private dung heap' outweighed the general health of the community.

This seems ludicrous to us now, as it would have seemed ludicrous to our imagined M.P. of 1951. By his day, government had assumed responsibility in nearly every sphere of life: education, employment, health, poverty, trade and industry. The dangers of which Sibthorpe had warned in respect of the loss of individual freedom were still recognised (see Steel Nationalisation debates 1949–56), but the balance of the argument had clearly swung away from the principles of individualism being defended, at all costs, to individualism as far as was consistent with the general good. In one respect it could be said that in the twentieth century Benthamism came of age. (You may recall that his ideas were becoming influential in

199

1815, page 16.) The idea of the general good of the greatest number had replaced the eighteenth century political notion of a balance of interests. The duty of the government to bring that greatest good about, instead of relying upon individual acts of charity, prompted by Christian beliefs or the sense of duty among members of the upper class, which might (or might not) be induced by a classically based education, was unquestioningly accepted by 1951. In other spheres too, the life experience of Britain was profoundly altered between 1815 and 1951.

The advance in *communications* had opened up new vistas and had brought to an end a life essentially parochial and narrow. In 1815 the only forms of transport were on foot, by boat and by horse. By 1951 the railways, motor car and aeroplane had brought about ease of access to all parts of the country and the world.

It is important to remember, however, that even in 1951, cars were not widely owned and that air travel was the prerogative of the relatively wealthy. The absence of motorways also meant that there were still enclaves of quiet, hidden away in areas which might be described as remote, but the time traveller from 1815 would stand amazed at the speed with which Britain could be traversed and with which news could be disseminated by telephone, telegraph and radio, and for those who were up to the minute and in possession of such a miraculous device, by the television.

Population

The sheer numbers of people would also be a striking factor. Early nineteenth century Englishmen had felt alarmed by the increasing population of their own age, but the 12 million who comprised the nation in 1815 would seem a paltry figure to set beside the 54 million who lived in Britain in 1951. There was also the dispersal of the population into the towns and cities which had sprung up since his day, and the changed balance from country to town. Britain's character, in fact, as an urbanised and industrialised country, would have been noteworthy and the fact that, contrary to Malthus's prediction, these millions were not on the verge of starvation, would be a further source of interest.

Malthus (see page 11), of course, had failed to realise the extent to which industrialisation and trade could enable the nation to feed by means of imports. Money could be made to purchase abroad the foodstuffs needed by an enlarged population which made demands upon native agriculture which could not be met. Industrialisation, a process in its infancy in 1815, was the key to most of the changes brought about in the century and a half under review. The improved standard of living, the wider availability of education, the altered view of the role which women should play in society, the broader political system and the affordability of the welfare state all stemmed from industrialisation. And William Cobbett, were he to be our traveller in time and were he to undertake a 'ride' through Britain in 1951 similar to that he took in the 1820s, whilst he would no doubt regret the loss of rustic beauty, could only applaud the greater humanity and the larger hopes of the nation in 1951.

Key Terms

Alienation Word used in the context of industrial society: describes emotional detachment from one's work and surroundings.

Balance of payments The ratio of a country's exports to its imports.

Capitalism The economic system by which individuals invest capital (money) in industry and receive a share of the profits; under **capitalism** plant and factories are controlled by the **capitalists** or their nominees.

Elementary education Taught 'elements' of education, reading, writing and arithmetic, to children between 5 and 11–12.

Evangelical Evangelicals were a religious group within the Anglican Church. The adjective derives from their moral outlook – emphasis on thrift, self-help, self discipline and hard work.

Franchise Right to vote; often interchangeable, with 'suffrage'.

Laissez faire Government policy of non-intervention.

Liberal Believing in a system of free enterprise, capitalism, free press and free institutions.

Luddites Machine-breakers; active 1811 onwards.

Nationalisation The take-over of a private industry by the state.

Nonconformist Not a member of the Church of England, the established church; sometimes called **Dissenter**.

Outdoor relief Payment of dole to the poor every week, as opposed to **indoor relief** which was the workhouse.

Philanthropist One actively concerned in promoting the welfare of others through good works.

Radical Description of a political persuasion favouring extension of the franchise and far-reaching social reforms.

Sectarian Member of independent religious group, usually nonconformist (e.g. Baptists, Quakers, Methodists, Unitarians).

Socialism Political point of view – egalitarian. Basic belief, more equal distribution of wealth, greater equality of opportunity, and state ownership of industry.

Status quo The state of affairs at the present.

Voluntary schools Schools run by independent body or organisation as opposed to the state.

Welfare State A country where the government provides for the basic social and economic needs of the people.

Whigs Political party whose followers favoured paternalism and moderate reform. Strong belief in rule by trained and responsible élite. By 1880 party more commonly known as Liberal Party.

Suggested Reading

This list is short because I have chosen only those books which treat subjects simply and concisely or recommended themselves on account of their readability.

England in 1815
R. J. White, *Waterloo to Peterloo* (Penguin Books)
Rural society
F. Huggett, *A Day in the Life of a Victorian Farm Worker* (Allen and Unwin)
T. May, *Agriculture and Rural Society in Britain 1846–1914* (Arnold, Archive Series)
Flora Thompson, *Lark Rise to Candleford* (Penguin Books)
The poor
J. J. and A. J. Bagley, *The English Poor Law* (Macmillan)
R. Blythe, *The Age of Illusion* (Penguin)
George Orwell, *The Road to Wigan Pier* (Penguin Books)
R. D. H. Seaman, *The Liberals and the Welfare State* (Arnold, Archive Series)
Industrial society
Sir Arthur Bryant, *English Saga 1840–1940*
Communications
T. Coleman, *The Railway Navvies* (Penguin Books)
M. Robbins, *The Railway Age* (Penguin Books)
L. Bailey, *B.B.C. Scrapbooks*
Factory reform
R. L. and B. Hammond, *Lord Shaftesbury*
The changing status of women
M. James, *Emancipation of Women in Great Britain* (Arnold, Archive Series)
T. Lloyd, *Suffragettes International* (Macdonald)
Education
Asa Briggs, *Victorian People* (Penguin Books)
Local government
Asa Briggs, *Victorian Cities* (Penguin Books)

Index

Adulteration of Foods Act (1860), 169

agriculture, 26–47
  Act (1921), 35
  Depression (1870), 34
  gangs, 38
  unions, 45–6
  wages, 39–40

Akenfield, 31, 40, 42–4, 160

Amalgamated Society of Engineers, 134

anaesthetics, 122

Anti-Corn Law League, 33, 60, 61

Applegarth, Robert, 134

Arch, Joseph, 45–6

Arnold, Thomas, 164–6

Ashley (Lord), 85, 108–11, 113–14, 116

Astor (Lady), 151

Attwood, Thomas, 58–9

Austen, Jane, 10, 142

Austin, Sir Herbert, 103

aviation, 104–5

Balfour's Education Act (1902), 161

Beale, Dorothea, 146

Beck, Lydia, 150

Bentham, Jeremy, 16, 110

Besant, Annie, 135

Bevin, Ernest, 139

Birmingham Political Union, 58

Black Friday, 137

blanketeers, 23–5

Bondfield, Margaret, 151

Booth, Charles, 63

Brandreth, Jeremiah, 23, 25

B.B.C., 106

British Sugar Corporation, 72

British and Foreign Schools Society, 154, 157–8

Brunel, Isambard Kingdom, 97

Butler, Josephine, 55, 144

capital punishment, 126–7
  Amendment Act (1868), 127

Cato Street Conspiracy, 23–4

Central Board of Health (1848), 118

Central Coal Board, 72

Central Electricity Board, 72

Chadwick, Edwin, 41, 52, 118

C.O.S., 55

Chartists, 57–62, 93, 102, 110, 157
  Charter, 58

child labour, 11, 40–1, 80, 84–5, 114–16
  mortality, 92, 121
  prostitution, 126

children, 88, 112, 121, 123
  Children's Charter (1909), 67

Citrine, Sir Walter, 139

Combination Acts, 132

Co-operative movement, 56, 109

Corn Laws, 14–15, 19, 22, 33, 36, 81

Corn Production Act, 35–6

corresponding societies, 21

Criminal Law Amendment Act (1871), 135, (1885), 125

crop rotation, 26, 30

dame schools, 153

Davison, Emily, 151

death rate, 11, 91–2

disease, 91–2, 117

Disraeli, Benjamin, 58, 80, 82–3, 110, 119

Dockers' strike (1889), 114, 136
Doherty, John, 132
drainage, 28–9

education, 16, 153–66
   Acts: (1870), 146, 158–9
      (1876), 159
      (1880), 160
      (1902), 161
      (1918), 161 2
      (1936), 163
   female, 146–7
Eliot, George, 37, 142, 153
Employers' and Workmen's Act
   (1875), 114
enclosure, 9, 26–8
endowed schools, 155
   Act, 163
evangelicals, 49

factory conditions, 79, 81–2
   reform in non-textiles
      industries, 113
   see also textile industry (Acts)
Fawcett, Millicent, 150
female: education, 146–7
      labour, 87–8
      suffrage, 148–52
fertiliser, 26, 30–1
Fielden, Robert, 110, 112
First World War, impact on:
   agriculture, 34
   industry, 68–9
   trade unions, 137
   women, 148
Fisher's Education Act (1918),
   161–2
Food and Drugs Act (1875), 119
Ford, Henry, 102–3
Forster's Education Act (1870),
   146, 158–9, 163
Free Trade, 13, 71
friendly societies, 39, 44, 46,
   55–6, 66, 134

Gag Acts (1819), 24
Galsworthy, John, 65
Gangs Act (1868), 38
Gaskell (Mrs), 28, 58, 83, 89,
   90–3, 143
General Strike: (1926), 71, 106,
   138
   proposed: by Chartists (1839),
      60
      by Owen (1833),
      133
Gold standard, 71
Grammar School Act (1840), 163
Guardianship of Infants Act, 145

Habeas Corpus Act: suspended
   (1819), 24
Hadow Report, 162–3
Hampden clubs, 21
high farming, 34
Hill, Octavia, 55
housing, rural, 40–2
   Acts (1875 and 1890), 169–70
   urban, 89–91
Hume, Joseph, 132
Hunt, Henry or Orator, 23–5
Huskisson, William, 14

industry:
   crime, 92–3, 131
   effect of railways on, 98
   industrial society, 78–93
   living conditions, 89
   organisation, 83–4
   reform, see factory conditions
      and textile industry (Acts)
   scale, 83
   schools, 154
   working conditions, 81–5
Intermediate Schools Act (1889),
   161
iron industry, 78, 83

Jex Blake, Sophia, 144

Junta, 134

Keynes, John Maynard, 70

Labour exchanges (1909), 65
laissez faire, 13–16, 35, 54, 67,
    111, 118
Lancaster, Thomas, 154
level of prosperity, 80, 93
    political attitudes, 20
Licensing Acts (1872, 1874), 125
Lister, (Lord), 122
literacy rates, 160
Lloyd George, David, 67, 70
local government, 167–70
    Acts: (1888), 168
        (1929), 170
        (1933), 168, 170
London Working Men's Associa-
        tion, 58
Lovett, William, 58
lower classes, 17
    disturbances, 21–4
Luddites, 21, 132

Malthus, Thomas, 11–12, 51
Mann, Thomas, 135
Marconi, 105
marketing boards, 36, 72
Married Women's Property Acts,
    145–6
May, Sir George, 70, 74
means test (1931), 74, 76
mechanisation, 22
    in agriculture, 31–2
medical officers of health, 119,
    123
mercantilism, 12–13
Metcalf, Jack, 9

Nightingale, Florence, 123

Peel, Sir Robert, 108

Peel, Sir Robert (Home Secretary,
        later Prime Minister), 126,
        129–30
Penal Servitude Act (1857), 128
Pentrich Revolution (1817), 23–4
People's Budget, 67–8
Peterloo, 23, 132
Place, Francis, 132
Playfair, Dr Lyon, 89
police, 116, 129–31
Poor Law, 11, 16, 50–4, 170
    Amendment Act (1834), 52–3,
        57
    Board, 54
    Commissioners, 40
    Hamilton Commission (1905),
        63
population, 11, 33, 81, 89, 124
prison, 128
    Act (1835), 128
prostitutes, 125–6
public health, 16, 117–21, 169
    Acts: (1848), 62, 118
        (1872, 1875), 119
public schools, 155
    Act (1868), 164

railways, 34, 94–100
Reformatory Schools Act (1867),
    129
Reith, J. C. W. (later Lord), 106
Representation of the People Act
    (1918), 151
Ricardo, David, 12
Rowntree, Joseph, 63, 120
Royal Agricultural Society, 29
Royal College of Agriculture, 29

Sadler, Michael, 85, 108, 110–11
    Commission (1831), 85, 108
Samuel Commission, 138
Senior, Nassau, 52
Settlement Laws, 50

Sex Disqualification (Removal)
  Act (1919), 148
Shaftesbury (Lord), see Lord
  Ashley
Shaw, George Bernard, 65, 147
Sheffield outrages, 134
Shop Hours Act (1912), 66
Simpson, Sir James, 122
Smith, Adam, 12–13
Spa Field Riots, 22, 24–5
Speenhamland system, 16, 50–1
Spenceans, 21
steamships, 10, 100–1
Stephenson, George, 80, 95
Stephenson, Robert, 95
Sunday schools, 155
syndicalism, 137

Taff Vale Case, 136
Taunton Commission, 163–4
telegraph, 101–2
Telford, 9
Temperance Movement, 125
Ten Hours Movement, 110
  Act (1847), 110, 112
textile industry, 78, 84–5
  Acts: (1802), 108
    (1819), 108
    (1833), 110–11, 154
    (1844), 112
    (1847), 112
    (1853), 112
    (1856), 112
    (1874), 112
  child labour in, 85–6
Thistlewood, Arthur, 23, 25
Thompson, Flora, 36, 37, 39,
  42–3, 84

Thring, E. W., 165
Tillett, Ben, 125, 136
Tolpuddle Martyrs, 7, 45, 133
towns, 11, 84, 88
Trade Boards Act (1909), 66
Trade Imports Act (1932), 71
trade unions, 62, 66, 109–10, 114,
  133–9
  Acts: (1871), 135
    (1875), 135
    (1906), 136
    (1913), 136
    (1927), 139
  agricultural, 45–6
Trevithick, Richard, 94–5
Triple Alliance, 137–8
Trollope, Anthony, 43, 142, 149
truck system, 82
Turnpike Trusts, 9–10, 16

unemployment, 53, 79
upper classes, 17–20

wages, agricultural workers', 39
  handloom weavers, 79
  miners, 85
  women's and children's (in
    textiles), 85
Wall Street crash, 69
Wheat Act (1930), 72
wireless, 105–6
Women's Social and Political
  Union, 150
Wollstonecraft, Mary, 140
workhouse, 50
Workmen's Compensation Act
  (1906), 66, 114

Young, Arthur, 27

Examination Hints

Introduction
This section is devoted to the preparation for and the taking of examinations. For most people taking an examination is not a very pleasant experience and in many respects is not unlike a visit to the dentist. It arouses all kinds of anxiety, and fears gradually build up until the day and then it is all quickly over. Much worry is caused by various examination myths. You may have heard, for example, a great deal about 'exam technique', a magical quality which alone can bring success – or so it is said. This is nonsense. The knack of answering examination questions has no value whatsoever unless you **know and understand the subject which you are writing about**. Knowledge and understanding must come first for without them a candidate will do badly however skilful or polished an examination technique he or she possesses. Alongside tales about exam technique are various stories about examination papers. Some believe that by carefully looking through papers which have been set in the past, they can discover what will be asked in the future. Having combed all the past papers they will confidently announce, 'I know that this question and that will come up next time.' This can **sometimes** be true but not always and therefore anyone who decides to study only those topics which he or she feels certain will appear on the paper is making a reckless gamble and may easily be disappointed. Certain important topics do occur regularly in papers and it is clearly worthwhile to make a careful study of them, but *not* to the exclusion of other topics which may not appear so frequently.

There is another commonly-held belief about examination papers which concerns the way in which they are set. This usually expresses itself in the idea that papers are somehow devised to confuse, trick or 'trip up' candidates. Again, this is nonsense. Examination questions are posed in the hope that they will enable those taking the exam to show what they know, in other words to give the candidates the best opportunity to display their knowledge and understanding.

Preparing for the examination

(1) Textbooks
The purpose of textbooks is to provide readers with information

and ideas. Each of the first twelve chapters in this revised edition is based on a particular theme – public health and medicine, the status of women, etc. – and the progress of each topic traced throughout the whole period. Two entirely new chapters, while covering these themes, deal chronologically with the period 1939–1951. Many proceed entirely chronologically, that is, splitting the total period covered by the book into divisions of time. Thus a chapter might be headed '1815–30: Unrest and Recovery' and would deal with all aspects of life during that time. Under such a chapter heading you would doubtless find accounts of the 1815 Corn Law, the disturbances of the next five years, Sir Robert Peel's legal reforms and so on.

How a history textbook handles its period, i.e. whether chronologically or by the separate examination of major topics, is unimportant as long as it contains the basic information required for the examination. When studying a period or a subject it is usually convenient and useful to read through all that part of your book which specifically deals with it. If you are seeking information about the suffragettes you should of course read through the section on the Status of Women to find out who they were and what they did in order to understand the part they played in the wider movement for the emancipation of women.

There are however certain subjects and persons which cannot be adequately covered in one chapter irrespective of whether it deals with a theme or a period of time. Take for instance the Corn Law of 1815, which influenced economic and social life in many different ways for the next thirty years. It was a source of grievance in the years after it had become law and in the 1840s became one of the central issues of the debate about Free Trade. The Anti-Corn Law League was the spearhead of the Free Trade movement and the repeal of the Corn Law in 1846 was rightly regarded as a victory for this movement as well as an acknowledgement of the power of industry over agriculture. The Law and its repeal naturally had an effect on British farming. So the Corn Law and its effects are subjects which cut across many different topics over a long period. To fully understand such a subject as this it is necessary to use the book's index.

In the index all the individuals and subjects included in the book are listed alphabetically. To find out all about the Corn Law you would look under 'c' until you found the relevant entry, then refer to each of the pages listed. In this way you would build up a comprehensive picture of the ways in which the Corn Law influenced economic and social life.

Using the index is therefore very useful, especially if the subject spans a longish period, since it enables you to follow through the progress of various topics and individuals.

For a more general impression, it is advisable to read through a whole chapter without pausing, to get an idea of the way in which a theme develops or a period changes. At the end you will have gained an idea of what this particular subject entails and then you may approach it in greater detail.

(2) Other sources of information

Whilst you must be businesslike in your reading of your textbook which, in a sense, is your basic tool, there are many interesting and enjoyable ways in which to increase your knowledge and understanding of the period.

Firstly, try some of the other books on one or more aspects of your set period. There are several covering 1815 to 1951 which are easy to read and will supplement the information contained in this textbook. The titles of some of these are included at the end of the main text on page 172 and more may be discovered at your local or school library (make enquiries to the librarian). If you are interested in crime and social conditions you would find Kellow Chesney's *The Victorian Underworld* a fascinating and readable account of the less well-known aspects of life in the mid-nineteenth century. This book captures something of the flavour of life in the larger towns in Victorian times and describes some of the scoundrels who lived in them. On a different subject, George Orwell's *The Road to Wigan Pier* is a first-hand account of day-to-day life in northern England during the 1930s which again conveys something of the 'feel' and savour of the time. Ronald Blythe's *Akenfield*, which consists of the reminiscences and observations of Suffolk villagers, gives a vivid and very often moving picture of rural life from the end of the last century. Here, as in the other two books, the people of the time come alive, they cease to be statistics and appear as human beings. History is, after all, about people and the more you can discover about individuals the more you will understand them and their world.

Throughout this book there are various references to contemporary novels. The novels of the nineteenth and twentieth centuries tell us much about the people who wrote them and read them. At first sight many of them appear daunting for they are invariably long; when first published they were often in three volumes known as 'three deckers', or else they appeared as serials in magazines. If you can read one or more of those referred to in the text you will find it a pleasant and historically valuable exercise. You will come into close contact with the men and women of the time, hear them talk and follow their thoughts. There are also modern novels which deal with historical subjects, though many are grossly inaccurate and should be treated with care. Of those which cover nineteenth-century subjects, two stand out both as novels and as historical entertainment. The first is T. H. White's *Farewell, Victoria* which tells the story of a man whose single passion in life was a love of horses. It covers the period from the 1850s until the years following the Great War when the hero sees the horse superseded by the motor car. Within the span of his life he is conscious of much change, and the background of the story ranges from the great country house to the Zulu War. Robert Graves' *They Hanged My Saintly Billy* is a less easy book to read but the story which it tells, of Dr Palmer the poisoner, provides a colourful and revealing picture of sporting and middle-class life in the 1840s and 1850s which is both fascinating and sometimes very funny.

Much may be learned about this period from photographs and films. The first photographs were taken in Britain during the early 1840s and the earliest moving films date from the mid-1890s, from which dates the famous and frequently-shown film of Queen Victoria's Diamond Jubilee. Nowadays many books exist with wide selections of old photographs and from time to time local and national galleries hold exhibitions of them so they may be studied at leisure. Of great value are those unposed views of streets and the countryside with their inhabitants busy going about their business. Whether the photograph shows the London of the 1890s with streets jammed with horse-drawn vehicles, the curious countryman with his wife in a 'poke' bonnet squinting at the strange device which is recording their likenesses, or the sturdy working men, lined up and posed before some piece of machinery, it says something about the people and time. Look closely at the clothes, the hands and faces, see if they are clean or dirty (many clothes, coats especially, were rarely cleaned at this time) and most men, until the safety razor of the 1890s, seldom shaved more than once or twice a week. The moving film of the period is equally revealing and sometimes appears on television historical documentaries.

Films about the period vary immensely, like novels. Some are careful reconstructions which scrupulously record the background, costume and dress of the time, and others are often wildly inaccurate. The B.B.C. costume dramas are usually scrupulously accurate and the film *The Go-Between*, which is set in Norfolk in 1900, is a delightful and sympathetic picture of rural life of the time and would be worth seeing for this reason alone.

Lastly, much can be understood by just looking around. Between 1815 and 1839 the landscape changed and the features imposed on it by industrial society survive. The factories, mines and railways still remain and even when they are derelict they say something about the men and women who built them and worked in them. Perhaps one of the most interesting historical exercises is to take a train from any one of the large industrial cities. The station will often be the same building that was set up in the heyday of the railways, vast and cathedral-like. As the trains leave the station they will pass through the industrial heart of the city, with workshops and businesses surrounded by narrow streets of mean houses where the servants of industry used to live. Some will have been demolished and in their place will be new housing and very often blocks of flats. Further away will be the commuters' suburbs, radiating out from the railway line, and beyond them new estates and factories, with lighter industries and less solidly-constructed buildings than the old ones. So in a few miles the train will have passed a hundred years of economic and social history.

You may ask what all this has to do with preparing for and passing an examination. Whilst it is possible to gain enough information and appreciation of a period without straying from the textbook, the sources mentioned above will all add to your knowledge, supply you with additional material and deepen your understanding of the period you are studying. In brief these supplementary sources will benefit your chances of success by enabling you to establish a 'rapport' with the period.

(3) Learning and revision

Your examination will take place at the end of a course of reading, class discussion and essay writing. It is sometimes alleged that what really matters is how you revise. The final weeks are of course important, but it would be mistaken and foolish to believe that all the work needed for the examination can be crammed into that brief time.

The actual process of learning is a personal one and students' methods vary. You should find the method which suits you best and keep to it. There are however certain points worth remembering which may be useful to you in both learning and revision. Firstly, it is helpful to make notes as you work through the period for they will be of direct value when you come to revise. How you compile these notes is again a personal matter, though they should of course be written in such a way that when you later come to read over them they make sense. Whether in a book or a file they should be compiled according to a system, and one which makes it easy for you to find what you want. If your notes are muddled and difficult to follow they will probably reflect muddled thinking and uncertainty. Remember that your notes should contain the essential points, the skeleton of the subject.

Whether you choose to learn from your own notes, or those in this book, or else to work directly from the chapters of the textbook, you must first aim to gain a clear general understanding. If a subject is not clear in your own mind it is unlikely that you will be able to write clearly about it in the examination. The key to learning is understanding: here class discussion is helpful, especially if you can ask questions. Once you have mastered the essential points of a subject you may proceed to learn the details which illustrate the points. For instance, once you understand why the railways were first built, why they spread and the changes they brought, you can build up a knowledge of details which illustrate these points. In many ways learning a subject like this is rather like painting a landscape. First you outline the general features, hills and valleys, etc., so as to show the structure of the land, then you fill in the details of trees and fields. But remember the details cannot exist except in a wider context. It is of no great value to know all the ins and outs of the 1911 Insurance Act without being able to say why it was important and how it changed people's lives.

Revision, like learning, is a personal matter. You will be well aware of those areas where your knowledge and understanding is weak and those about which you feel more confident. You will quickly become aware of your own strengths and weaknesses once you go over your textbook and notes. Again, as with your initial learning **you must isolate what is crucial**, the **key issues** and the

central facts. Once you have done this and appreciated why they are important then you can remind yourself of the supporting details.

How and when you do your revision is something which you must work out for yourself. It is however essential that you draw up some kind of timetable, allocating to each topic a certain amount of time and working into the timetable some kind of reasonable progression. In other words, do not jump from subject to subject but try to follow a coherent pattern. It is easier to pass from the nature of the industrial revolution to factory reform and trade unions than it is to move from agriculture to public health to women's rights and then to education. You may of course test yourself, devise questions and attempt to answer them, but do not attempt to memorise passages from books. This takes a lot of effort and such extracts are easily recognisable in the examination answer. Moreover, **what you have so painstakingly learnt by heart may not fit into the answers of any of the questions you are asked**.

To sum up, make every effort in your learning and revision **to understand the subject you are studying**. Just to learn facts is not enough. You must know why they are important, how they relate to each other and understand their wider implications.

Taking the examination

(1) The examination paper
Examination papers are in two parts, (1) the instructions to candidates (this is sometimes called the **rubric**), and (2) the questions. The rubric will give you detailed instructions, which you may have been given before by your teachers, as to how many questions you should answer and the time allowed for the paper. Some boards issue papers with two or more sections and you should read the instructions carefully in order to discover how many questions you are supposed to answer from each section. If you answer more questions than you need to, you will have wasted effort and gained no extra marks, so **read the instructions carefully**. Make a note of the time you are allowed and the number of questions which you have to answer within that time. **Timing is important**: allow yourself enough time to read the paper, prepare your answers, write them down and then have a few minutes to spare for checking over what you have just written. Occasionally something may go wrong with your timing and you may be left with insufficient time in which to answer your last question: should this be an essay,

your best tactic is to answer the question in outline using notes. As long as the meaning is clear such an answer will not be unduly penalised.

(2) The questions

Read each question carefully. Some candidates, in a panic, glance through the questions in the desperate hope that a subject which they have prepared has come up, light on a word or a group of words (say, 'the Chartists') sigh with relief and start to write down all they know about the prepared topic. In nine cases out of ten they will not have bothered to look at the exact wording of the question, which probably does not require a general account of the Chartists but instead requires an essay about one particular aspect of them.

On reading the paper, keep uppermost in your mind the thought 'What does this question mean?' You should be on the lookout for seven crucial words: 'How', 'Why', 'What', 'Discuss', 'Describe', 'Contrast' and 'Changes'. These are invariably the **key words in a question** and once they have been recognised and isolated, you are on your way to understanding the way in which a question should be answered. **Understanding the meaning of a question is of the greatest importance.**

If a question asks 'how' something happened, the answer must obviously be descriptive. If, for instance, someone asked you 'How do you get to school?', you would answer with a description of the way in which you travel and the route you follow. **In questions which ask 'why'** something happened, the examiners are looking for **explanations** and therefore the answers should contain reasons. **The same is true of those involving 'what'**: if you were asked 'What makes you happy?' you would presumably list and describe those things which give you pleasure. '**Describe**' naturally demands a description of some kind and usually questions based on this instruction are straightforward, e.g. 'Describe the main features of transport in the first quarter of the twentieth century'.

'**Discuss**', as in 'Discuss the part played by Trade Unions in improving wages and working conditions between 1850 and 1914', calls firstly for an account of the ways in which unions were responsible for improvements in wages and working conditions. As you describe the part they played you must expand your remarks. It would be of little use just to state that the Dockers' Union made pay and labour conditions better in the London docks in the 1880s.

You must go further and 'discuss' why this was so, explaining perhaps why conditions were bad in the first place and how the dockers enlisted public sympathy. When the words '**contrast**' and '**changes**' occur in a question certain rules must be followed. If you are required to show how the role of women in society changed between 1815 and 1914 you must begin by stating exactly what the role of women in 1815 was, and then you can go on to show how that changed over the next hundred years. **When asked to 'contrast'** two things you must first describe them and then show the ways in which they were different from each other. So if you were asked 'to contrast the life of an urban worker with that of an agricultural labourer in 1815', you would place aspects of the life of each alongside one another. The nature of factory work could be contrasted with that of the farm; the housing and diet could similarly be compared. Questions of this sort, which seek comparisons or accounts of what changed and why, are to some extent more complicated than the more readily understood 'What happened . . .?' and 'Why did . . .?' kind and therefore require specially careful thought and planning.

To demonstrate the importance of the wording of questions, the three following examples should be studied:

(i) Who were the Chartists and what did they want?
(ii) What were the causes of Chartism? Why did it fail?
(iii) 'Disunited and disorganised, the Chartist movement was doomed to failure.' Discuss.

All these questions are about Chartism but **each requires a different kind of treatment**. Question (i) divides into two parts, the first being concerned with the **identity** of those who supported Chartism and the second with an account of the **demands they put forward**. Therefore your answer should be in two parts: the first will list the types of people who joined the movement and if you know them, the names of their leaders; the second section will explain the two kinds of Chartism, violent and non-violent, and then describe its political objectives. By approaching the question in this way, you will have supplied a direct answer to each part. Question (ii) is also in two parts: the first requires you to **describe the circumstances which gave rise to the Chartist movement** and the second requires a **list of the reasons for its failure**. You may also pause to explain what you think is meant by 'failure': here it must mean **failure of the movement to secure its objectives**. As a general rule 'success' and 'failure', wherever they are referred to in examination questions, must be related to

216

objectives. If you have to write about the success or failure of a person, a movement or an idea, you must first make clear what the person, movement or idea set out to achieve.

The last question may appear to be more difficult. Here you are given an opinion about the Chartist movement and are asked to comment on it. This kind of question is quite common and requires careful consideration. In the first place, make sure that you understand what the quotation means. Here it is quite clear and breaks down easily; **the Chartist movement lacked unity, was poorly organised** and **therefore was likely to fail**. In your answer you must examine each point: you must say (a) whether the movement was without unity, (b) whether it was disorganised and (c) whether it was likely to fail. You will of course have to illustrate each point you make with some evidence, for instance the disagreements between those Chartists who looked to revolution as the means of gaining their ends and those who wished to achieve the same ends through peaceful persuasion.

So whilst all three of the questions quoted above are about Chartism, each requires a different approach and a different type of essay. It is therefore very important to **read the questions carefully, understand what they mean**, and provide the **sort of answer required for the particular question chosen.** Always ask yourself, **'What does this question ask?'**

(3) Writing the answers

When you come to write your answers you must remember that you are writing for a stranger, the examiner. **He can only judge you on what you have written.** You must therefore write legibly and clearly, preferably in a **dark ink**. Bad hand-writing makes it difficult for the examiner to read what you have written and you will not be given credit for work that is unreadable.

Before preparing your answer you will have looked at the question and found out what it means. Often the wording of the question will dictate the form of the answer. If you are asked to 'give an account of the career and achievements of the Earl of Shaftesbury', your answer should be a description of each stage of his public life with comments on what he achieved. On the other hand if you are asked 'How did the position of women change between 1870 and 1928?' your answer might well begin, 'The position of women in society changed in the following ways between these years . . .'. Afterwards, you would describe the position of women in society in 1870 and then list and describe the changes of the next sixty years.

Before you write your essay you must **draw up a plan**, an outline of what you are going to say. You must have a beginning, in which you introduce the subject, a middle, which will contain the bulk of your answer, and a conclusion (which should be brief) which sums up the material in your answer. This is best explained with reference to a specific question, for example: '*Describe the spread of railways in Britain between 1830 and 1850. What changes did they bring?*'

Bearing in mind what has been already said about reading the question, note that this one divides into two halves, one concerned with an account of the spread of railways, the other with the changes they brought. It is logical to answer the first part first, then the second. Before putting pen to paper, quickly write down your main points on a piece of scrap paper. They might be: the first railway from Liverpool to Manchester in 1830 – its success encourages others – demand for rail links between cities and towns – then the areas joined together – the availability of money and public enthusiasm. The time available means that you can include only what you consider the important features of the spread of railways. In setting out these features you would be wise to say why you think they are important: 'In 1830 the first major railway was built between Liverpool and Manchester. Its success encouraged the building of more railways.' Here the point about the first railway is made and at the same time its importance and relevance to the question is emphasised.

In the next paragraph you might continue: 'As more railways were built, joining major cities like Birmingham and London, the potential profits of railways stimulated further investment and building.' Soon the question of how much should be included will arise. Since you were asked to **describe** the spread of railways it would be reasonable to describe the building of them. However, had the question asked **why** the railways spread, a long account of the work of the navvies would not assist the explanation and would therefore be irrelevant. Irrelevant work gains no marks and may often lose them.

Once you have given a balanced account of the spread of railways, saying where they were built, how they were built and why, you should attempt the second part. Here you are concerned with changes and again you should briefly note the outstanding ones – cheaper transport of goods and finished products, easy private travel, mobility of labour, etc. Then you can put them into sentences and paragraphs.

Every sentence should make a useful point and make it **clearly**. When you are nearing the end of the answer you should look at the question and then look at what you have just written. **Ask yourself 'Am I still answering the question?'** or 'Am I wandering off the subject?' Too many people fail to do well in examinations because they wander off the point or fail to answer the question. For example, if asked about the slump in the 1920s and 1930s they write all about the General Strike. However excellent their essays on the General Strike, they will earn only a minimum of marks if the question is about the Depression. Similarly, if the question asked is 'Give an account of the problems faced by the coal industry between 1918 and 1939' and the candidate devotes over half his answer to the General Strike, again he will get few marks. To over-concentrate on one aspect of a subject at the expense of others is harmful and you should always aim to produce a balanced answer.

(3) Style and approach
Here the commonest errors are in spelling and expression. Spelling is a vexed subject, and for many a troublesome one but where possible avoid obvious errors. If you mis-spell a word which actually appears on the exam paper (e.g. 'Listur' for Lister), you will create a bad impression, especially since such mistakes are easily avoided. The other most common error is the meaningless sentence which is no more than a string of words signifying nothing, e.g. 'The General Strike of 1926 caused a great deal of unemployment while it lasted.' Well, obviously if men are on strike they are not working and are therefore unemployed! Similarly, avoid using the word 'things' when another more specific word can be used. 'In 1819 things got bad so there were riots': here the 'things' are or should be food shortages and unemployment. Another word often used without thought is 'they'. 'The government was worried so they took hard measures': 'it' should be used in place of 'they' when referring to the government ('they', if it **is** to be used, must refer back to some persons recently mentioned). So avoid (a) sentences which say nothing and (b) words which are vague.

In written answers you should leave no doubt as to what you mean: always be clear, so that the examiner can instantly understand what you are saying.

(4) Non-essay questions
Many examination papers contain non-essay questions. These are in two forms, short notes and extracts.

(a) **Short notes**

The short-notes questions consist of a number of topics such as the Six Acts, Lord Lister, the *Titanic*, etc. on which you must write short notes. They are invariably short subjects which can be briefly handled but **they will always demand precise knowledge**. You should therefore attempt these questions only if you have a full knowledge of the subject. Just to say 'Lord Lister introduced antiseptics' will gain minimal marks. You must do three things: (i) place the subject in context, (ii) describe it thoroughly, and (iii) say why it was important:

'Lord Lister was a distinguished surgeon who in 1865 first introduced antiseptics for the treatment of wounds. Before that date large numbers of patients had died from sepsis, especially after operations in which unsterilised instruments had been used. Lister, aware of the studies of bacteria recently undertaken by the French scientist Louis Pasteur, realised that germs in the wounds were the cause of death. Therefore he insisted on the use of carbolic acid to treat wounds and ensured that doctors and nurses in operating theatres sterilised their instruments. He even had the air sprayed with carbolic acid in the belief that germs existed and lived in the air. His measures were successful and many thousands of lives were subsequently saved. Surgery was therefore able to make further advances.'

(b) **Extract questions**

Extract questions consist of a passage (usually from a historical document) of about twenty lines or more and a set of short questions which refer to the various points raised in it. They call for a detailed knowledge of the subject, for although the questions are short, they require precision and care in answering. The marks allocated to each answer are shown alongside the question, so if one question carries 2 marks and another 10 candidates will know that the latter obviously needs a longer and more detailed answer. The following extract question, dealing with unrest amongst the poor in 1822, will serve as an example.

'Discontented paupers: a letter to the Home Secretary'

13 November 1822

Sir,

I have the honour to inclose a statement which has this morning been made before me by Mr. John Flurry, Overseer

5   of the Poor of the Parish of Burwash whose barn and stacks
were maliciously set on fire the night of Saturday last. Mr.
Flurry is a man of respectability and in public conduct has
acted meritoriously and it does not appear at any time that he
has been guilty of any improper conduct towards the poor of
10   Burwash. Yet it is supposed that this act was perpetrated
by a Combination of Paupers. In this area there are full two
thousand persons out of profitable employ and the price of
labour has been reduced to sixpence the day and even less.
The poor rates are in some cases actually increasing whilst the
15   Farmers are daily becoming more unable to pay them.
The cultivation of Hops has filled this district with inhabitants and hop planters are generally speaking in a state of
Ruin.

E. G. Curteis, One of His Majesty's Justices of the Peace.

(marks)

(a) Describe the duties of the Overseer of the Poor (lines 4–5).   3

(b) What do you think is meant by the phrase 'a man of
respectability' (line 7)?   2

(c) The writer refers to large numbers 'out of profitable
employ' (line 12), low wages (line 13), rising poor rates and
the inability of the farmers to pay them (lines 14–15). Describe
the system of poor relief then in force and show how it was
affected by these circumstances.   9

(d) What do you think is meant by 'a Combination of Paupers'
(line 11)? Why do you think they had resorted to the burning
of a barn?   3

(e) What kind of action did a local magistrate at this time take
to deal with this type of situation?   3

When faced with a question of this sort, you must first read the
passage through carefully. It is not a difficult piece of writing: there
has been a fire, presumably started by men on poor relief, and the
local magistrate is naturally anxious so he seeks advice from the
Home Office. Now look at the questions. Each refers to a part of
the passage and since the lines of the passage are numbered, reference to it is easy. Question *(a)* asks you to give the duties of an
Overseer of the Poor and links with *(c)*, which asks for a description of the Poor Relief System 'then in force'. The date 1822 gives
the obvious clue, for it is before the well-known Poor Law Amendment Act of 1834. **Always in extract questions look for the**

date and the identity of the author of the passage, for they may well have a bearing on the questions. Here, once you realise that the Speenhamland System is being applied, you will be able to explain what the Overseer's duties were, and for question *(c)* give a fuller account of the levying of rates which were used to increase low wages. Obviously *(c)* requires a full factual answer for it carries nine marks, whilst *(a)* will only need reference to the Overseer's collection and distribution of money.

Question *(b)* asks you to explain the phrase 'a man of respectability'. Here you must use your commonsense. He is a man who is looked up to locally and, you might add, was probably a farmer – after all, he has a barn. In *(d)* you are asked to explain 'a Combination of Paupers'. The paupers were the poor, the men and women who took relief payments, and the word 'combination' was then used to describe an alliance or union of persons. The 'Combination Laws' which were repealed in 1825 made illegal any such groups, which were usually formed by working men to better their conditions and pay. The last question, *(e)*. asks you to make a judgement of your own: how did the local authorities react? There was no police force (remember the date), so troops might have to be used for police work. These might be the local volunteer cavalry, the yeomanry. Then you might imagine that one of the arsonists would have to be punished as an example to others, and you might mention the penalties (such as hanging or transportation) which the guilty might suffer. Here you will have to draw on your wider knowledge of the handling of unrest in the period 1815–30.

The **important points** to remember when answering these questions are: (i) **read the extract and questions carefully**; (ii) **give longer answers where the marks are higher**, and (iii) as with essays, **shape your answers to the question**. Thus in answer to *(d)* you might write:
'A Combination of Paupers was a union of the poor formed to further their interests. They would have resorted to burning a barn for two possible reasons: either because they had no other way of making their feelings known, or as an act of revenge on the Overseer.'

Conclusion
The history O-level examination is a test of knowledge and understanding. You will be asked not only to demonstrate what you know, but to show that you can use your knowledge intelligently. If you just learn the facts off by heart like Victorian school-

children and then repeat them parrot-fashion, you will not get very far. You should **understand what you are writing about** and show this by the way in which you tackle the questions. The essential points to keep in mind are therefore:

1. answer the question directly;
2. keep to the point;
3. answer clearly and concisely;
4. write legibly.

Other study aids in the **keyfacts** series

KEY FACTS CARDS

Latin
Julius Caesar
New Testament
German
Macbeth
Geography Regional
English Comprehension
English Language
Economics
Elementary Mathematics
Algebra
Modern Mathematics

British History (1815-1914)
British History (1914-1951)
Chemistry
Physics
Biology
Geometry
Geography
French
Arithmetic & Trigonometry
General Science
Additional Mathematics
Technical Drawing

KEY FACTS COURSE COMPANIONS

Economics
Modern Mathematics
Algebra
Geometry
Arithmetic &
   Trigonometry
Additional Mathematics

Geography
French
Physics
Chemistry
English
Biology

KEY FACTS A-LEVEL BOOKS

Chemistry
Biology

Pure Mathematics
Physics

KEY FACTS O-LEVEL PASSBOOKS

Biology
Chemistry
Economics
English
French
Geography

History (*Social and Economic*)
History (*Political and Constitutional*)
Modern Mathematics
Physics
Regional Geography (*British Isles*)
Technical Drawing

KEY FACTS O-LEVEL MODEL ANSWERS

Modern Mathematics
English History
   (1815-1939)
Biology
Chemistry

Physics
Geography
French
English

KEY FACTS REFERENCE LIBRARY

O-Level Trad. & Mod. Mathematics
O-Level History (1815-1914)
O-Level Geography

O-Level Biology
O-Level Physics
O-Level Chemistry

KEY FACTS A-LEVEL PASSBOOKS

Physics
Biology
Geography
Economics

Chemistry
Pure Mathematics
Pure & Applied Mathematics
Applied Mathematics

KEY FACTS DICTIONARIES

Biology
Chemistry

Mathematics
Physics